Who's Up for Some Bonding?

Other FoxTrot Books by Bill Amend

FoxTrot • Pass the Loot • Black Bart Says Draw • Eight Yards, Down and Out
Bury My Heart at Fun-Fun Mountain • Say Hello to Cactus Flats • May the Force Be with Us, Please
Take Us to Your Mall • The Return of the Lone Iguana • At Least This Place Sells T-shirts
Come Closer, Roger, There's a Mosquito on Your Nose • Welcome to Jasorassic Park
I'm Flying, Jack . . . I Mean, Roger • Think iFruity • Death by Field Trip
Encyclopedias Brown and White • His Code Name Was The Fox
Your Momma Thinks Square Roots Are Vegetables

Anthologies

FoxTrot: The Works • FoxTrot *en masse* • Enormously FoxTrot • Wildly FoxTrot
FoxTrot Beyond a Doubt • Camp FoxTrot • Assorted FoxTrot • FoxTrot: Assembled with Care

Who's Up for Some Bonding?

**A FoxTrot Collection
by Bill Amend**

**Andrews McMeel
Publishing**

Kansas City

FoxTrot is distributed internationally by Universal Press Syndicate.

Who's Up for Some Bonding? copyright © 2003 by Bill Amend. All rights reserved. Printed in the United States of America. No part of this book may be used or reproduced in any manner whatsoever without written permission except in the case of reprints in the context of reviews. For information, write Andrews McMeel Publishing, 4520 Main Street, Kansas City, Missouri 64111.

03 04 05 06 07 BBG 10 9 8 7 6 5 4 3 2 1

ISBN: 0-7407-3806-2

Library of Congress Control Number: 2003106494

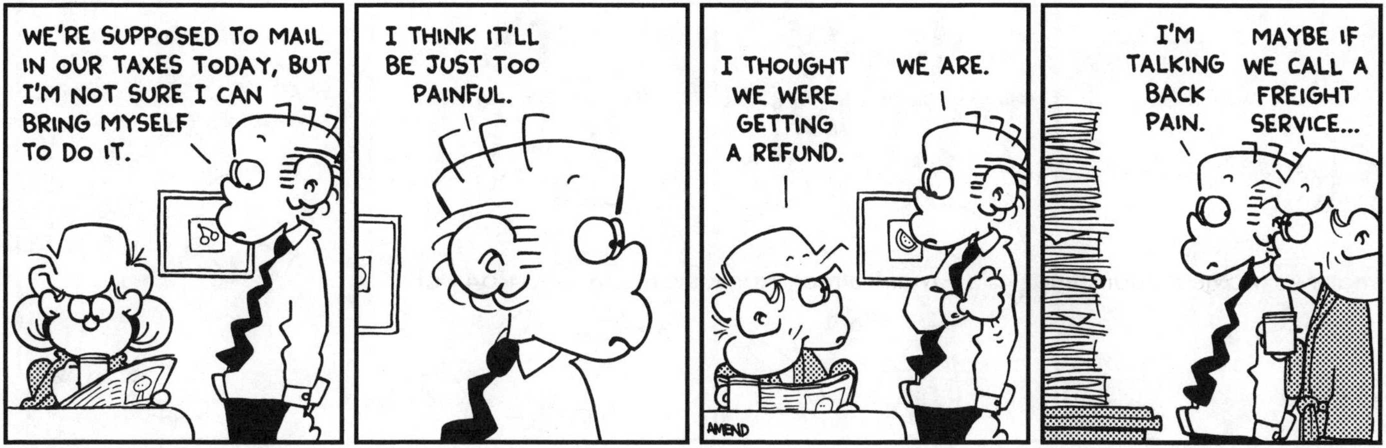
WE'RE SUPPOSED TO MAIL IN OUR TAXES TODAY, BUT I'M NOT SURE I CAN BRING MYSELF TO DO IT.
I THINK IT'LL BE JUST TOO PAINFUL.
I THOUGHT WE WERE GETTING A REFUND.
WE ARE.
I'M TALKING BACK PAIN.
MAYBE IF WE CALL A FREIGHT SERVICE...
AMEND

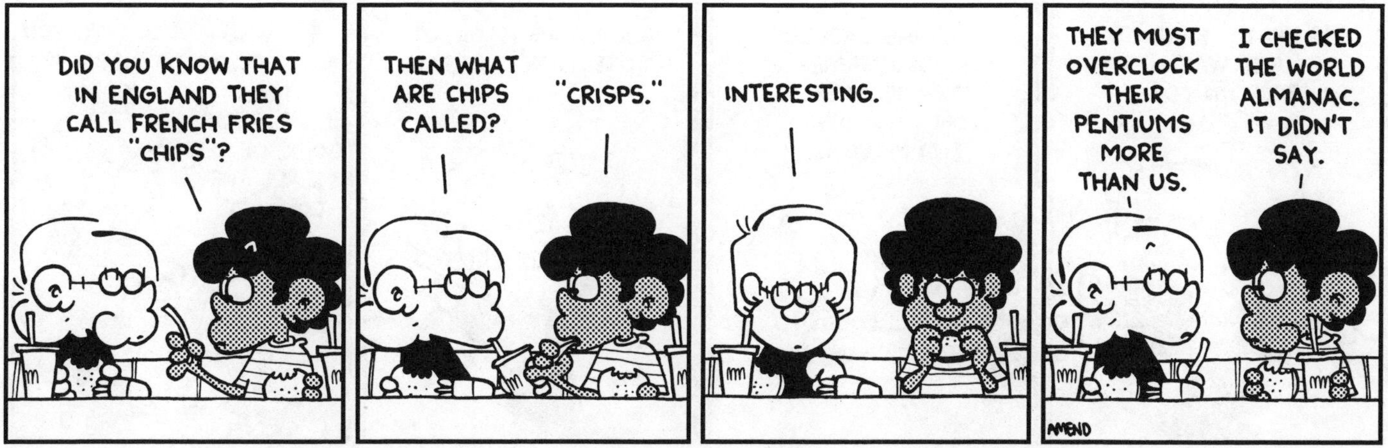
DID YOU KNOW THAT IN ENGLAND THEY CALL FRENCH FRIES "CHIPS"?
THEN WHAT ARE CHIPS CALLED?
"CRISPS."
INTERESTING.
THEY MUST OVERCLOCK THEIR PENTIUMS MORE THAN US.
I CHECKED THE WORLD ALMANAC. IT DIDN'T SAY.
AMEND

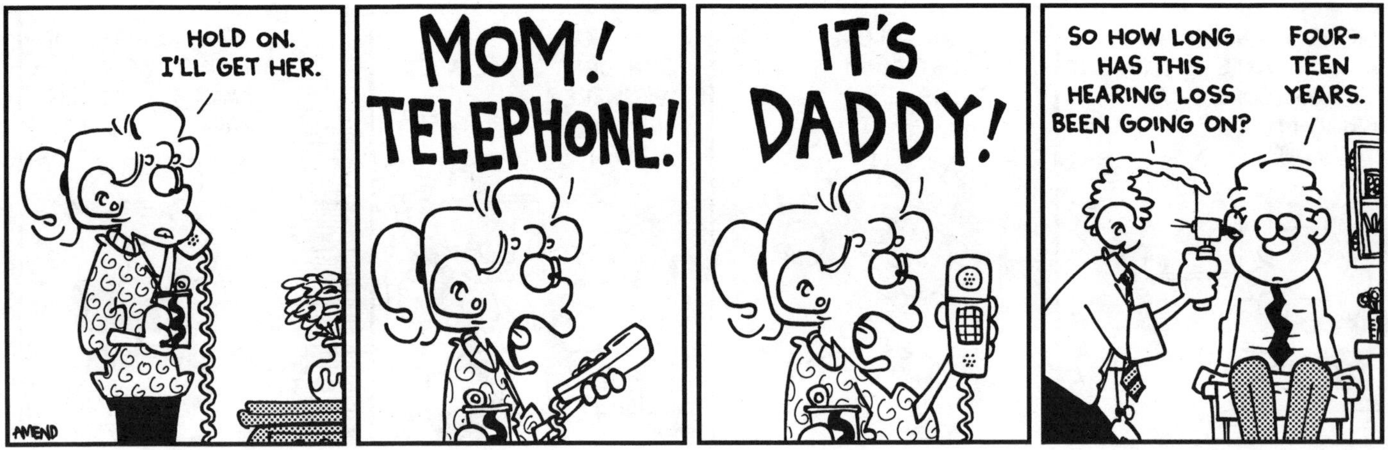
AMEND
HOLD ON. I'LL GET HER.
MOM! TELEPHONE!
IT'S DADDY!
SO HOW LONG HAS THIS HEARING LOSS BEEN GOING ON?
FOUR-TEEN YEARS.

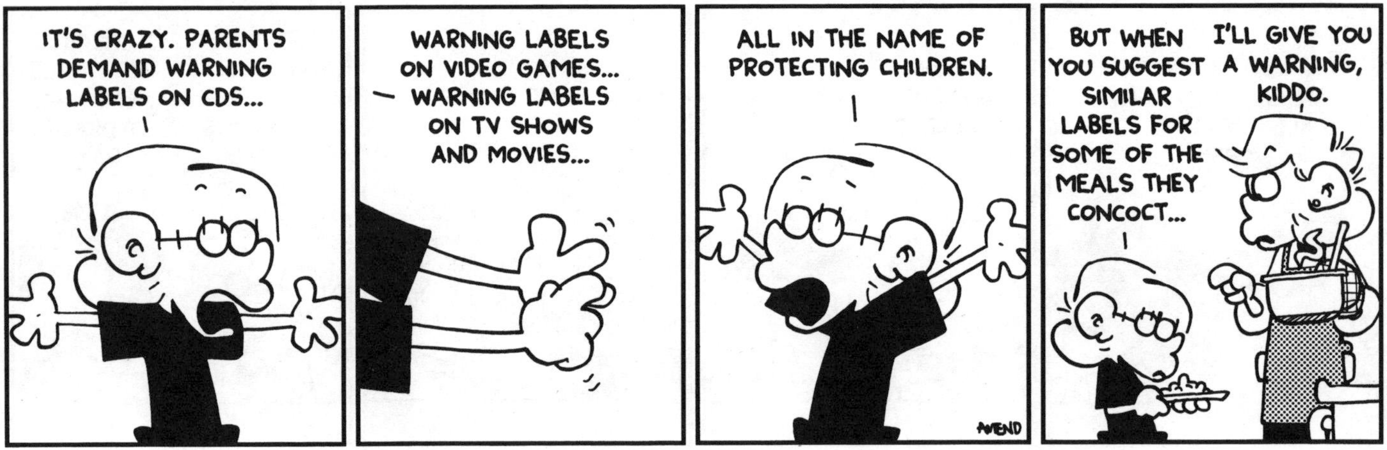
IT'S CRAZY. PARENTS DEMAND WARNING LABELS ON CDS...
WARNING LABELS ON VIDEO GAMES... WARNING LABELS ON TV SHOWS AND MOVIES...
ALL IN THE NAME OF PROTECTING CHILDREN.
AMEND
BUT WHEN YOU SUGGEST SIMILAR LABELS FOR SOME OF THE MEALS THEY CONCOCT...
I'LL GIVE YOU A WARNING, KIDDO.

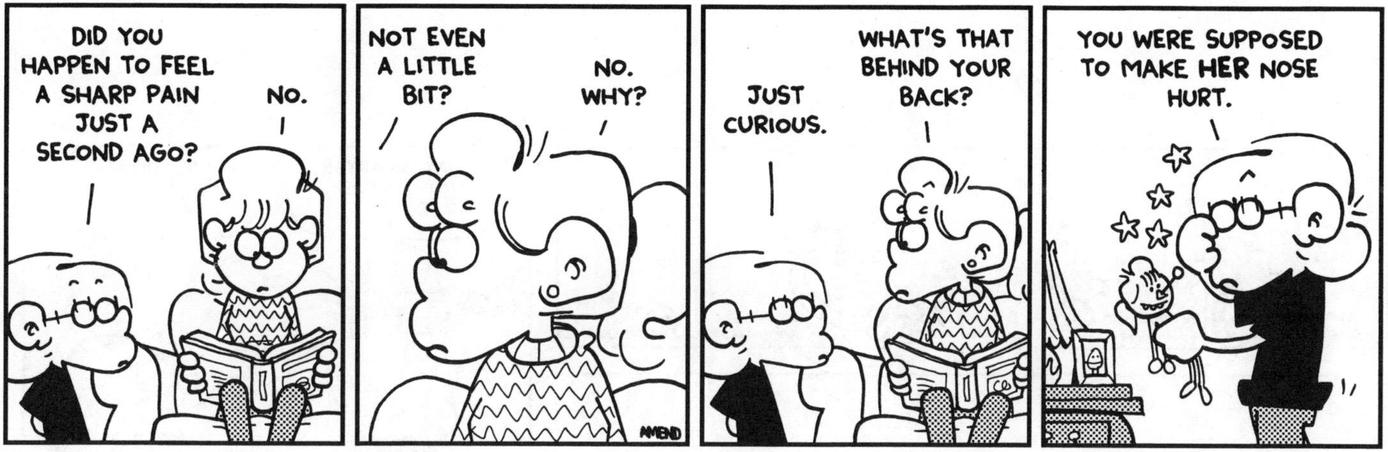
DID YOU HAPPEN TO FEEL A SHARP PAIN JUST A SECOND AGO?
NO.
NOT EVEN A LITTLE BIT?
NO. WHY?
JUST CURIOUS.
WHAT'S THAT BEHIND YOUR BACK?
YOU WERE SUPPOSED TO MAKE HER NOSE HURT.
AMEND

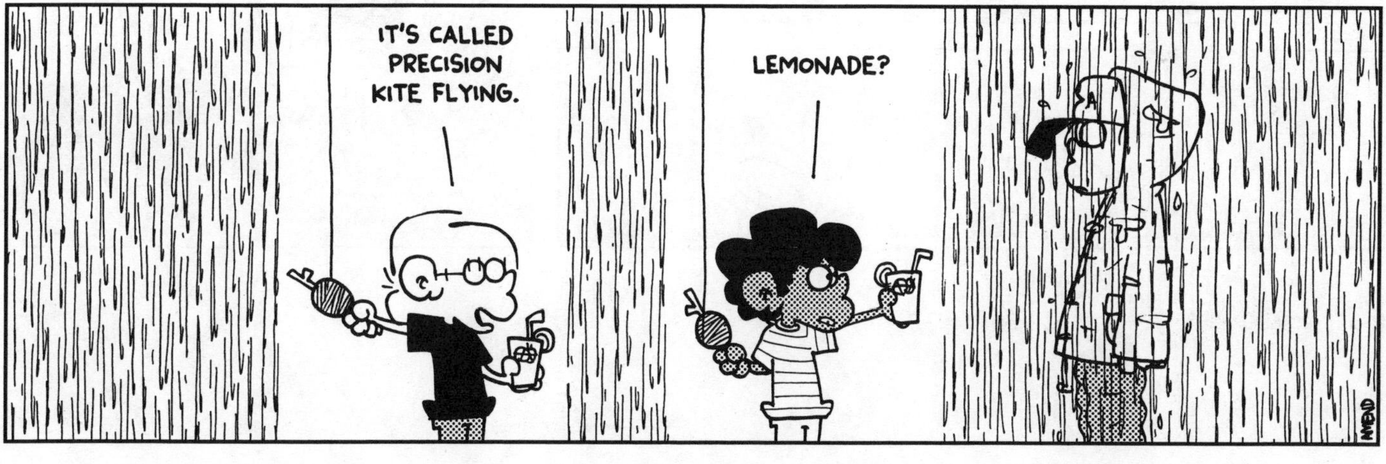
IT'S CALLED PRECISION KITE FLYING.
LEMONADE?
AMEND

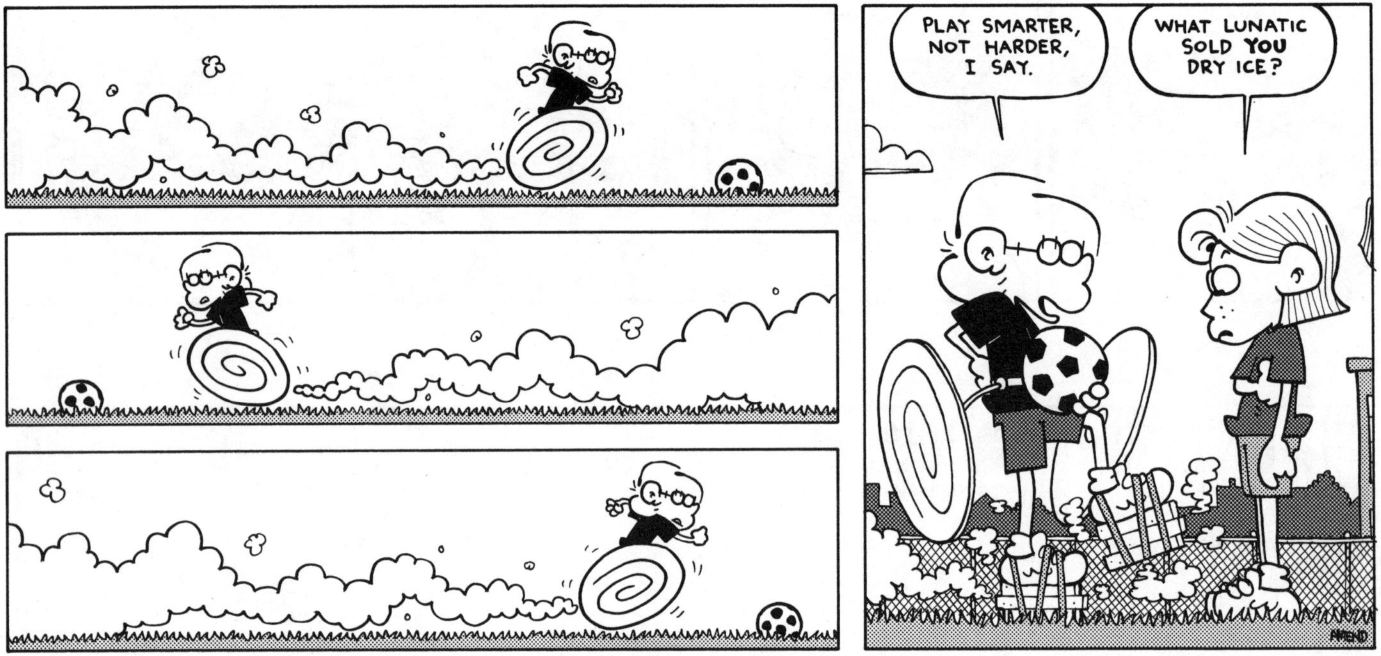
PLAY SMARTER, NOT HARDER, I SAY.
WHAT LUNATIC SOLD YOU DRY ICE?

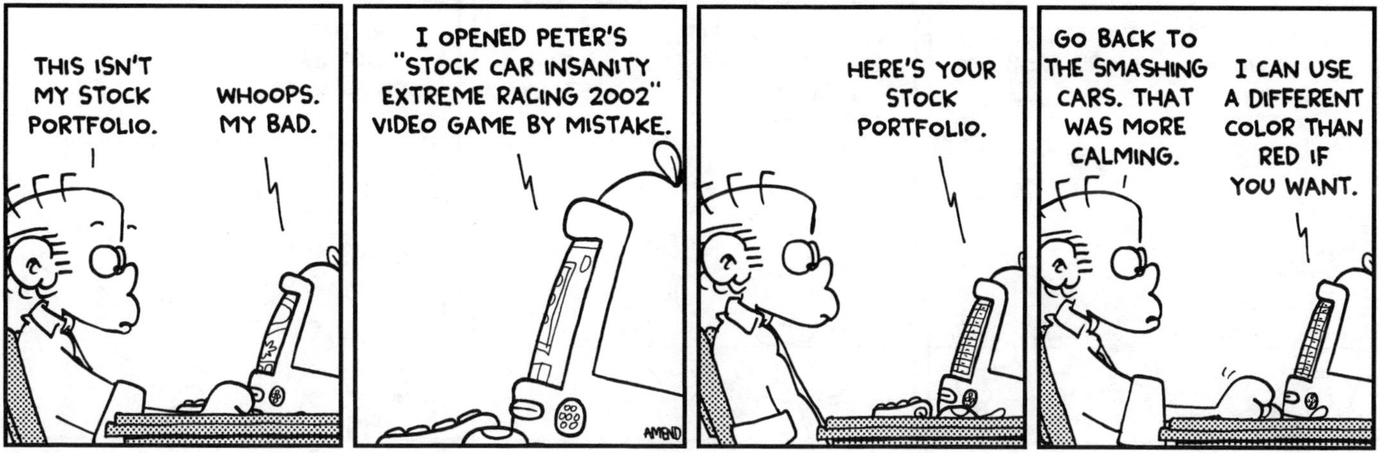
THIS ISN'T MY STOCK PORTFOLIO.
WHOOPS. MY BAD.
I OPENED PETER'S "STOCK CAR INSANITY EXTREME RACING 2002" VIDEO GAME BY MISTAKE.
AMEND
HERE'S YOUR STOCK PORTFOLIO.
GO BACK TO THE SMASHING CARS. THAT WAS MORE CALMING.
I CAN USE A DIFFERENT COLOR THAN RED IF YOU WANT.

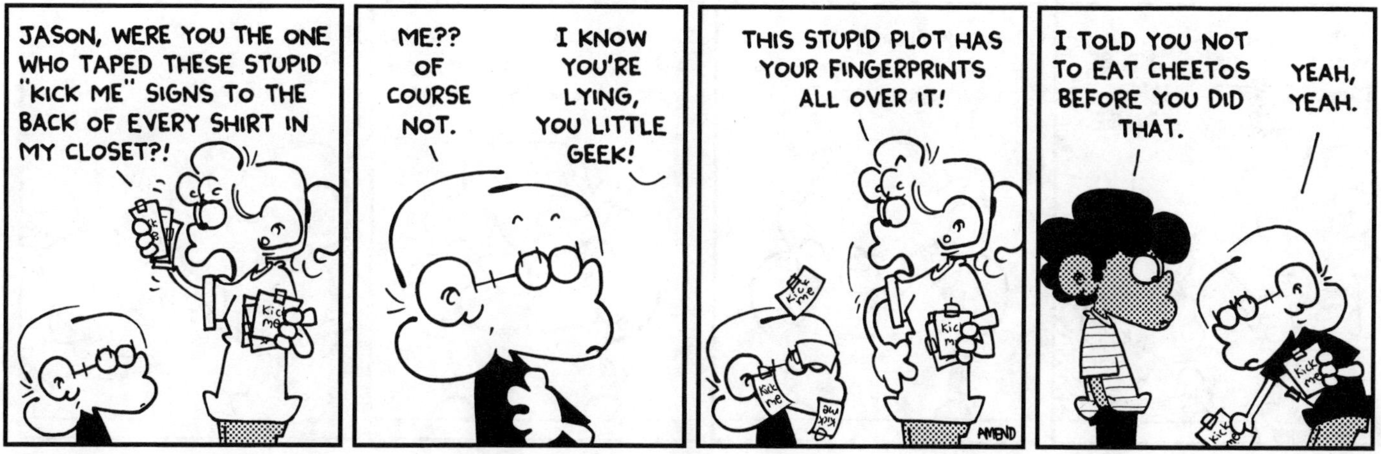
JASON, WERE YOU THE ONE WHO TAPED THESE STUPID "KICK ME" SIGNS TO THE BACK OF EVERY SHIRT IN MY CLOSET?!
ME?? OF COURSE NOT.
I KNOW YOU'RE LYING, YOU LITTLE GEEK!
THIS STUPID PLOT HAS YOUR FINGERPRINTS ALL OVER IT!
AMEND
I TOLD YOU NOT TO EAT CHEETOS BEFORE YOU DID THAT.
YEAH, YEAH.

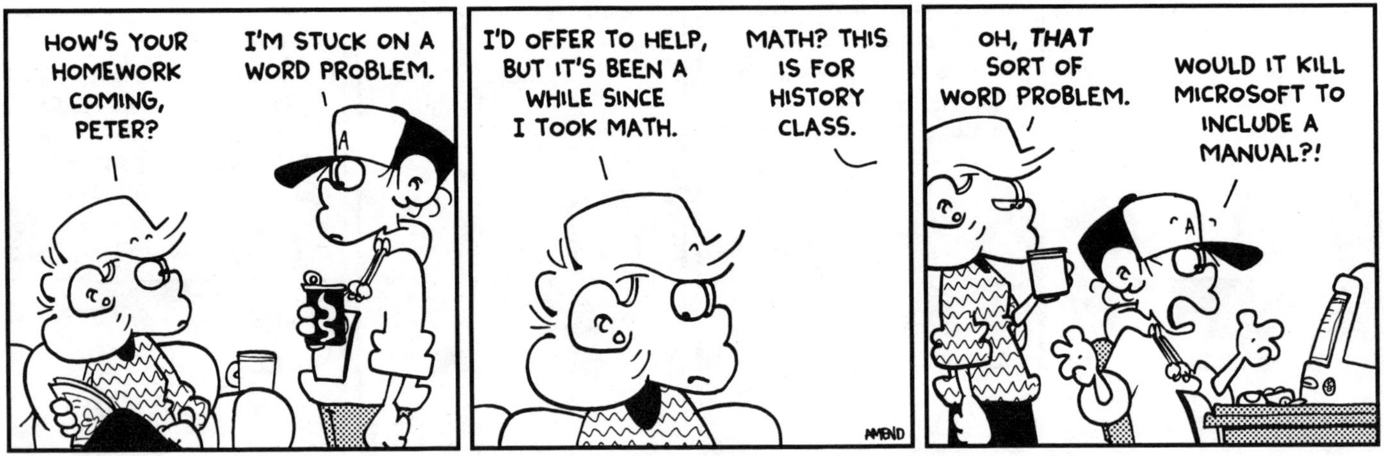
HOW'S YOUR HOMEWORK COMING, PETER?
I'M STUCK ON A WORD PROBLEM.
I'D OFFER TO HELP, BUT IT'S BEEN A WHILE SINCE I TOOK MATH.
MATH? THIS IS FOR HISTORY CLASS.
OH, *THAT* SORT OF WORD PROBLEM.
WOULD IT KILL MICROSOFT TO INCLUDE A MANUAL?!
AMEND

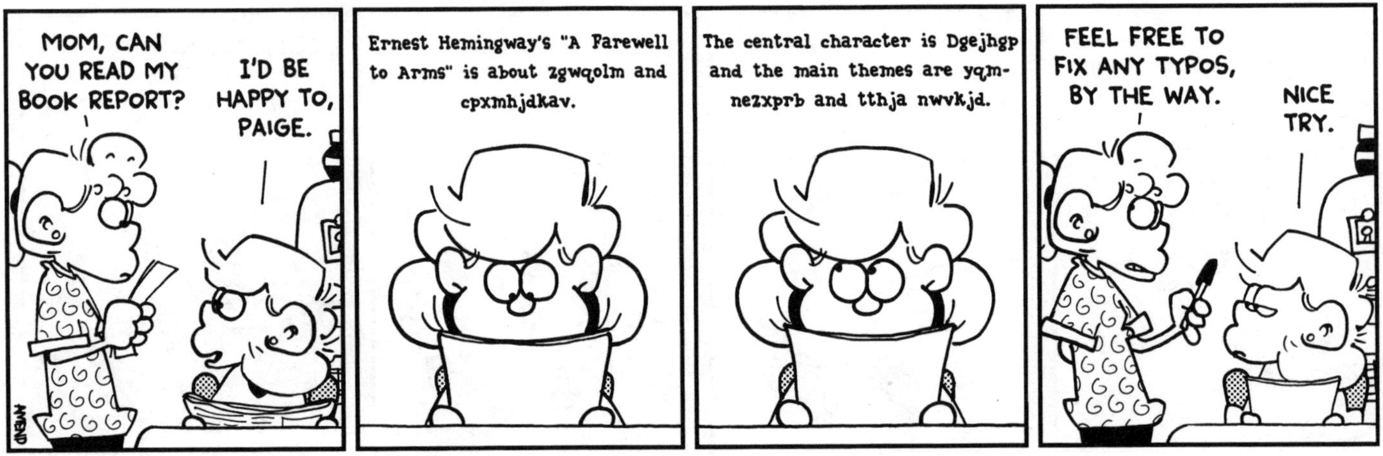
MOM, CAN YOU READ MY BOOK REPORT?
I'D BE HAPPY TO, PAIGE.
AMEND
Ernest Hemingway's "A Farewell to Arms" is about zgwqolm and cpxmhjdkav.
The central character is Dgejhgp and the main themes are yqm-nezxprb and tthja nwvkjd.
FEEL FREE TO FIX ANY TYPOS, BY THE WAY.
NICE TRY.

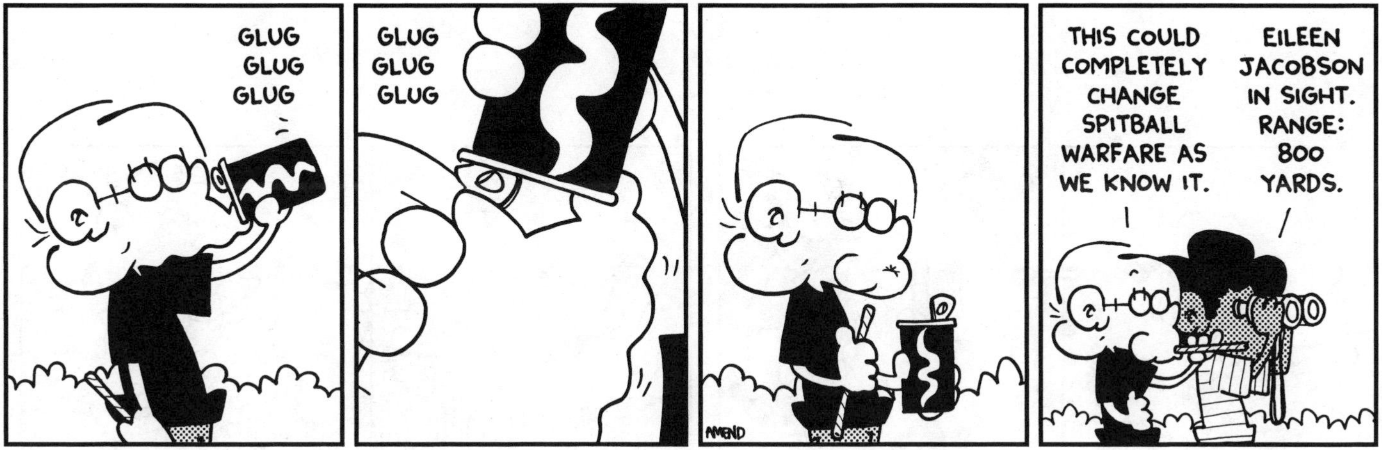
GLUG
GLUG
GLUG
GLUG
GLUG
GLUG
AMEND
THIS COULD COMPLETELY CHANGE SPITBALL WARFARE AS WE KNOW IT.
EILEEN JACOBSON IN SIGHT. RANGE: 800 YARDS.

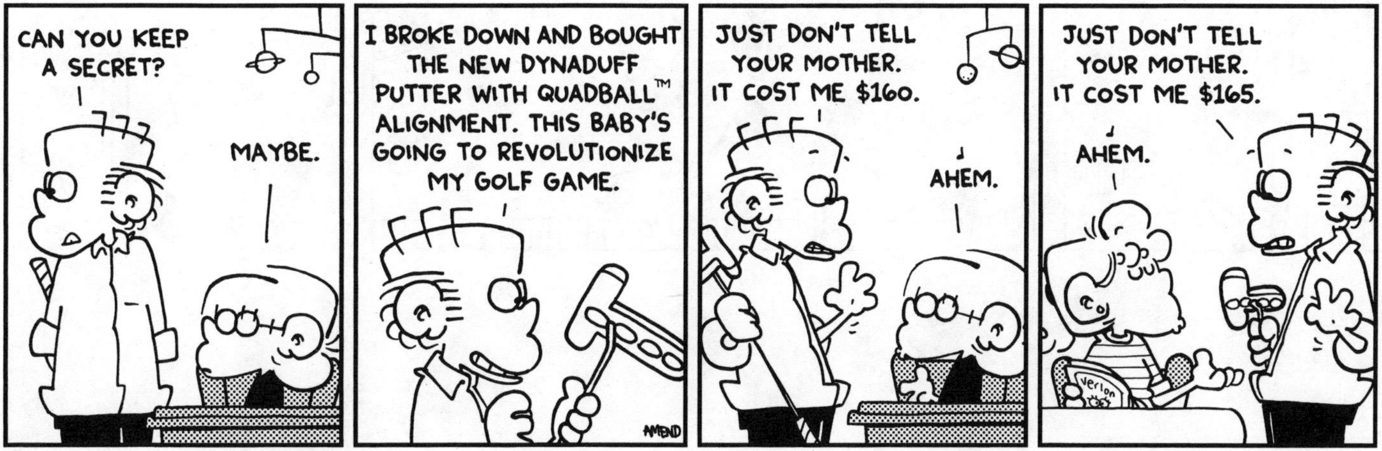
CAN YOU KEEP A SECRET?
MAYBE.
I BROKE DOWN AND BOUGHT THE NEW DYNADUFF PUTTER WITH QUADBALL™ ALIGNMENT. THIS BABY'S GOING TO REVOLUTIONIZE MY GOLF GAME.
AMEND
JUST DON'T TELL YOUR MOTHER. IT COST ME $160.
AHEM.
JUST DON'T TELL YOUR MOTHER. IT COST ME $165.
AHEM.
Verlon

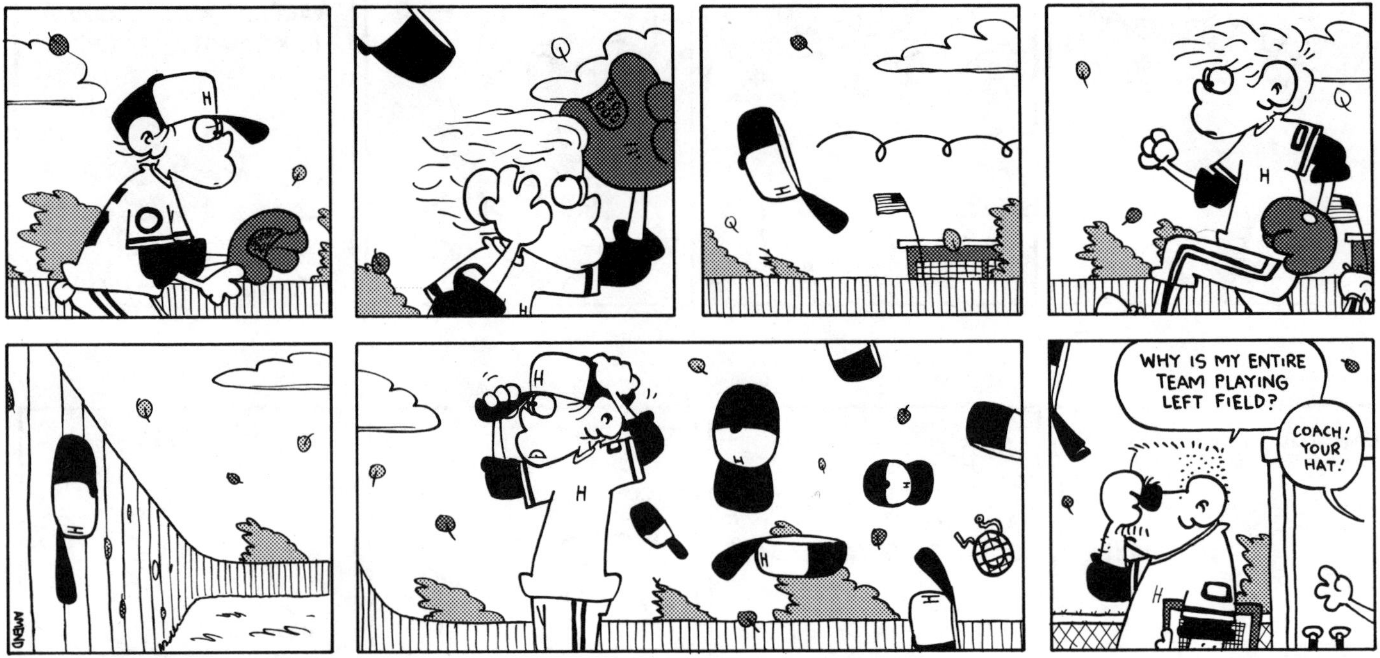

WHY IS MY ENTIRE TEAM PLAYING LEFT FIELD?
COACH! YOUR HAT!
AMEND

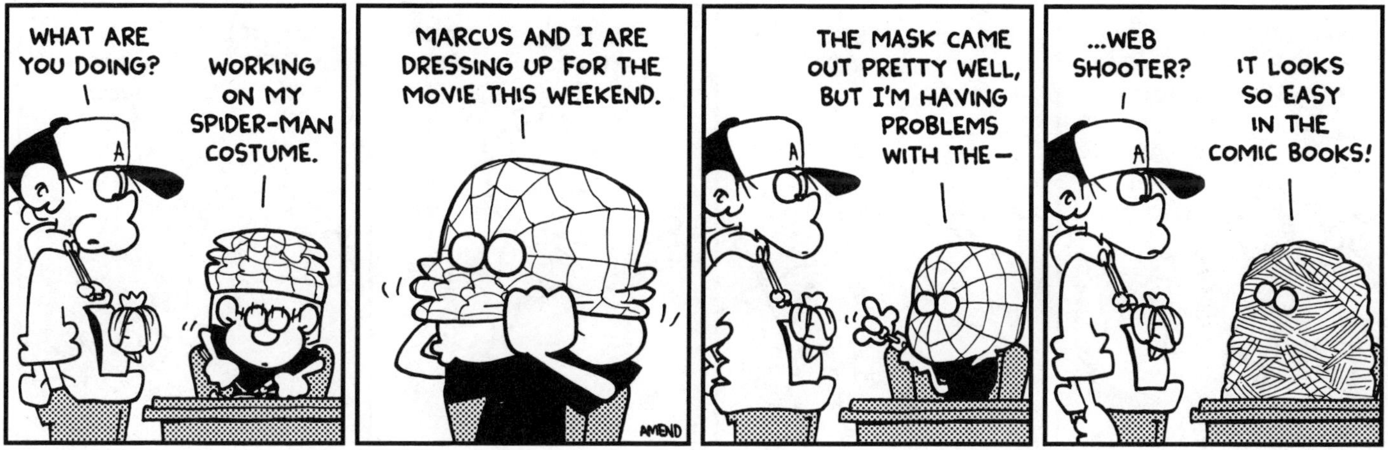
WHAT ARE YOU DOING?
WORKING ON MY SPIDER-MAN COSTUME.
MARCUS AND I ARE DRESSING UP FOR THE MOVIE THIS WEEKEND.
AMEND
THE MASK CAME OUT PRETTY WELL, BUT I'M HAVING PROBLEMS WITH THE—
...WEB SHOOTER?
IT LOOKS SO EASY IN THE COMIC BOOKS!

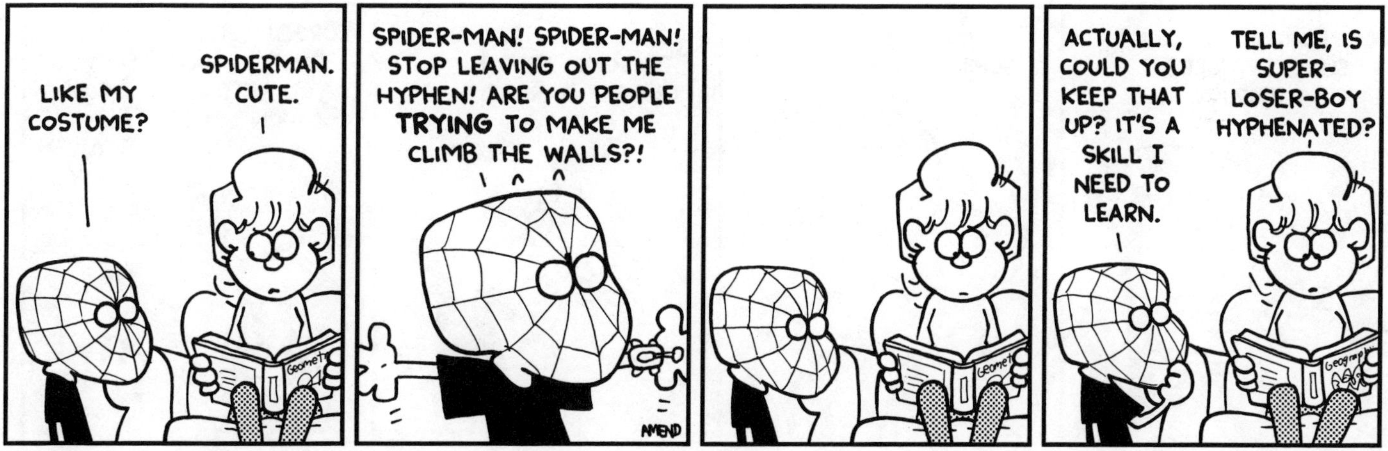
LIKE MY COSTUME?
SPIDERMAN. CUTE.
SPIDER-MAN! SPIDER-MAN! STOP LEAVING OUT THE HYPHEN! ARE YOU PEOPLE **TRYING** TO MAKE ME CLIMB THE WALLS?!
AMEND
ACTUALLY, COULD YOU KEEP THAT UP? IT'S A SKILL I NEED TO LEARN.
TELL ME, IS SUPER-LOSER-BOY HYPHENATED?

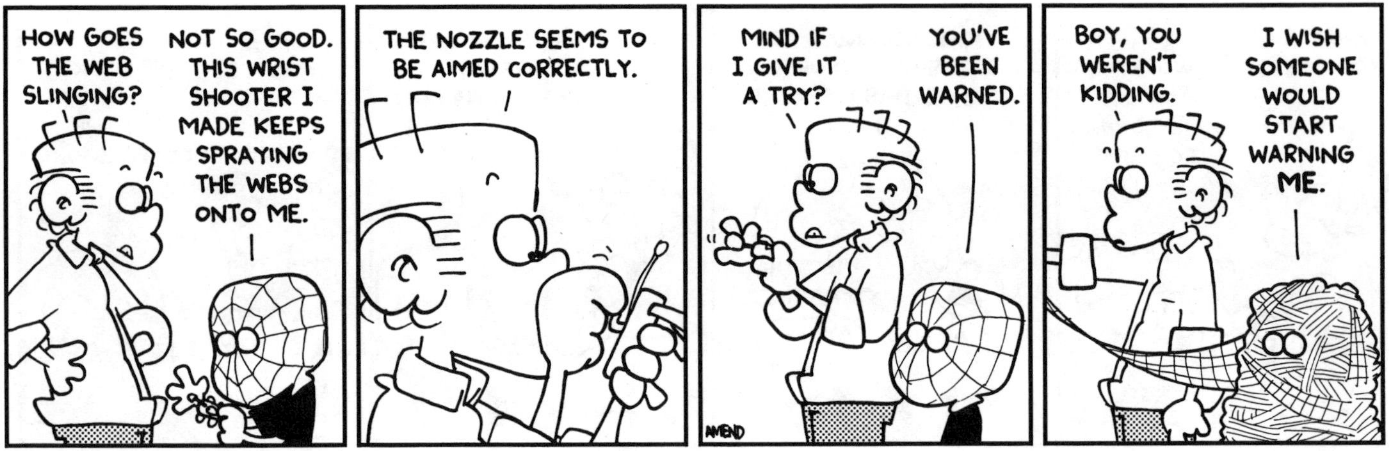
HOW GOES THE WEB SLINGING?
NOT SO GOOD. THIS WRIST SHOOTER I MADE KEEPS SPRAYING THE WEBS ONTO ME.
THE NOZZLE SEEMS TO BE AIMED CORRECTLY.
MIND IF I GIVE IT A TRY?
YOU'VE BEEN WARNED.
BOY, YOU WEREN'T KIDDING.
I WISH SOMEONE WOULD START WARNING **ME.**
AMEND

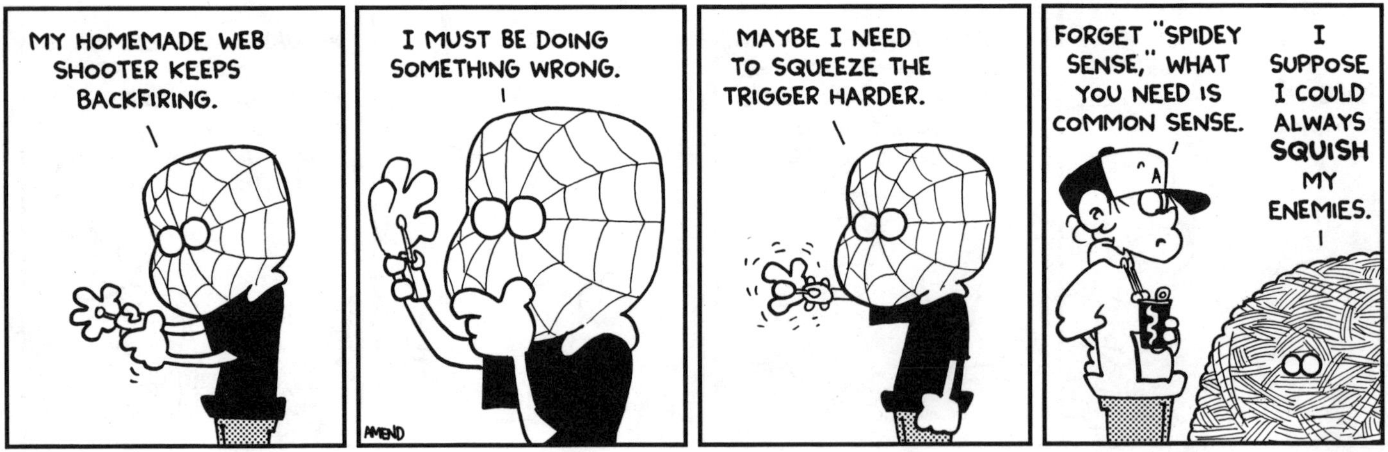
MY HOMEMADE WEB SHOOTER KEEPS BACKFIRING.
I MUST BE DOING SOMETHING WRONG.
AMEND
MAYBE I NEED TO SQUEEZE THE TRIGGER HARDER.
FORGET "SPIDEY SENSE," WHAT YOU NEED IS COMMON SENSE.
I SUPPOSE I COULD ALWAYS **SQUISH** MY ENEMIES.

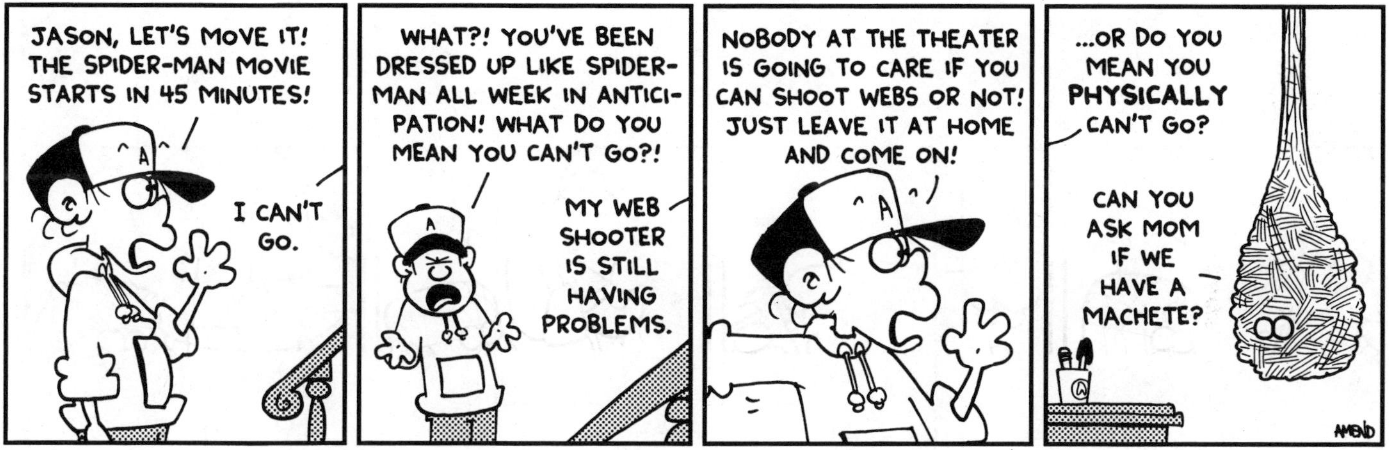
JASON, LET'S MOVE IT! THE SPIDER-MAN MOVIE STARTS IN 45 MINUTES!
I CAN'T GO.
WHAT?! YOU'VE BEEN DRESSED UP LIKE SPIDER-MAN ALL WEEK IN ANTICIPATION! WHAT DO YOU MEAN YOU CAN'T GO?!
MY WEB SHOOTER IS STILL HAVING PROBLEMS.
NOBODY AT THE THEATER IS GOING TO CARE IF YOU CAN SHOOT WEBS OR NOT! JUST LEAVE IT AT HOME AND COME ON!
...OR DO YOU MEAN YOU **PHYSICALLY** CAN'T GO?
CAN YOU ASK MOM IF WE HAVE A MACHETE?
AMEND

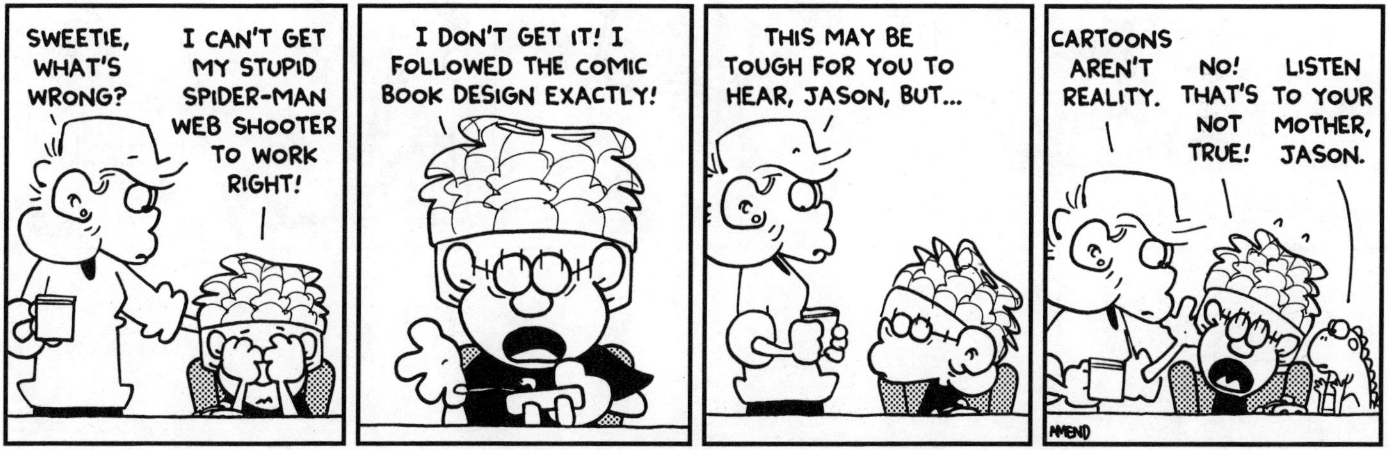
SWEETIE, WHAT'S WRONG?
I CAN'T GET MY STUPID SPIDER-MAN WEB SHOOTER TO WORK RIGHT!
I DON'T GET IT! I FOLLOWED THE COMIC BOOK DESIGN EXACTLY!
THIS MAY BE TOUGH FOR YOU TO HEAR, JASON, BUT...
CARTOONS AREN'T REALITY.
NO! THAT'S NOT TRUE!
LISTEN TO YOUR MOTHER, JASON.
AMEND

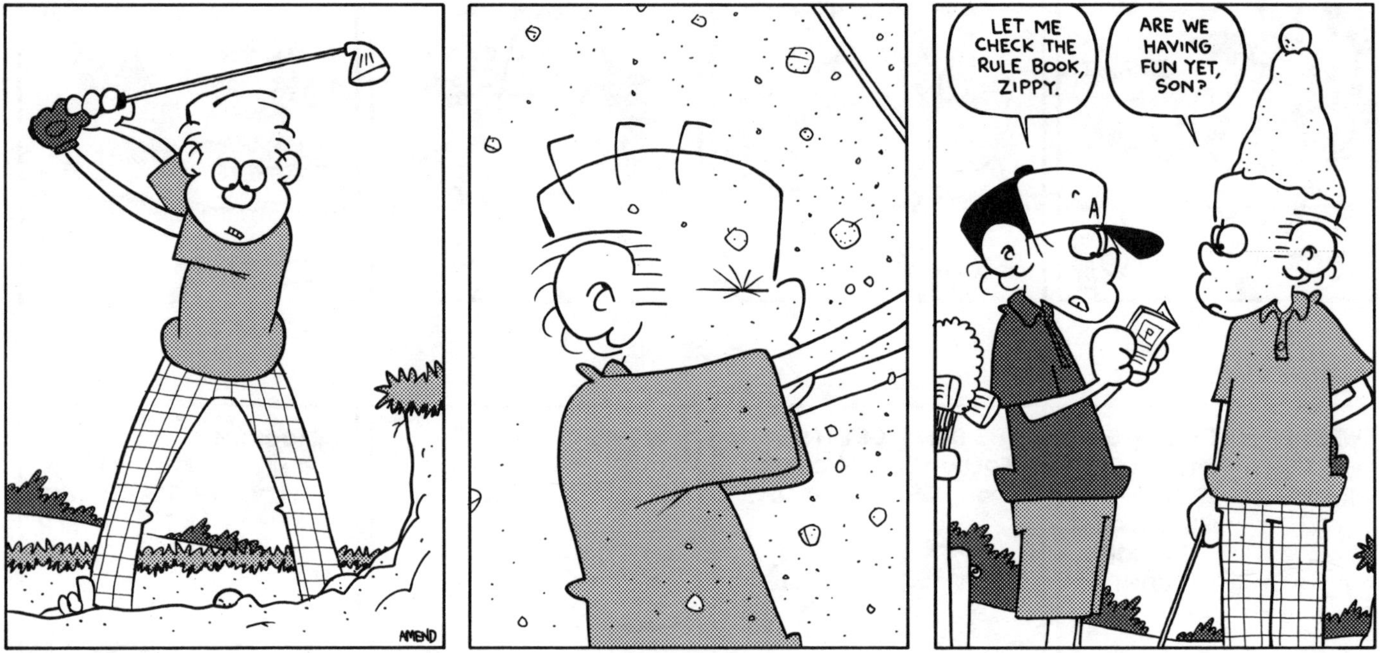
AMEND
LET ME CHECK THE RULE BOOK, ZIPPY.
ARE WE HAVING FUN YET, SON?

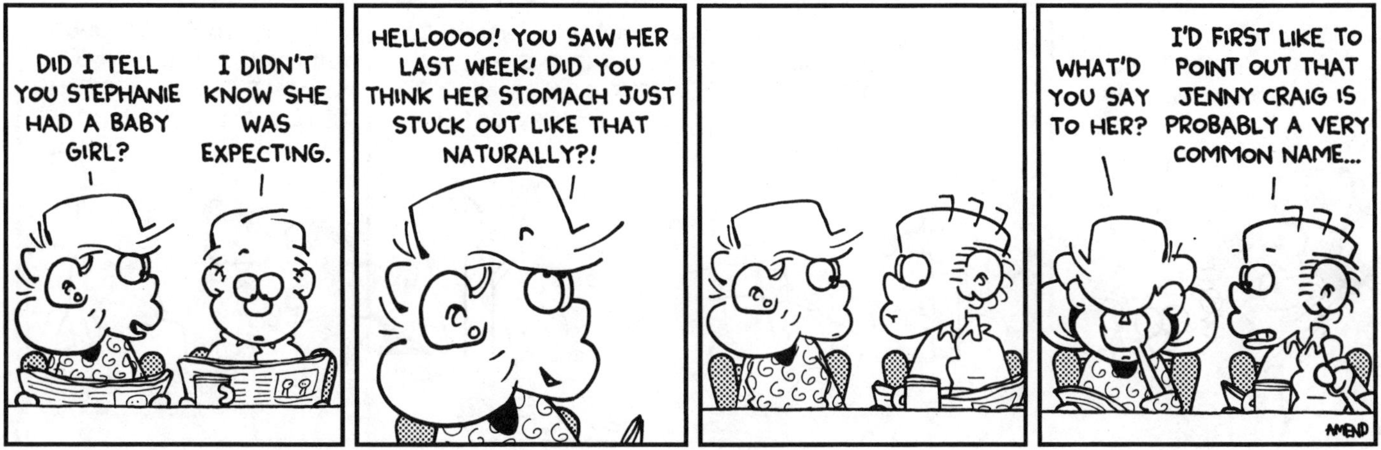
DID I TELL YOU STEPHANIE HAD A BABY GIRL?
I DIDN'T KNOW SHE WAS EXPECTING.
HELLOOOO! YOU SAW HER LAST WEEK! DID YOU THINK HER STOMACH JUST STUCK OUT LIKE THAT NATURALLY?!
WHAT'D YOU SAY TO HER?
I'D FIRST LIKE TO POINT OUT THAT JENNY CRAIG IS PROBABLY A VERY COMMON NAME...
AMEND

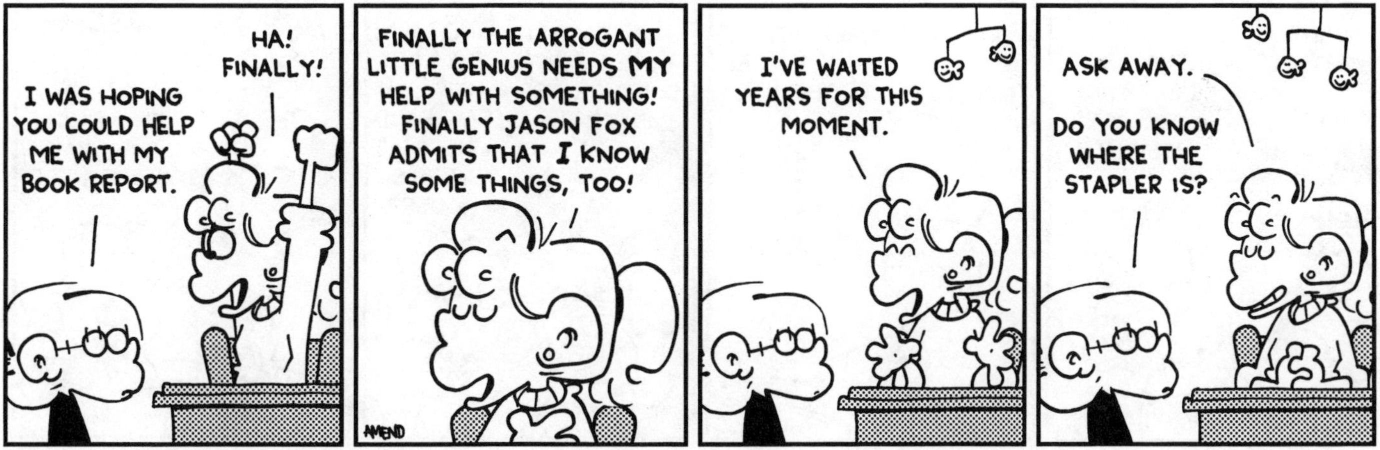
I WAS HOPING YOU COULD HELP ME WITH MY BOOK REPORT.
HA! FINALLY!
FINALLY THE ARROGANT LITTLE GENIUS NEEDS MY HELP WITH SOMETHING! FINALLY JASON FOX ADMITS THAT I KNOW SOME THINGS, TOO!
AMEND
I'VE WAITED YEARS FOR THIS MOMENT.
ASK AWAY.
DO YOU KNOW WHERE THE STAPLER IS?

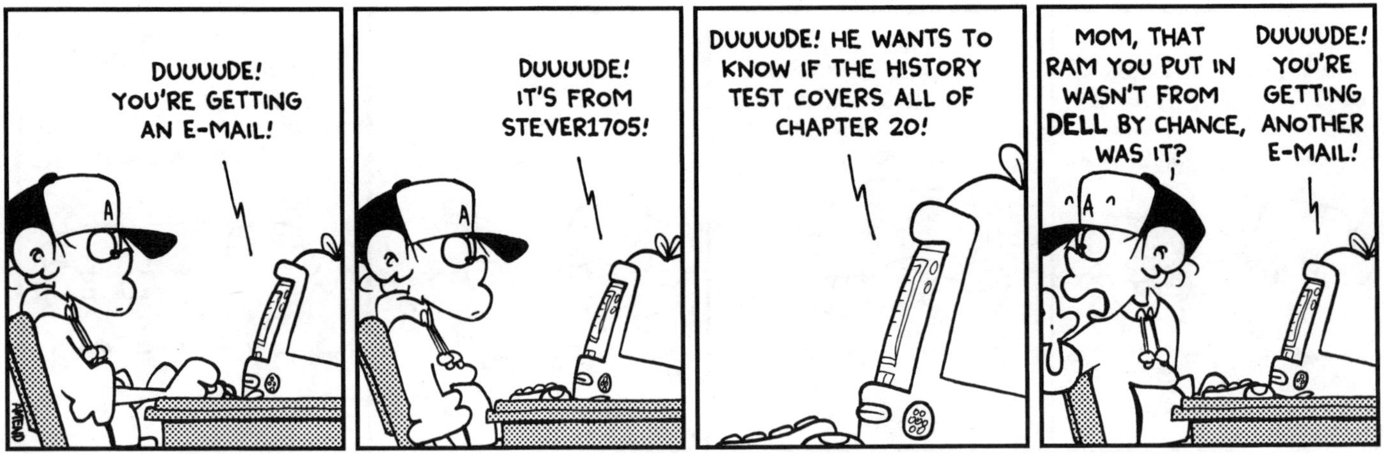
DUUUUDE! YOU'RE GETTING AN E-MAIL!
DUUUUDE! IT'S FROM STEVER1705!
DUUUUDE! HE WANTS TO KNOW IF THE HISTORY TEST COVERS ALL OF CHAPTER 20!
MOM, THAT RAM YOU PUT IN WASN'T FROM DELL BY CHANCE, WAS IT?
DUUUUDE! YOU'RE GETTING ANOTHER E-MAIL!

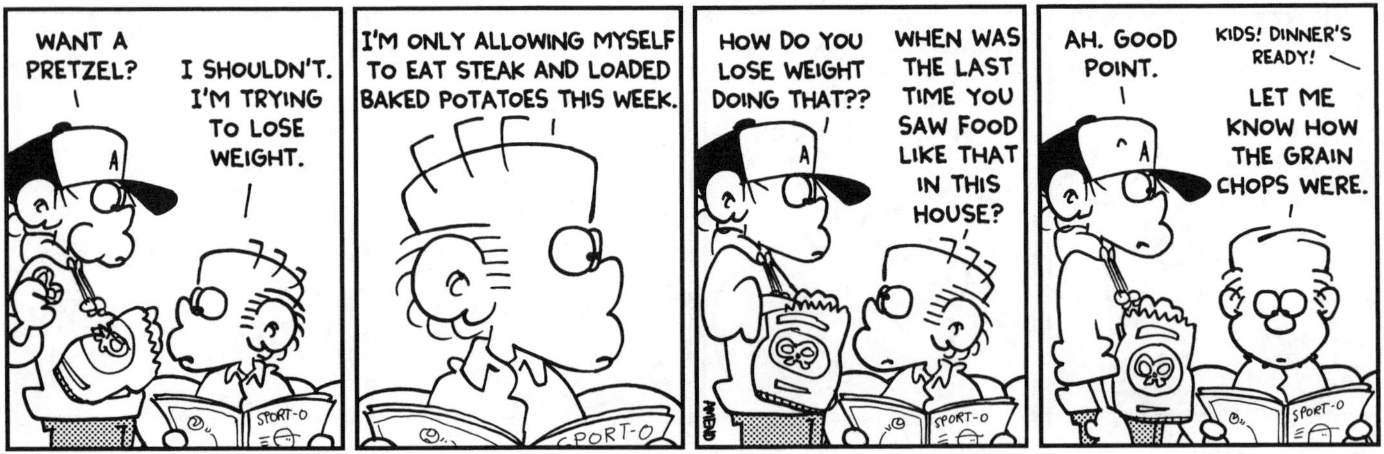
WANT A PRETZEL?
I SHOULDN'T. I'M TRYING TO LOSE WEIGHT.
SPORT-O
I'M ONLY ALLOWING MYSELF TO EAT STEAK AND LOADED BAKED POTATOES THIS WEEK.
SPORT-O
HOW DO YOU LOSE WEIGHT DOING THAT??
WHEN WAS THE LAST TIME YOU SAW FOOD LIKE THAT IN THIS HOUSE?
SPORT-O
AH. GOOD POINT.
KIDS! DINNER'S READY!
LET ME KNOW HOW THE GRAIN CHOPS WERE.
SPORT-O

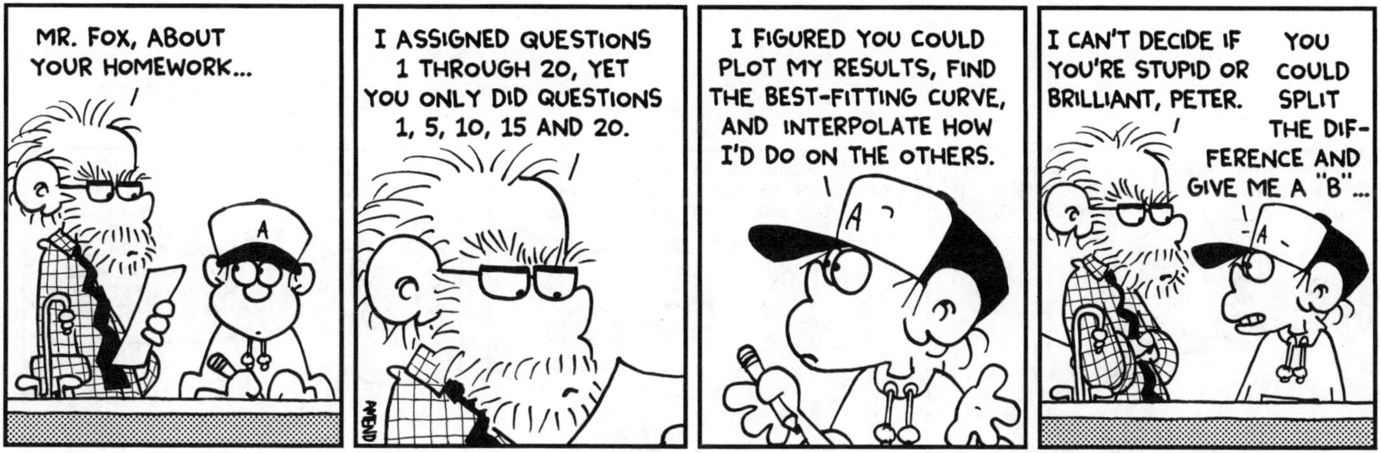
MR. FOX, ABOUT YOUR HOMEWORK...
I ASSIGNED QUESTIONS 1 THROUGH 20, YET YOU ONLY DID QUESTIONS 1, 5, 10, 15 AND 20.
I FIGURED YOU COULD PLOT MY RESULTS, FIND THE BEST-FITTING CURVE, AND INTERPOLATE HOW I'D DO ON THE OTHERS.
I CAN'T DECIDE IF YOU'RE STUPID OR BRILLIANT, PETER.
YOU COULD SPLIT THE DIF-FERENCE AND GIVE ME A "B"...
AMEND

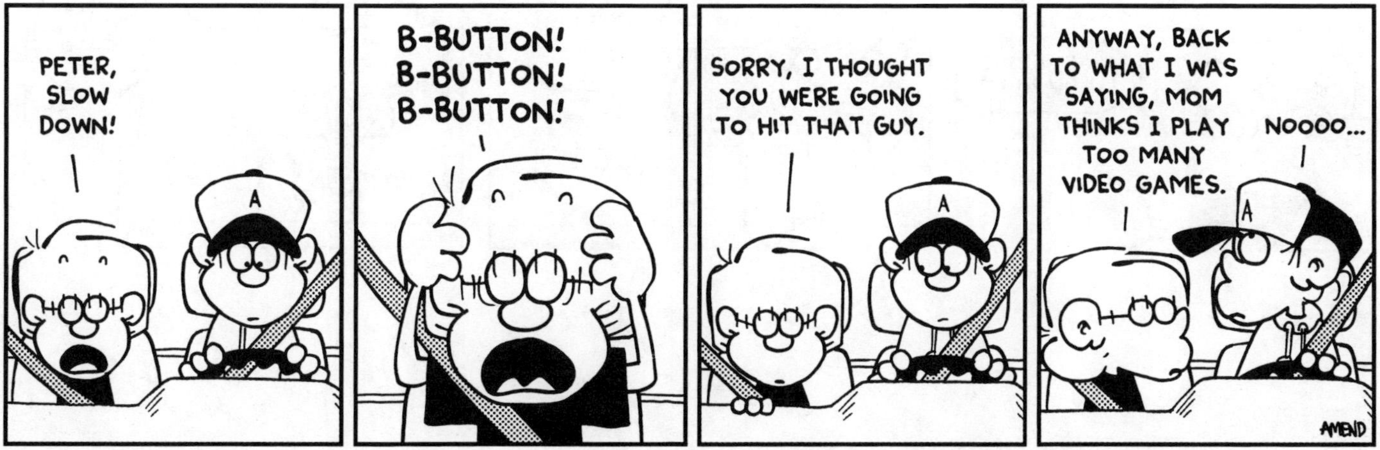
PETER, SLOW DOWN!
B-BUTTON! B-BUTTON! B-BUTTON!
SORRY, I THOUGHT YOU WERE GOING TO HIT THAT GUY.
ANYWAY, BACK TO WHAT I WAS SAYING, MOM THINKS I PLAY TOO MANY VIDEO GAMES.
NOOOO...
AMEND

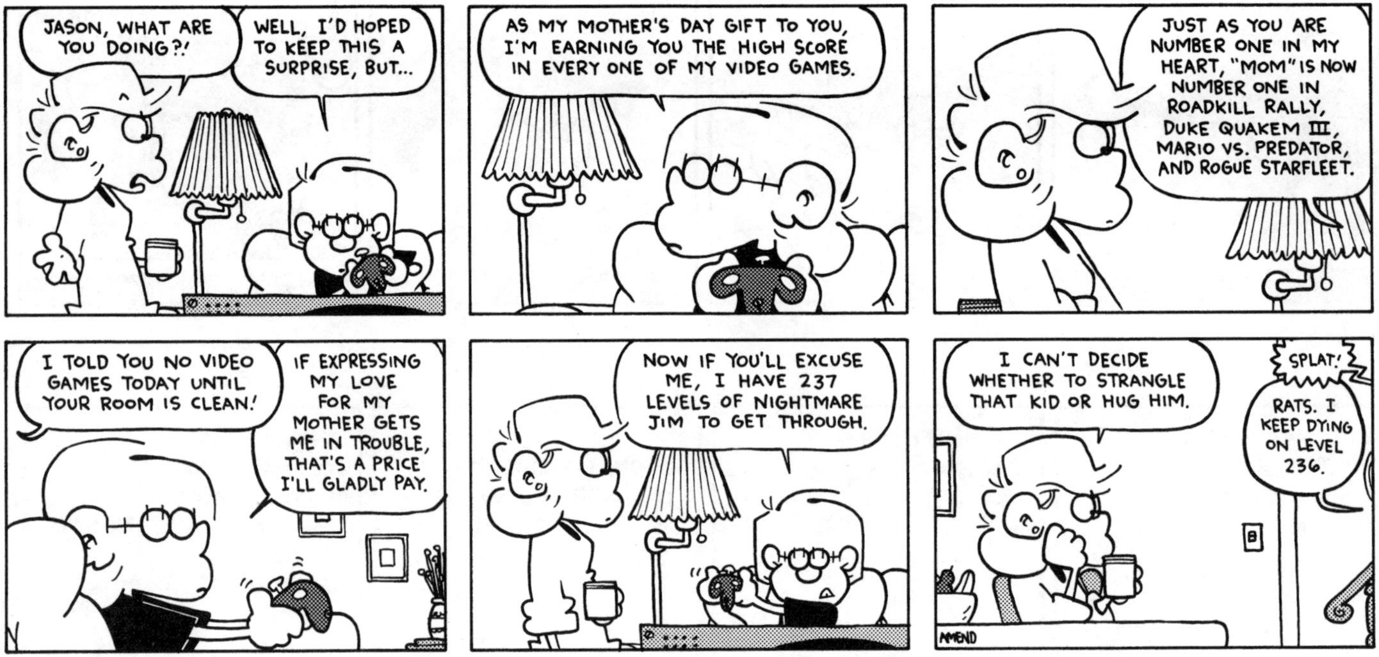

JASON, WHAT ARE YOU DOING?!
WELL, I'D HOPED TO KEEP THIS A SURPRISE, BUT...
AS MY MOTHER'S DAY GIFT TO YOU, I'M EARNING YOU THE HIGH SCORE IN EVERY ONE OF MY VIDEO GAMES.
JUST AS YOU ARE NUMBER ONE IN MY HEART, "MOM" IS NOW NUMBER ONE IN ROADKILL RALLY, DUKE QUAKEM III, MARIO VS. PREDATOR, AND ROGUE STARFLEET.
I TOLD YOU NO VIDEO GAMES TODAY UNTIL YOUR ROOM IS CLEAN!
IF EXPRESSING MY LOVE FOR MY MOTHER GETS ME IN TROUBLE, THAT'S A PRICE I'LL GLADLY PAY.
NOW IF YOU'LL EXCUSE ME, I HAVE 237 LEVELS OF NIGHTMARE JIM TO GET THROUGH.
I CAN'T DECIDE WHETHER TO STRANGLE THAT KID OR HUG HIM.
SPLAT!
RATS. I KEEP DYING ON LEVEL 236.
AMEND

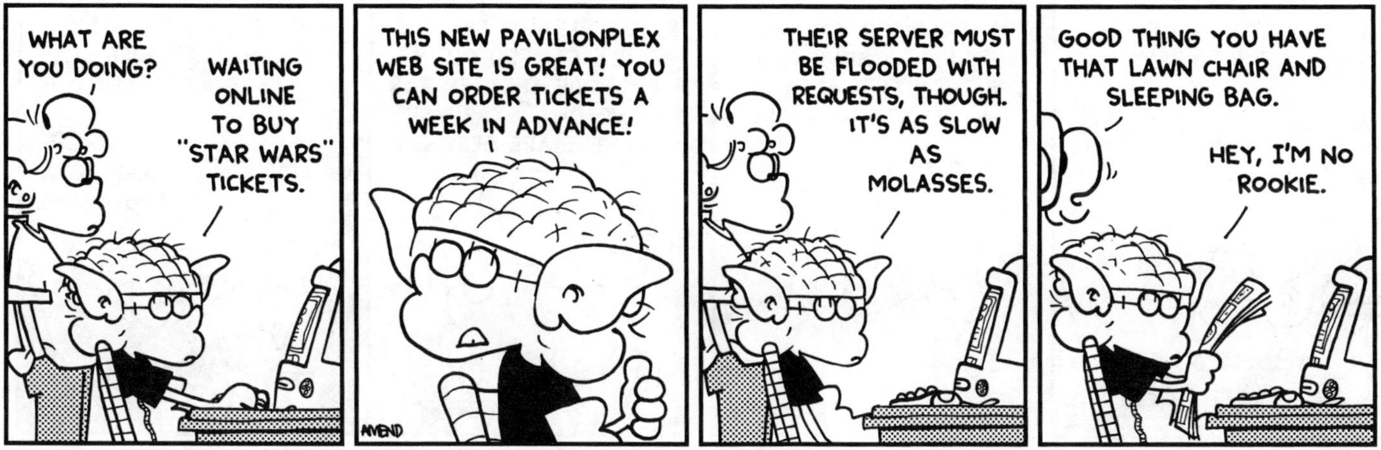
WHAT ARE YOU DOING?
WAITING ONLINE TO BUY "STAR WARS" TICKETS.
THIS NEW PAVILIONPLEX WEB SITE IS GREAT! YOU CAN ORDER TICKETS A WEEK IN ADVANCE!
AMEND
THEIR SERVER MUST BE FLOODED WITH REQUESTS, THOUGH. IT'S AS SLOW AS MOLASSES.
GOOD THING YOU HAVE THAT LAWN CHAIR AND SLEEPING BAG.
HEY, I'M NO ROOKIE.

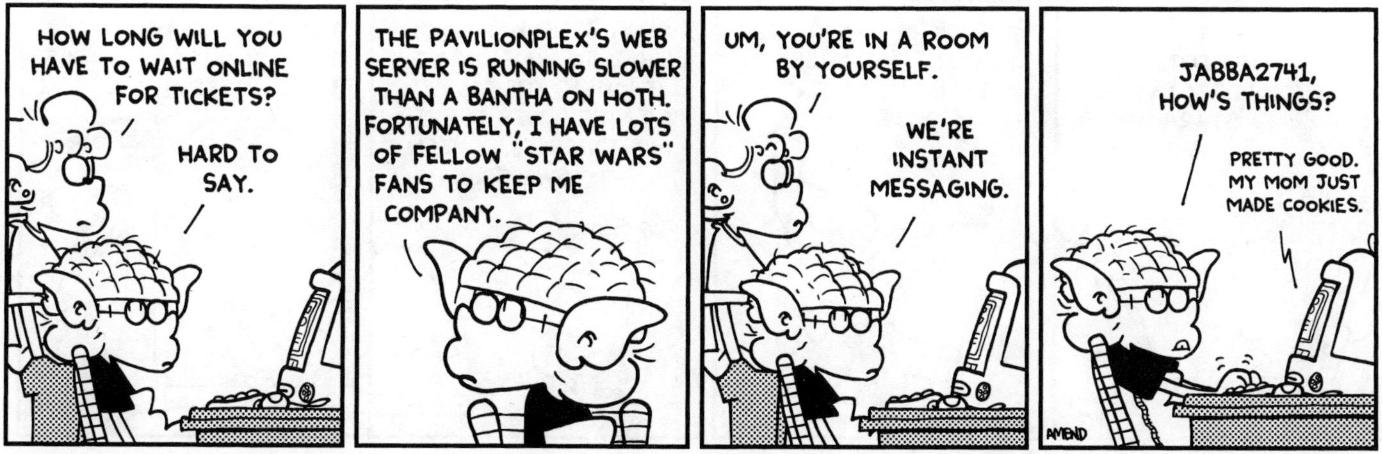
HOW LONG WILL YOU HAVE TO WAIT ONLINE FOR TICKETS?
HARD TO SAY.
THE PAVILIONPLEX'S WEB SERVER IS RUNNING SLOWER THAN A BANTHA ON HOTH. FORTUNATELY, I HAVE LOTS OF FELLOW "STAR WARS" FANS TO KEEP ME COMPANY.
UM, YOU'RE IN A ROOM BY YOURSELF.
WE'RE INSTANT MESSAGING.
JABBA2741, HOW'S THINGS?
PRETTY GOOD. MY MOM JUST MADE COOKIES.
AMEND

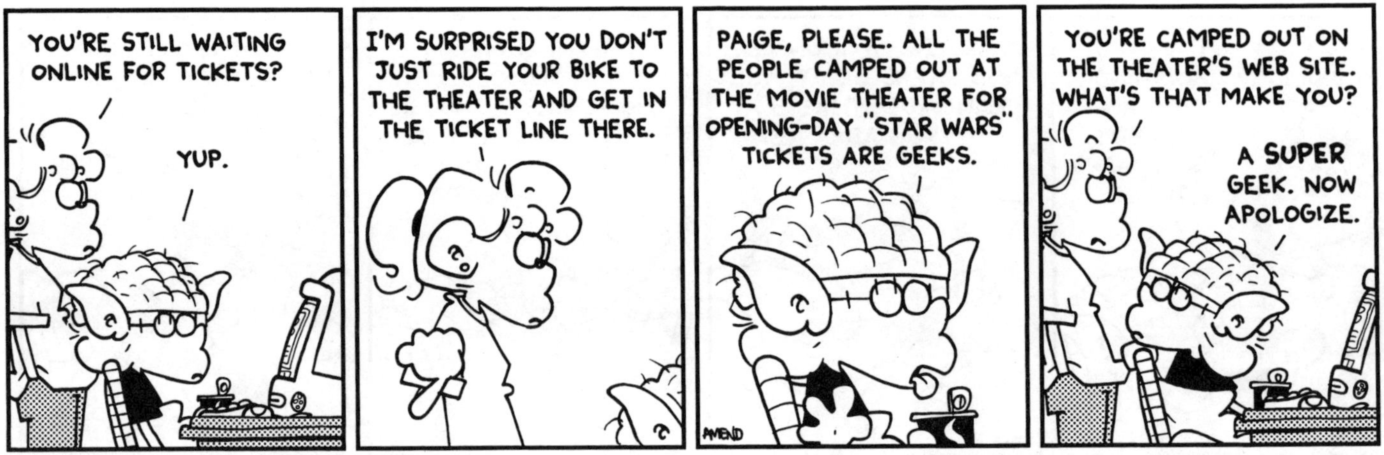
YOU'RE STILL WAITING ONLINE FOR TICKETS?
YUP.
I'M SURPRISED YOU DON'T JUST RIDE YOUR BIKE TO THE THEATER AND GET IN THE TICKET LINE THERE.
PAIGE, PLEASE. ALL THE PEOPLE CAMPED OUT AT THE MOVIE THEATER FOR OPENING-DAY "STAR WARS" TICKETS ARE GEEKS.
AMEND
YOU'RE CAMPED OUT ON THE THEATER'S WEB SITE. WHAT'S THAT MAKE YOU?
A **SUPER** GEEK. NOW APOLOGIZE.

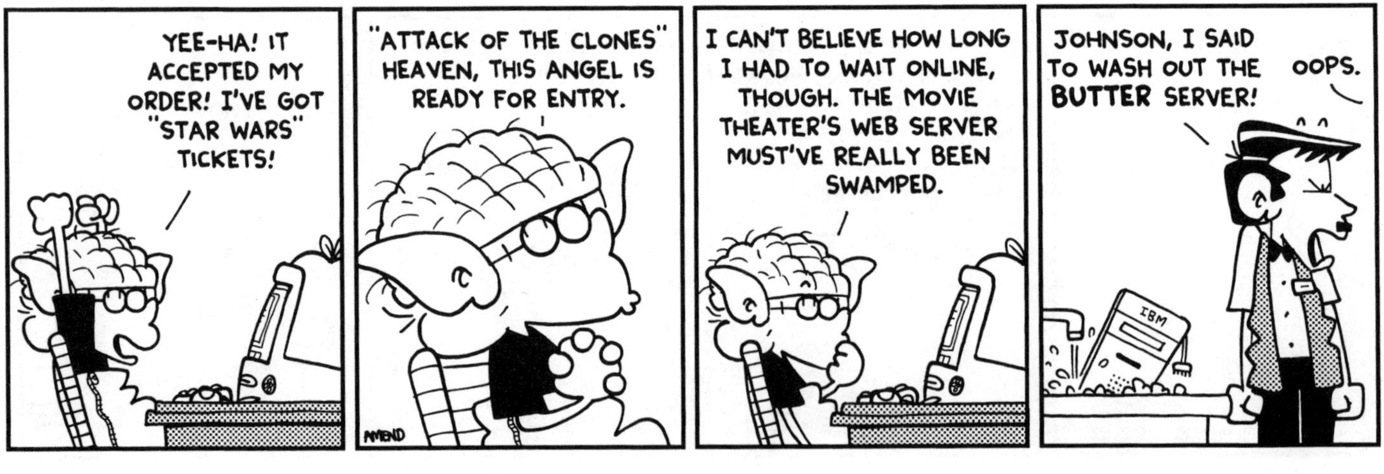
YEE-HA! IT ACCEPTED MY ORDER! I'VE GOT "STAR WARS" TICKETS!
"ATTACK OF THE CLONES" HEAVEN, THIS ANGEL IS READY FOR ENTRY.
AMEND
I CAN'T BELIEVE HOW LONG I HAD TO WAIT ONLINE, THOUGH. THE MOVIE THEATER'S WEB SERVER MUST'VE REALLY BEEN SWAMPED.
JOHNSON, I SAID TO WASH OUT THE **BUTTER** SERVER!
OOPS.
IBM

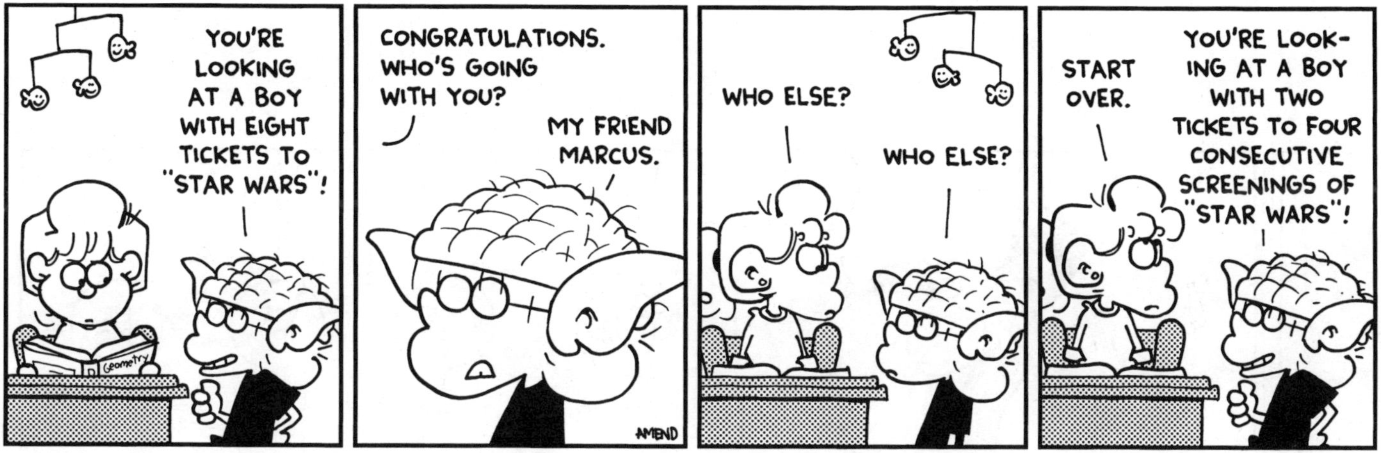
YOU'RE LOOKING AT A BOY WITH EIGHT TICKETS TO "STAR WARS"!
Geometry
CONGRATULATIONS. WHO'S GOING WITH YOU?
MY FRIEND MARCUS.
AMEND
WHO ELSE?
WHO ELSE?
START OVER.
YOU'RE LOOK-ING AT A BOY WITH TWO TICKETS TO FOUR CONSECUTIVE SCREENINGS OF "STAR WARS"!

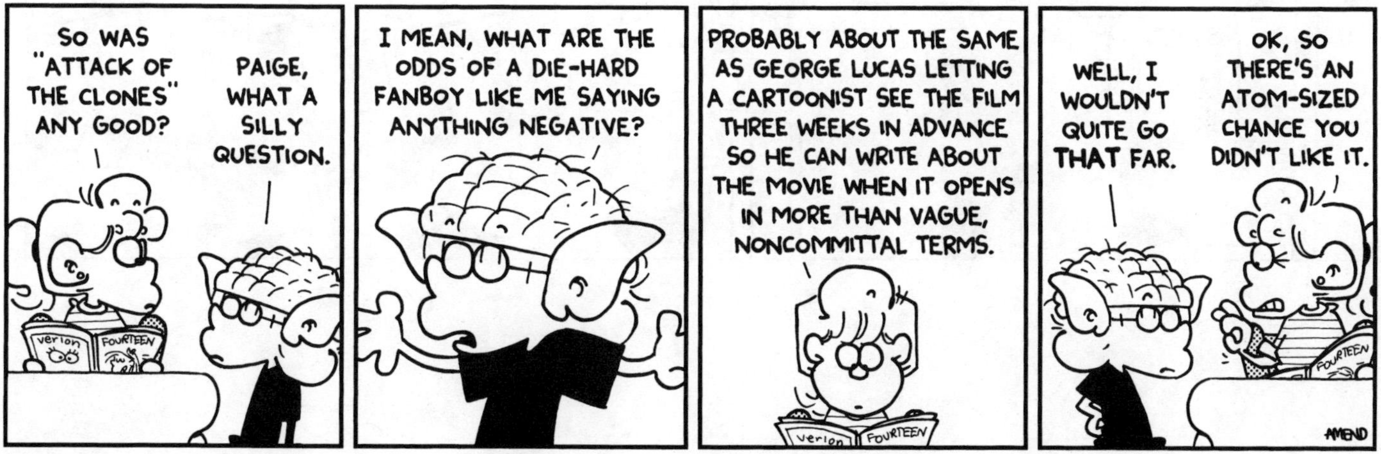
SO WAS "ATTACK OF THE CLONES" ANY GOOD?
PAIGE, WHAT A SILLY QUESTION.
I MEAN, WHAT ARE THE ODDS OF A DIE-HARD FANBOY LIKE ME SAYING ANYTHING NEGATIVE?
PROBABLY ABOUT THE SAME AS GEORGE LUCAS LETTING A CARTOONIST SEE THE FILM THREE WEEKS IN ADVANCE SO HE CAN WRITE ABOUT THE MOVIE WHEN IT OPENS IN MORE THAN VAGUE, NONCOMMITTAL TERMS.
WELL, I WOULDN'T QUITE GO THAT FAR.
OK, SO THERE'S AN ATOM-SIZED CHANCE YOU DIDN'T LIKE IT.
AMEND

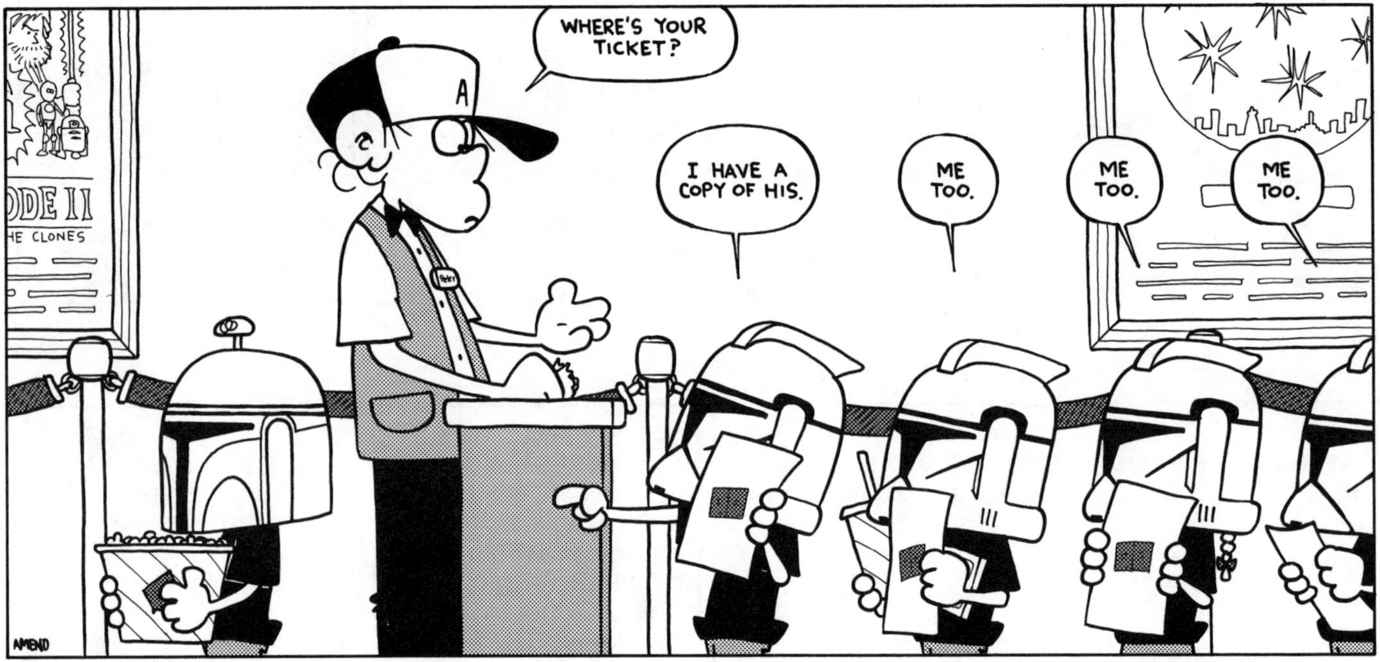
ODE II
HE CLONES
WHERE'S YOUR TICKET?
I HAVE A COPY OF HIS.
ME TOO.
ME TOO.
ME TOO.
AMEND

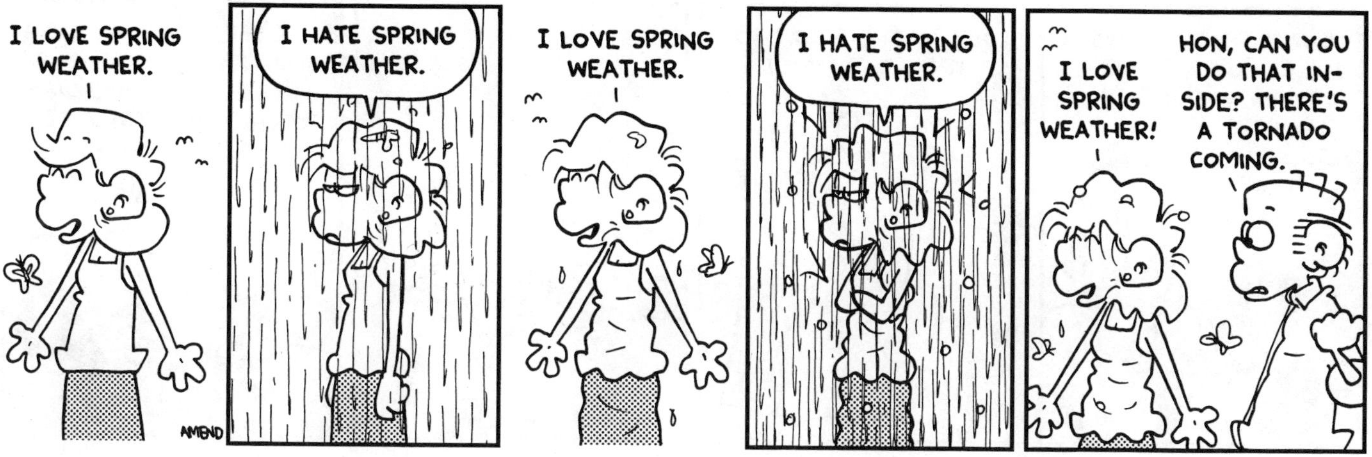
I LOVE SPRING WEATHER.
AMEND
I HATE SPRING WEATHER.
I LOVE SPRING WEATHER.
I HATE SPRING WEATHER.
I LOVE SPRING WEATHER!
HON, CAN YOU DO THAT IN-SIDE? THERE'S A TORNADO COMING.

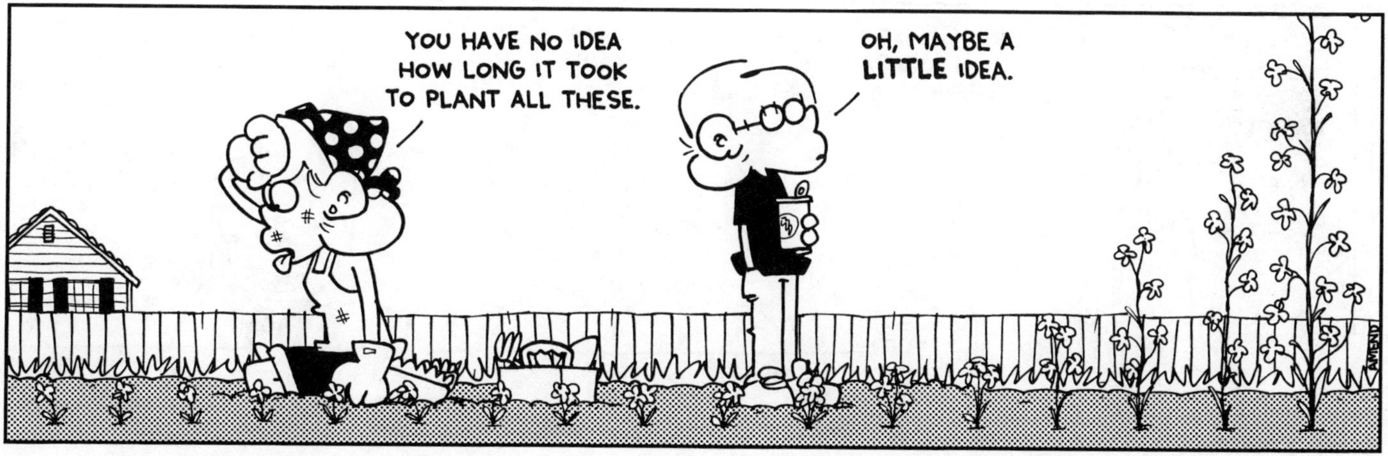
YOU HAVE NO IDEA HOW LONG IT TOOK TO PLANT ALL THESE.
OH, MAYBE A **LITTLE** IDEA.
AMEND

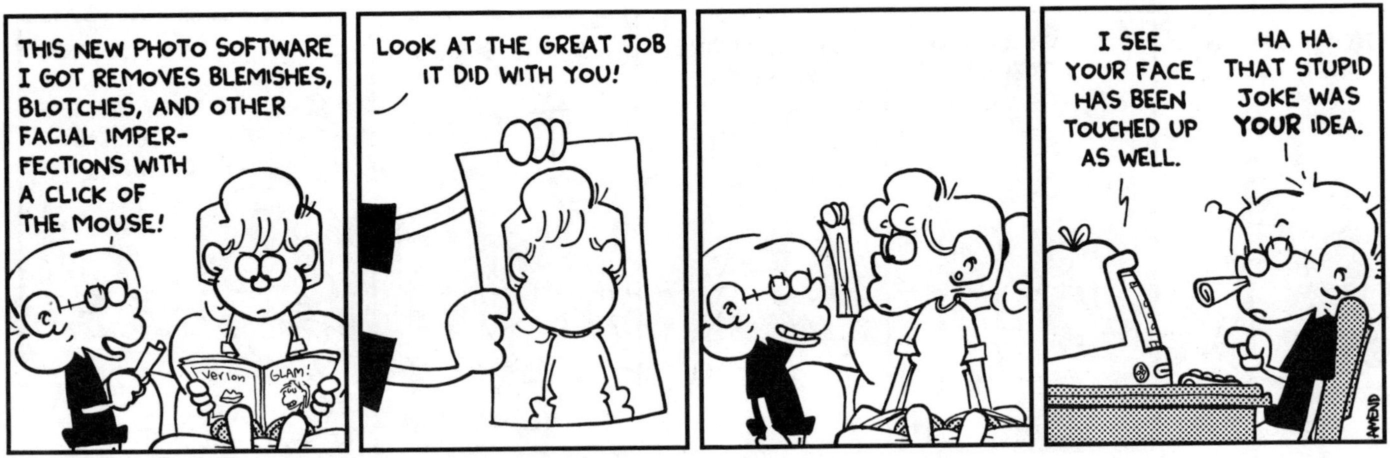
THIS NEW PHOTO SOFTWARE I GOT REMOVES BLEMISHES, BLOTCHES, AND OTHER FACIAL IMPERFECTIONS WITH A CLICK OF THE MOUSE!
Verlon
GLAM!
LOOK AT THE GREAT JOB IT DID WITH YOU!
I SEE YOUR FACE HAS BEEN TOUCHED UP AS WELL.
HA HA. THAT STUPID JOKE WAS YOUR IDEA.
AMEND

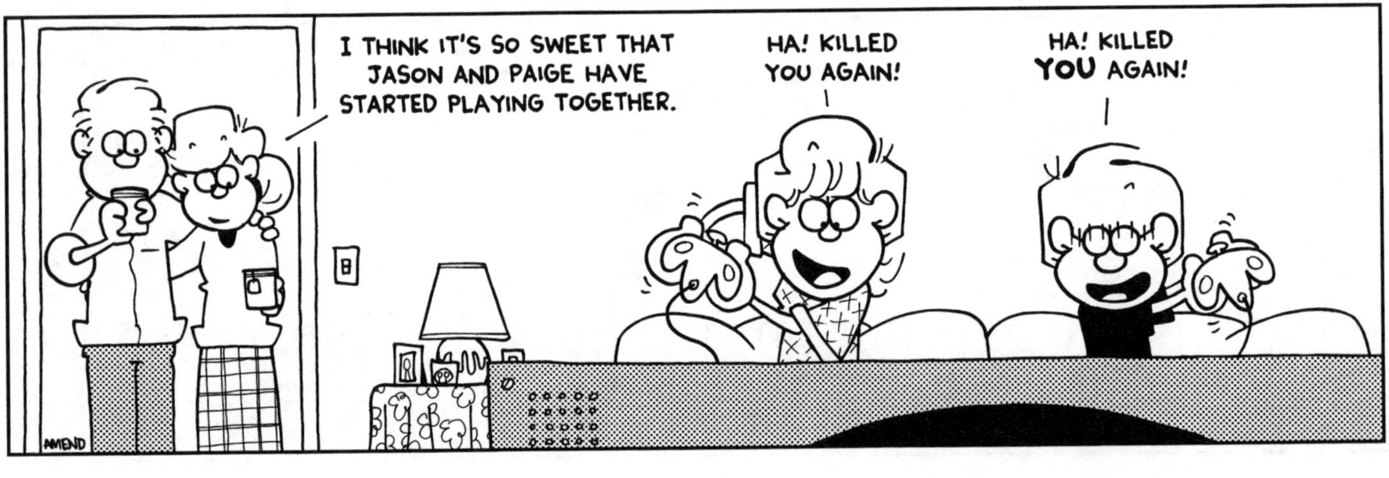
I THINK IT'S SO SWEET THAT JASON AND PAIGE HAVE STARTED PLAYING TOGETHER.
HA! KILLED YOU AGAIN!
HA! KILLED YOU AGAIN!
AMEND

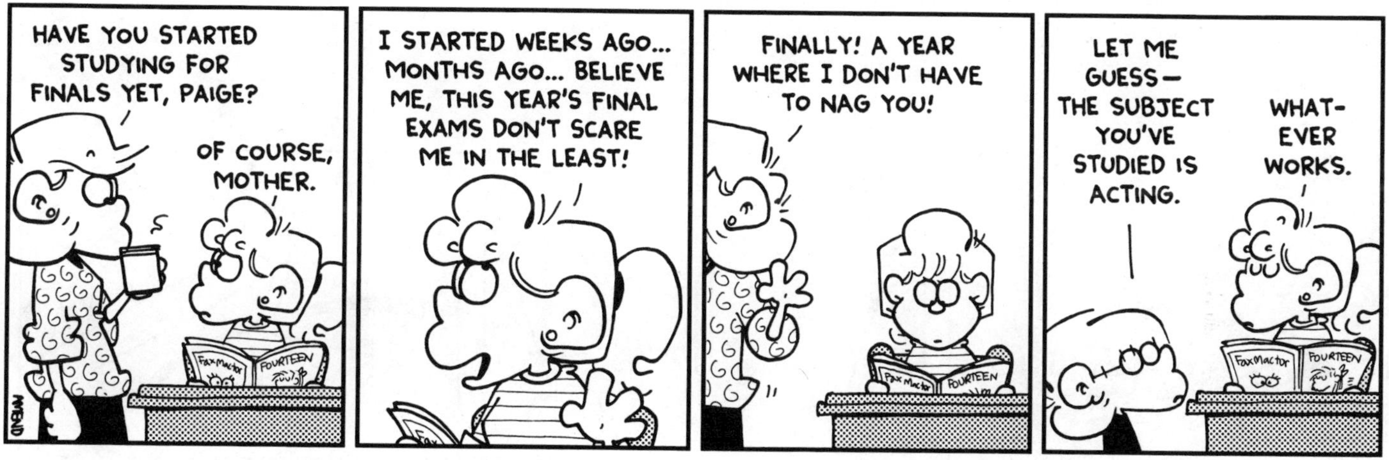
HAVE YOU STARTED STUDYING FOR FINALS YET, PAIGE?
OF COURSE, MOTHER.
I STARTED WEEKS AGO... MONTHS AGO... BELIEVE ME, THIS YEAR'S FINAL EXAMS DON'T SCARE ME IN THE LEAST!
FINALLY! A YEAR WHERE I DON'T HAVE TO NAG YOU!
LET ME GUESS— THE SUBJECT YOU'VE STUDIED IS ACTING.
WHAT-EVER WORKS.

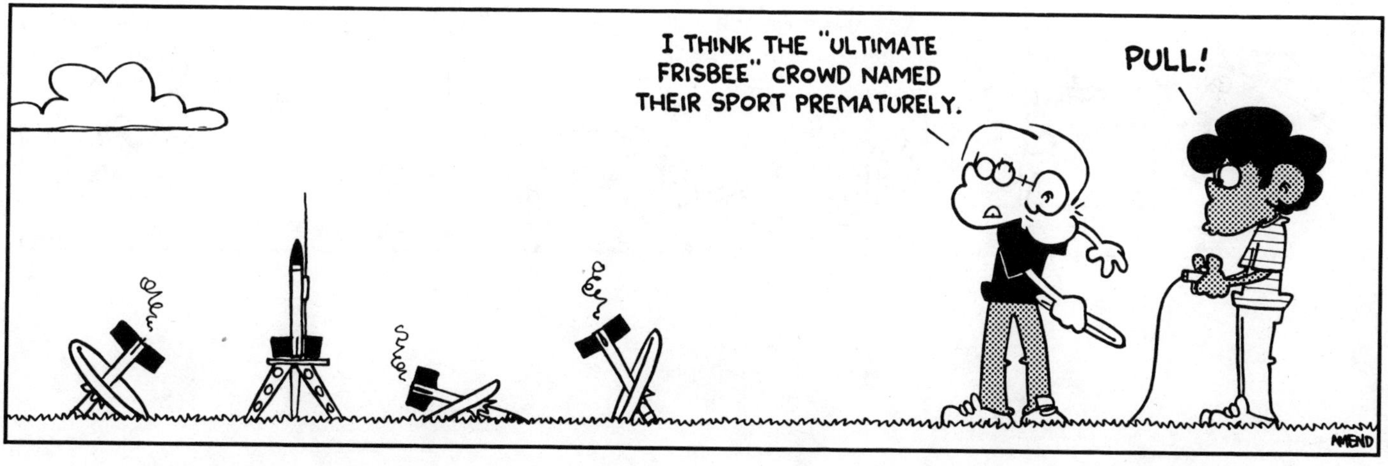
I THINK THE "ULTIMATE FRISBEE" CROWD NAMED THEIR SPORT PREMATURELY.
PULL!

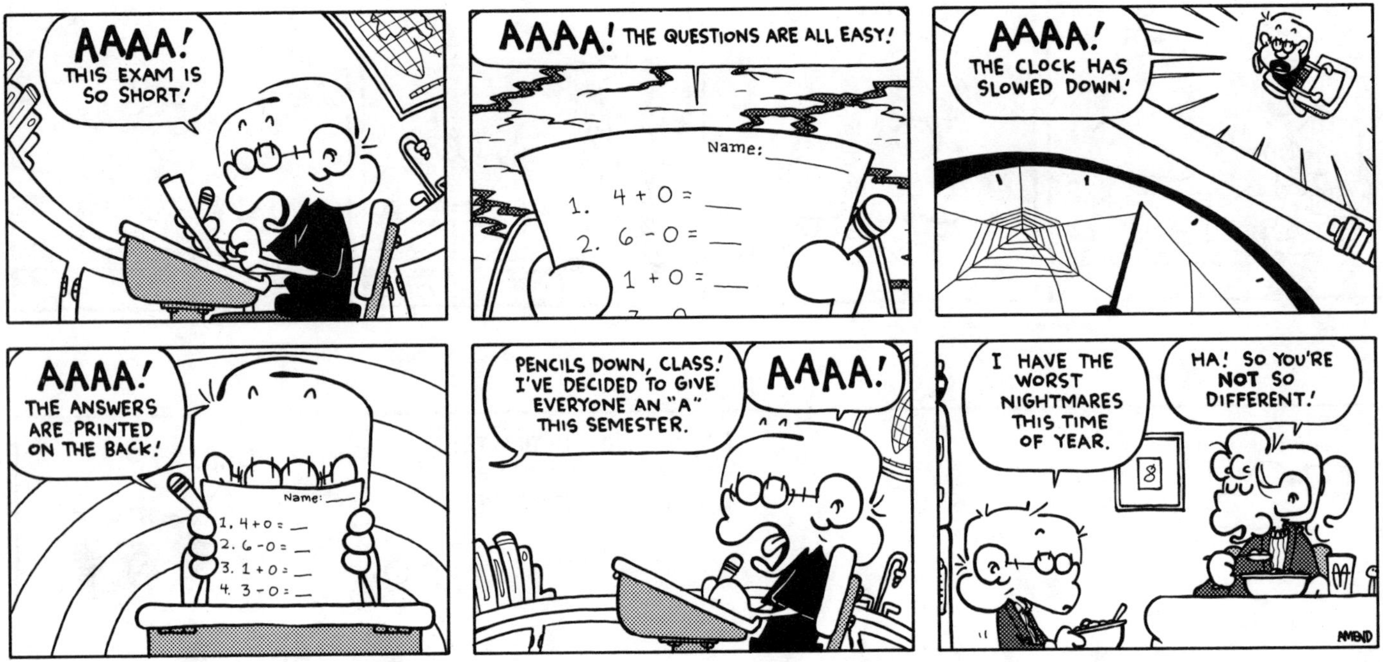
AAAA! THIS EXAM IS SO SHORT!
AAAA! THE QUESTIONS ARE ALL EASY!
Name:
1. 4 + 0 =
2. 6 - 0 =
1 + 0 =
AAAA! THE CLOCK HAS SLOWED DOWN!
AAAA! THE ANSWERS ARE PRINTED ON THE BACK!
Name:
1. 4 + 0 =
2. 6 - 0 =
3. 1 + 0 =
4. 3 - 0 =
PENCILS DOWN, CLASS! I'VE DECIDED TO GIVE EVERYONE AN "A" THIS SEMESTER.
AAAA!
I HAVE THE WORST NIGHTMARES THIS TIME OF YEAR.
HA! SO YOU'RE **NOT** SO DIFFERENT!
AMEND

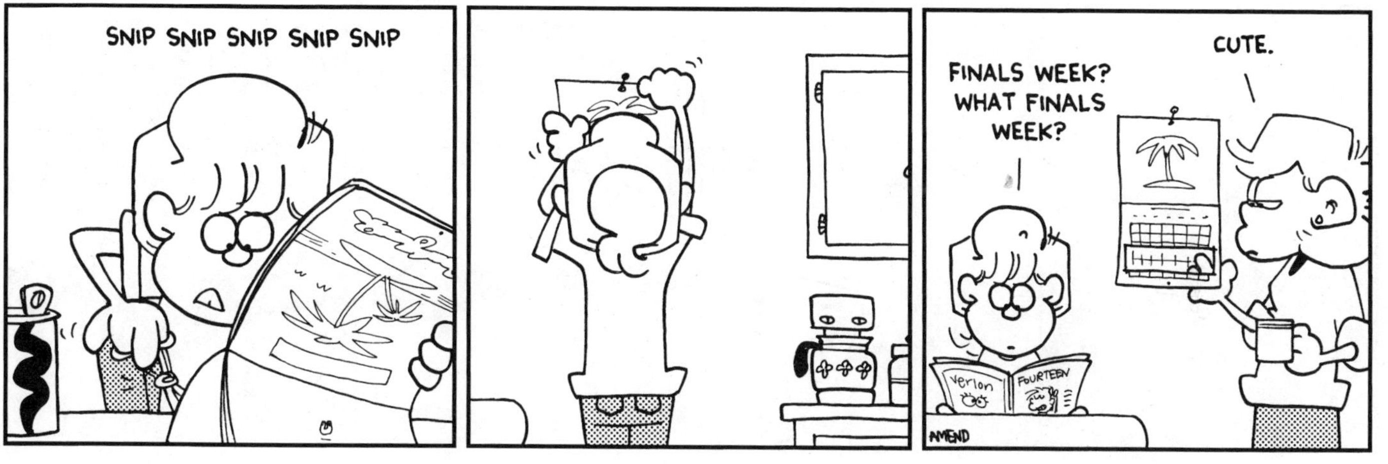
SNIP SNIP SNIP SNIP SNIP
FINALS WEEK? WHAT FINALS WEEK?
CUTE.
Verlon
FOURTEEN
AMEND

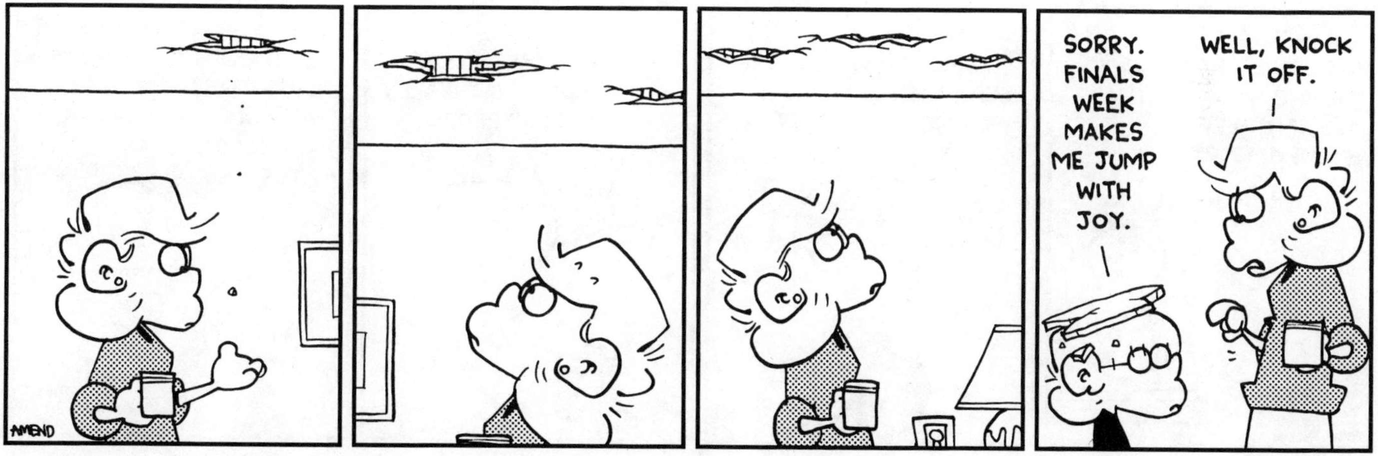
AMEND
SORRY. FINALS WEEK MAKES ME JUMP WITH JOY.
WELL, KNOCK IT OFF.

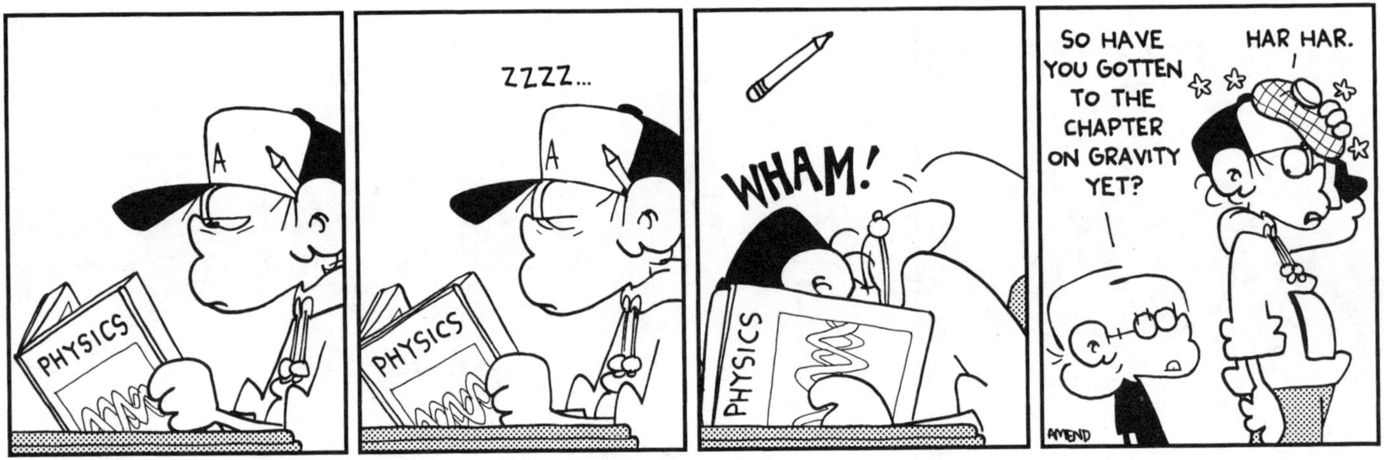
ZZZZ...
WHAM!
PHYSICS
SO HAVE YOU GOTTEN TO THE CHAPTER ON GRAVITY YET?
HAR HAR.
AMEND

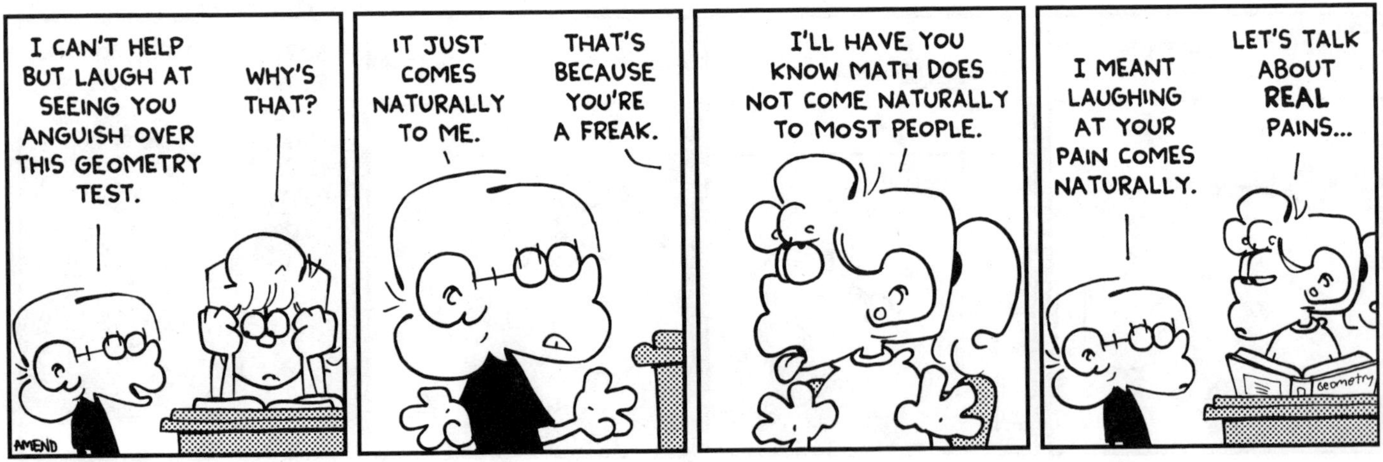
I CAN'T HELP BUT LAUGH AT SEEING YOU ANGUISH OVER THIS GEOMETRY TEST.
WHY'S THAT?
IT JUST COMES NATURALLY TO ME.
THAT'S BECAUSE YOU'RE A FREAK.
I'LL HAVE YOU KNOW MATH DOES NOT COME NATURALLY TO MOST PEOPLE.
I MEANT LAUGHING AT YOUR PAIN COMES NATURALLY.
LET'S TALK ABOUT **REAL** PAINS...
AMEND

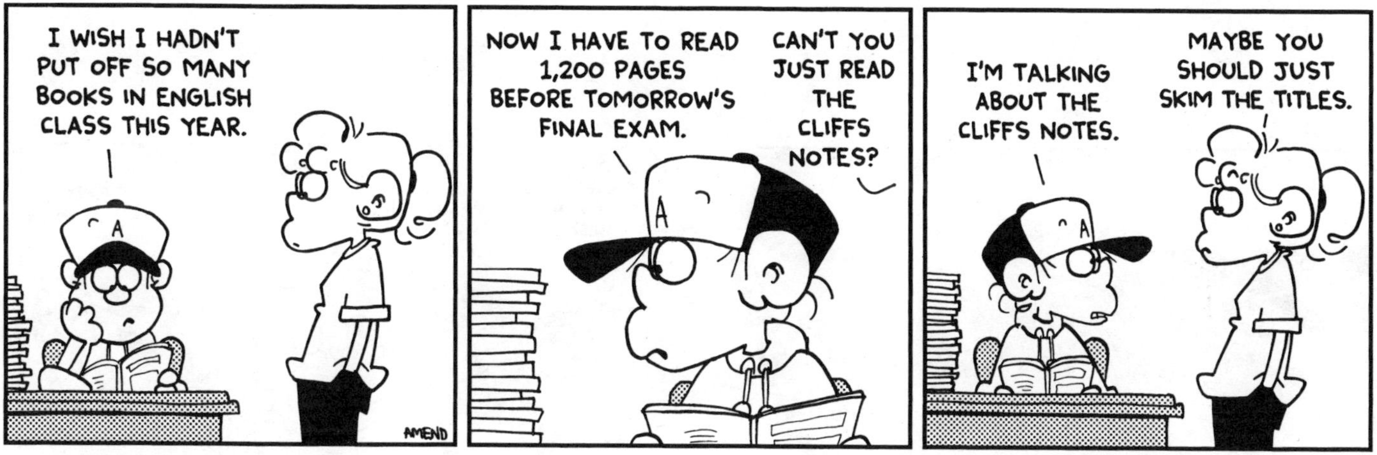
I WISH I HADN'T PUT OFF SO MANY BOOKS IN ENGLISH CLASS THIS YEAR.
NOW I HAVE TO READ 1,200 PAGES BEFORE TOMORROW'S FINAL EXAM.
CAN'T YOU JUST READ THE CLIFFS NOTES?
I'M TALKING ABOUT THE CLIFFS NOTES.
MAYBE YOU SHOULD JUST SKIM THE TITLES.
AMEND

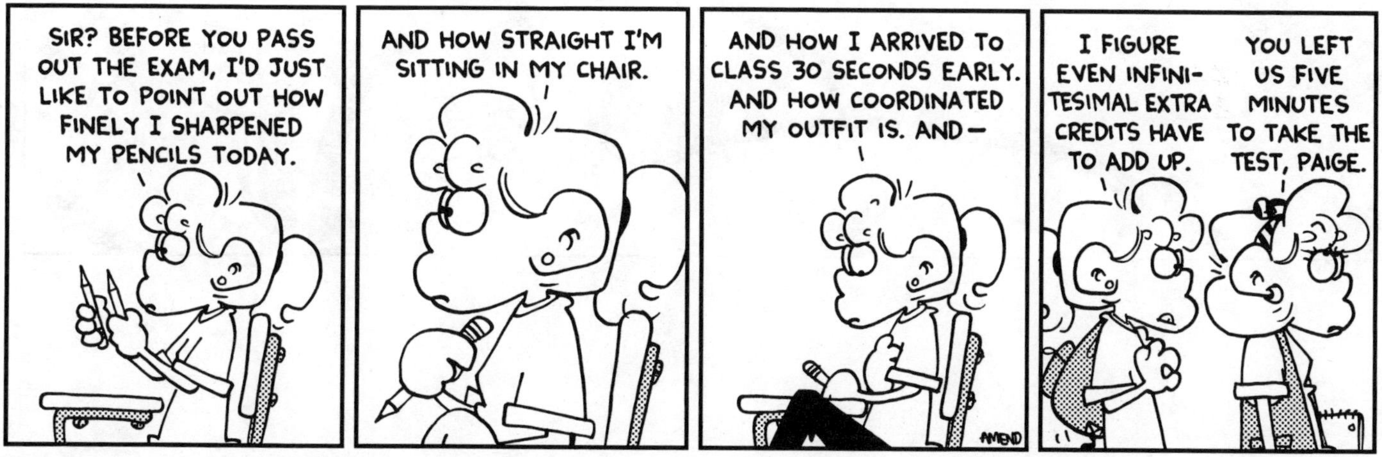
SIR? BEFORE YOU PASS OUT THE EXAM, I'D JUST LIKE TO POINT OUT HOW FINELY I SHARPENED MY PENCILS TODAY.
AND HOW STRAIGHT I'M SITTING IN MY CHAIR.
AND HOW I ARRIVED TO CLASS 30 SECONDS EARLY. AND HOW COORDINATED MY OUTFIT IS. AND—
AMEND
I FIGURE EVEN INFINITESIMAL EXTRA CREDITS HAVE TO ADD UP.
YOU LEFT US FIVE MINUTES TO TAKE THE TEST, PAIGE.

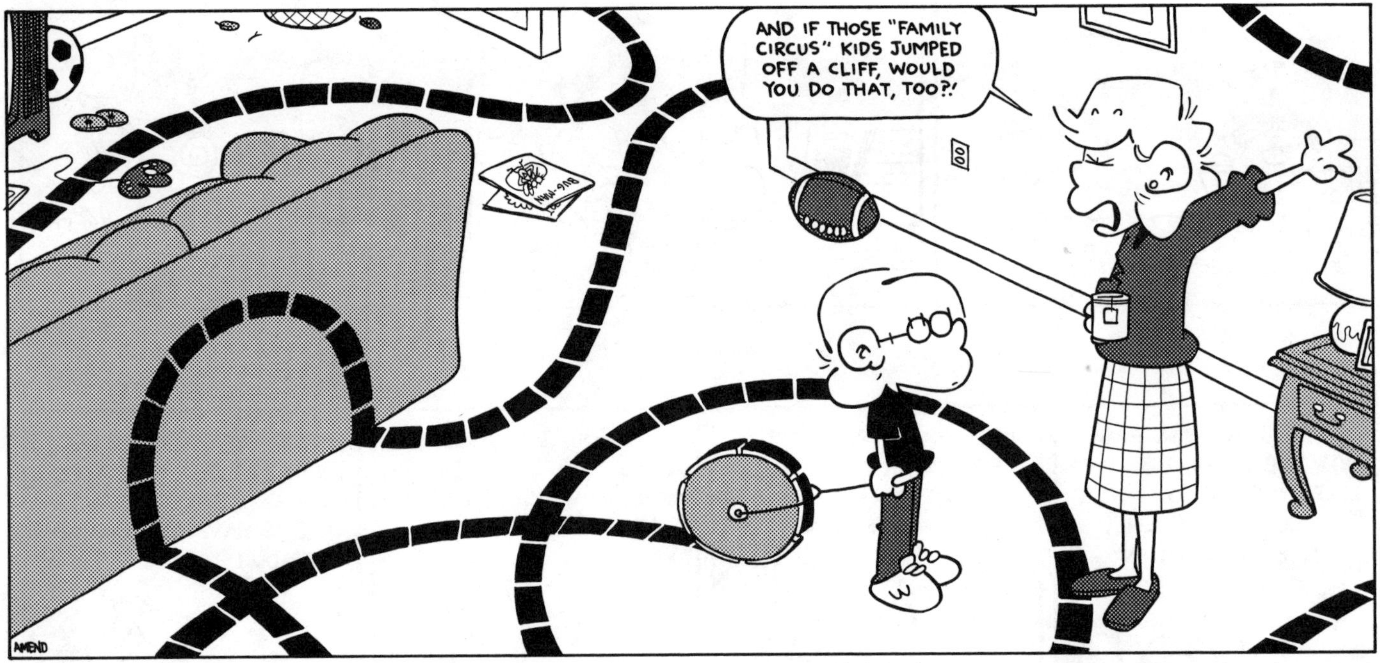
AND IF THOSE "FAMILY CIRCUS" KIDS JUMPED OFF A CLIFF, WOULD YOU DO THAT, TOO?!
BUG-MAN
AMEND

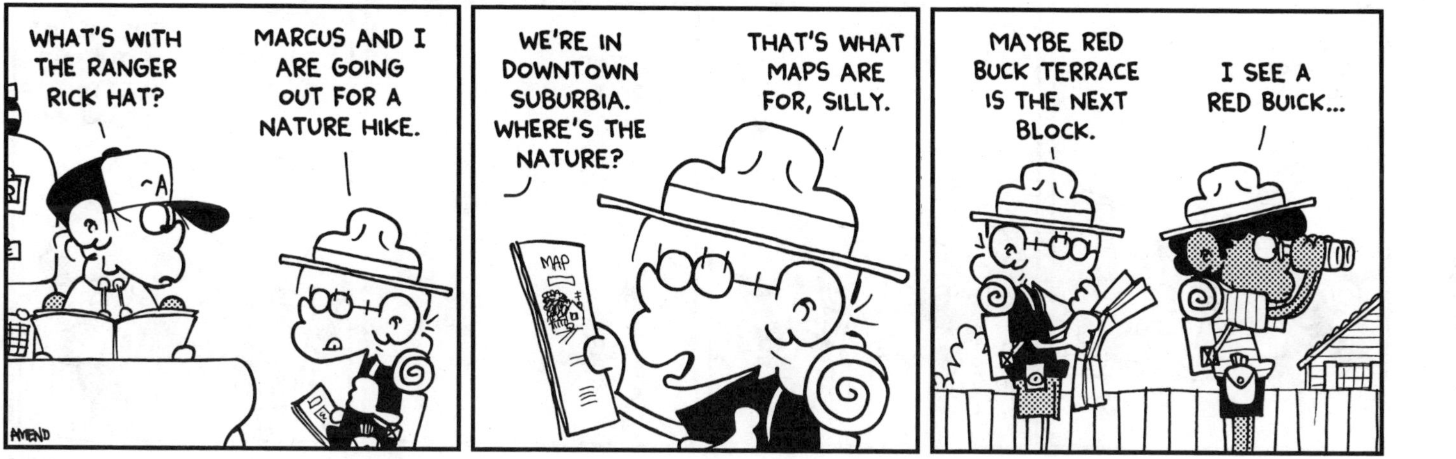
WHAT'S WITH THE RANGER RICK HAT?
MARCUS AND I ARE GOING OUT FOR A NATURE HIKE.
AMEND
WE'RE IN DOWNTOWN SUBURBIA. WHERE'S THE NATURE?
THAT'S WHAT MAPS ARE FOR, SILLY.
MAP
MAYBE RED BUCK TERRACE IS THE NEXT BLOCK.
I SEE A RED BUICK...

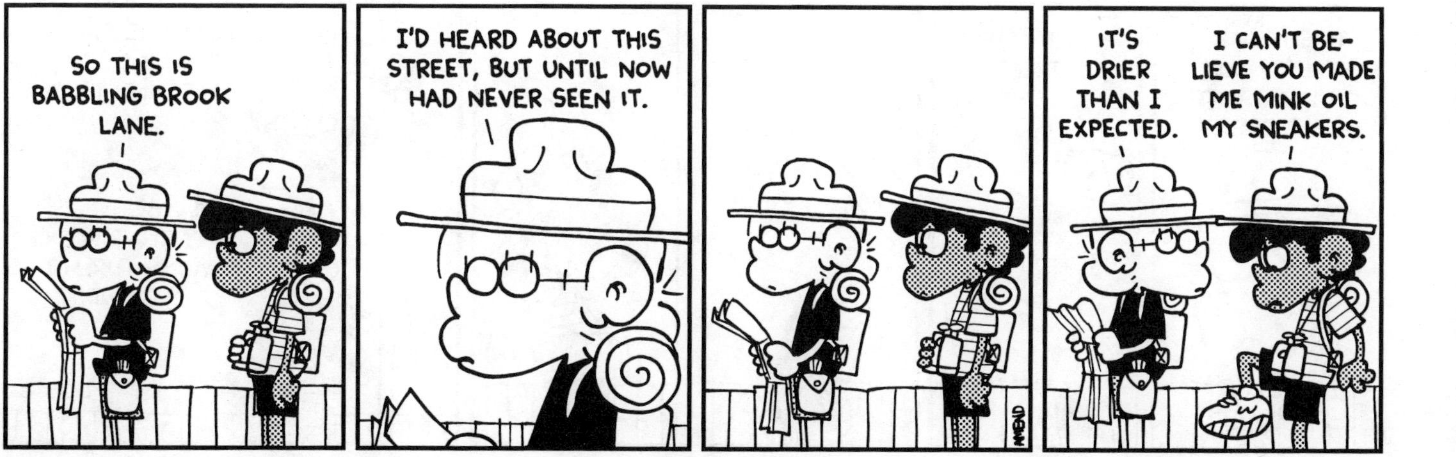
SO THIS IS BABBLING BROOK LANE.
I'D HEARD ABOUT THIS STREET, BUT UNTIL NOW HAD NEVER SEEN IT.
AMEND
IT'S DRIER THAN I EXPECTED.
I CAN'T BE-LIEVE YOU MADE ME MINK OIL MY SNEAKERS.

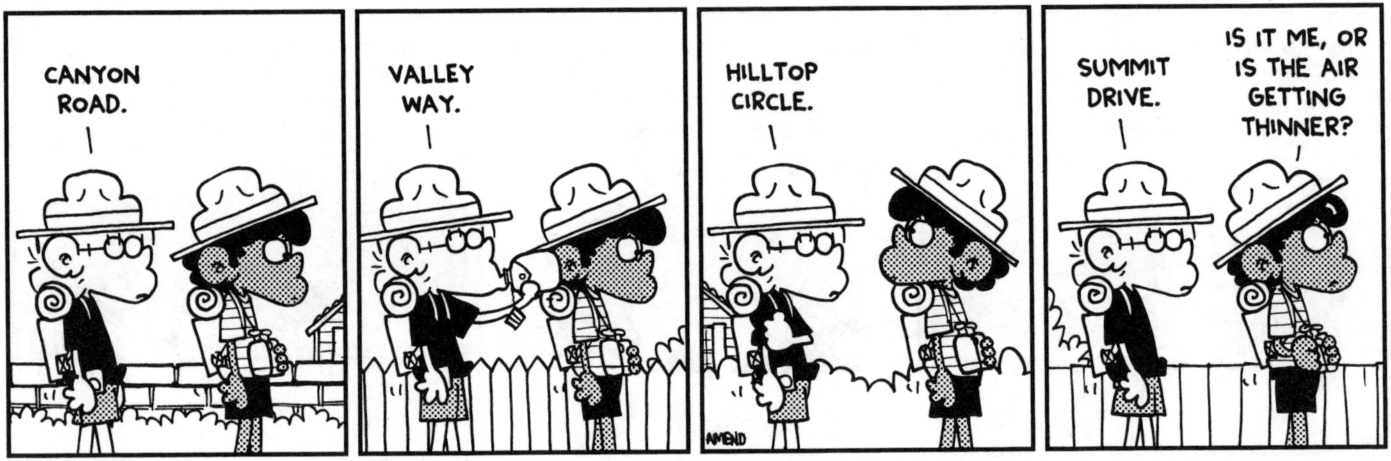
CANYON ROAD.
VALLEY WAY.
HILLTOP CIRCLE.
AMEND
SUMMIT DRIVE.
IS IT ME, OR IS THE AIR GETTING THINNER?

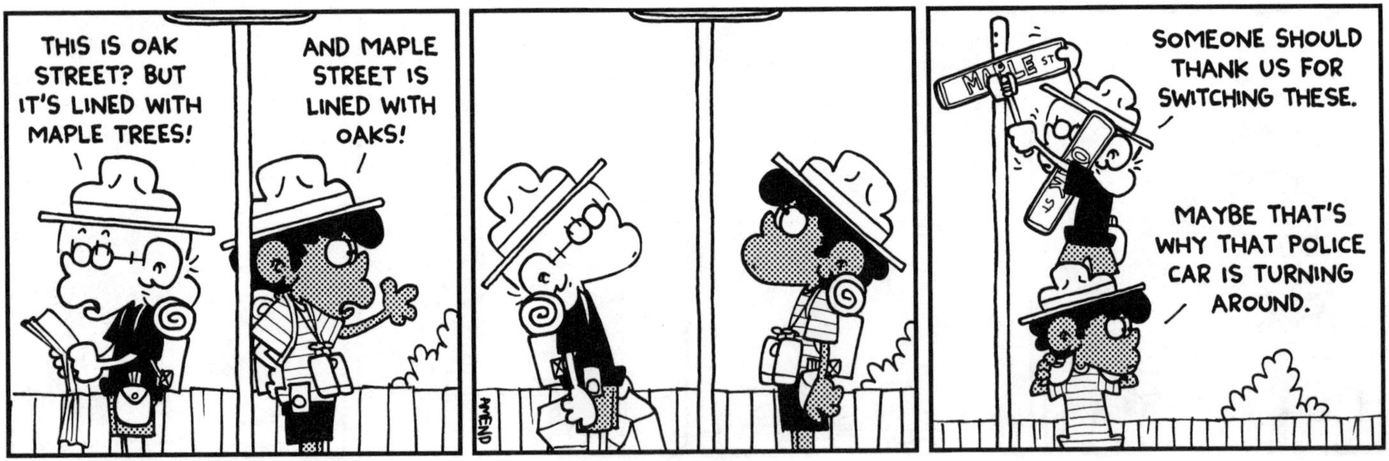
THIS IS OAK STREET? BUT IT'S LINED WITH MAPLE TREES!
AND MAPLE STREET IS LINED WITH OAKS!
AMEND
MAPLE ST
SOMEONE SHOULD THANK US FOR SWITCHING THESE.
MAYBE THAT'S WHY THAT POLICE CAR IS TURNING AROUND.

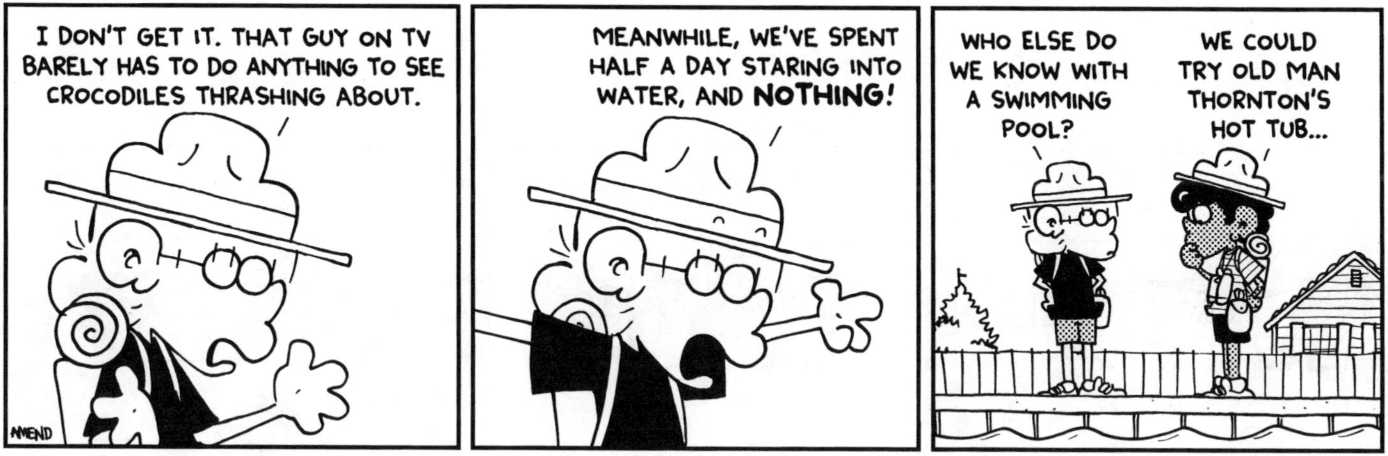
I DON'T GET IT. THAT GUY ON TV BARELY HAS TO DO ANYTHING TO SEE CROCODILES THRASHING ABOUT.
AMEND
MEANWHILE, WE'VE SPENT HALF A DAY STARING INTO WATER, AND NOTHING!
WHO ELSE DO WE KNOW WITH A SWIMMING POOL?
WE COULD TRY OLD MAN THORNTON'S HOT TUB...

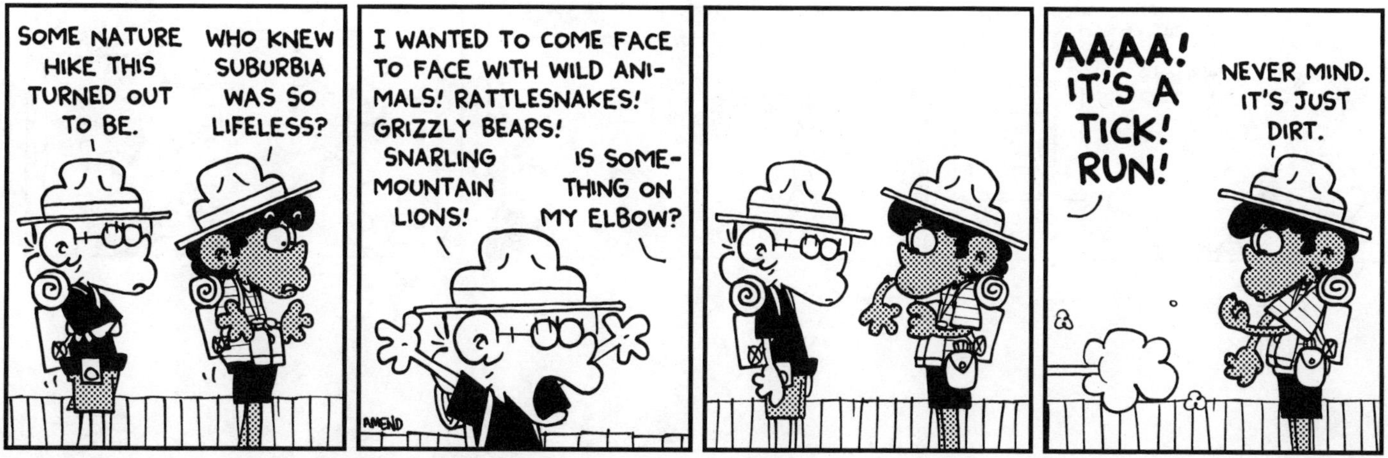
SOME NATURE HIKE THIS TURNED OUT TO BE.
WHO KNEW SUBURBIA WAS SO LIFELESS?
I WANTED TO COME FACE TO FACE WITH WILD ANIMALS! RATTLESNAKES! GRIZZLY BEARS!
SNARLING MOUNTAIN LIONS!
IS SOMETHING ON MY ELBOW?
AMEND
AAAA! IT'S A TICK! RUN!
NEVER MIND. IT'S JUST DIRT.

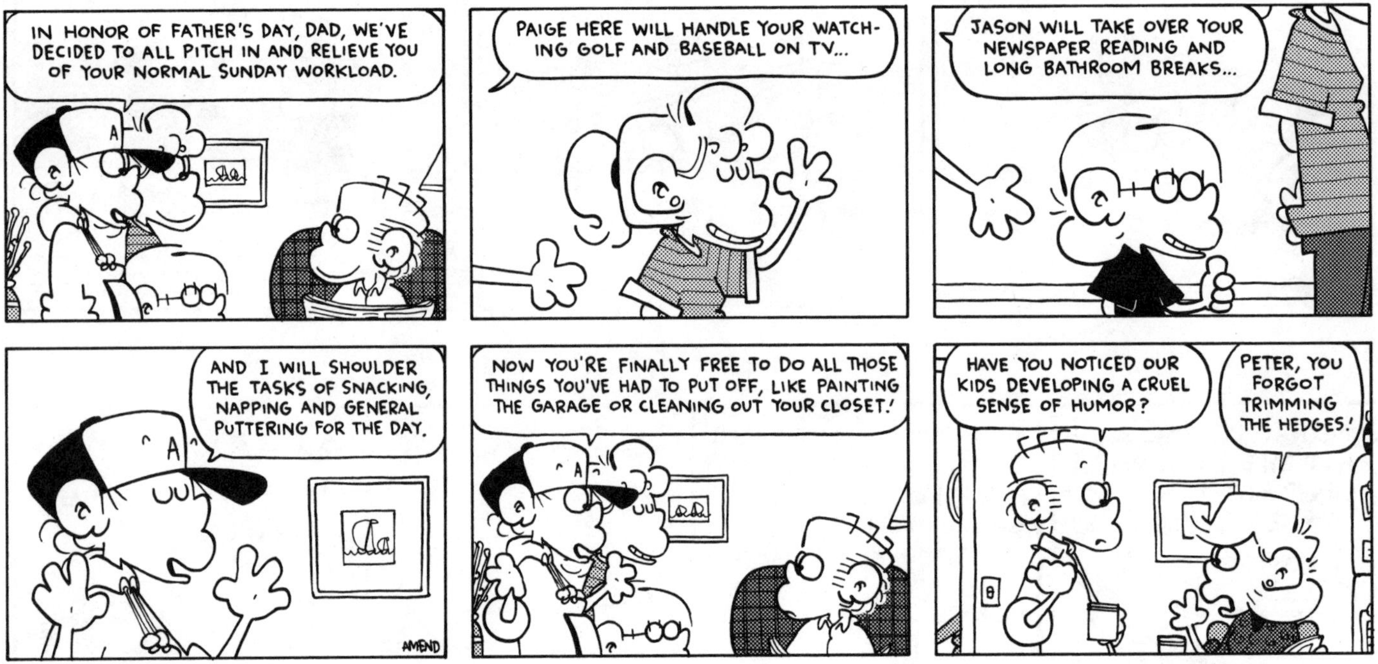
IN HONOR OF FATHER'S DAY, DAD, WE'VE DECIDED TO ALL PITCH IN AND RELIEVE YOU OF YOUR NORMAL SUNDAY WORKLOAD.
PAIGE HERE WILL HANDLE YOUR WATCHING GOLF AND BASEBALL ON TV...
JASON WILL TAKE OVER YOUR NEWSPAPER READING AND LONG BATHROOM BREAKS...
AND I WILL SHOULDER THE TASKS OF SNACKING, NAPPING AND GENERAL PUTTERING FOR THE DAY.
AMEND
NOW YOU'RE FINALLY FREE TO DO ALL THOSE THINGS YOU'VE HAD TO PUT OFF, LIKE PAINTING THE GARAGE OR CLEANING OUT YOUR CLOSET!
HAVE YOU NOTICED OUR KIDS DEVELOPING A CRUEL SENSE OF HUMOR?
PETER, YOU FORGOT TRIMMING THE HEDGES!

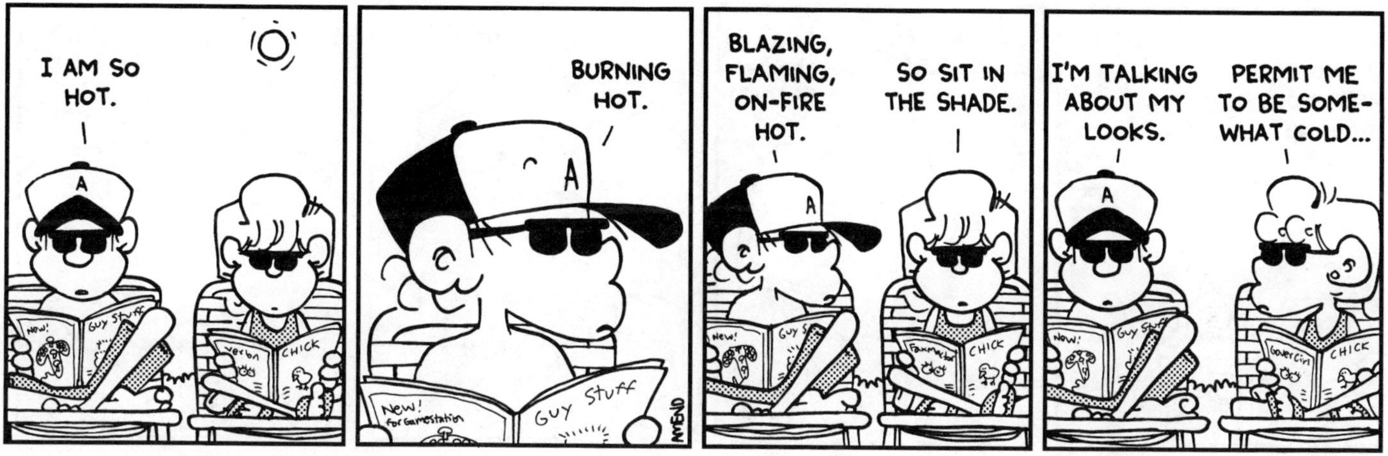
I AM SO HOT.
BURNING HOT.
BLAZING, FLAMING, ON-FIRE HOT.
SO SIT IN THE SHADE.
I'M TALKING ABOUT MY LOOKS.
PERMIT ME TO BE SOME-WHAT COLD...
GUY STUFF
CHICK
AMEND

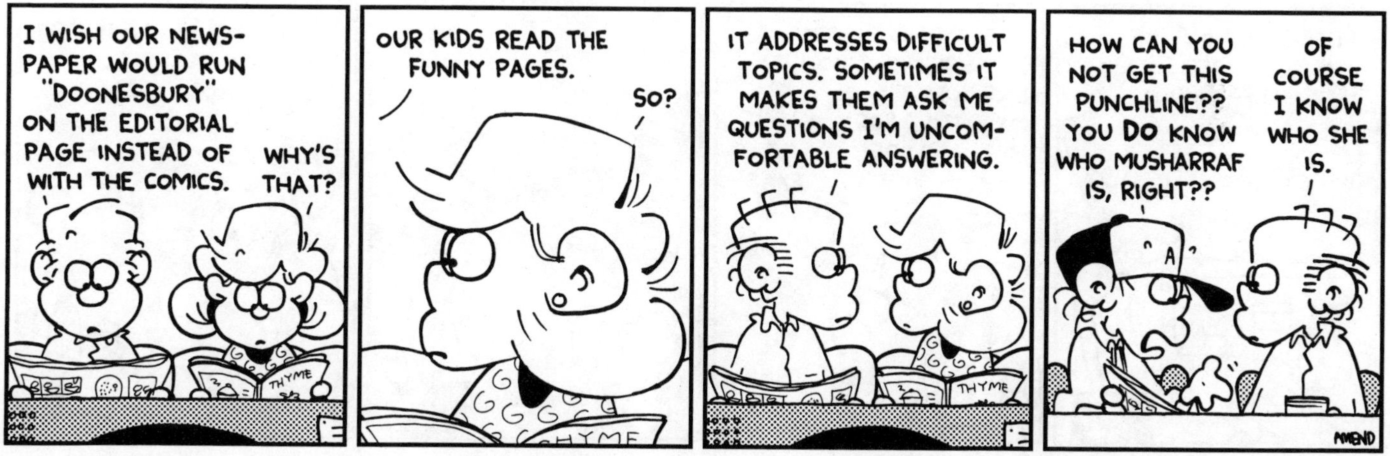
I WISH OUR NEWS-PAPER WOULD RUN "DOONESBURY" ON THE EDITORIAL PAGE INSTEAD OF WITH THE COMICS.
WHY'S THAT?
OUR KIDS READ THE FUNNY PAGES.
SO?
IT ADDRESSES DIFFICULT TOPICS. SOMETIMES IT MAKES THEM ASK ME QUESTIONS I'M UNCOM-FORTABLE ANSWERING.
HOW CAN YOU NOT GET THIS PUNCHLINE?? YOU DO KNOW WHO MUSHARRAF IS, RIGHT??
OF COURSE I KNOW WHO SHE IS.
THYME
AMEND

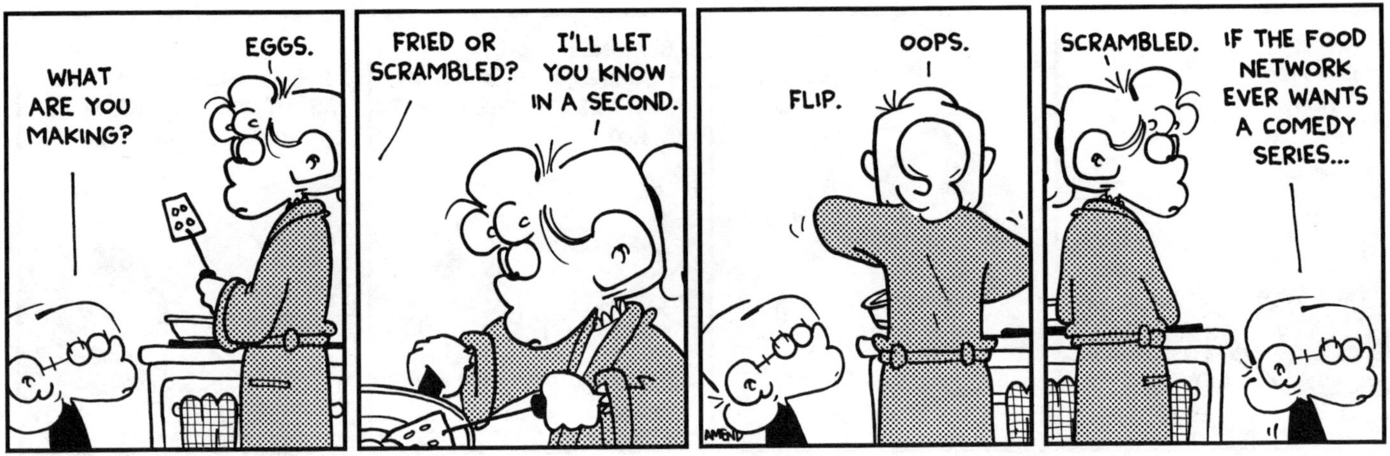
WHAT ARE YOU MAKING?
EGGS.
FRIED OR SCRAMBLED?
I'LL LET YOU KNOW IN A SECOND.
FLIP.
OOPS.
SCRAMBLED.
IF THE FOOD NETWORK EVER WANTS A COMEDY SERIES...
AMEND

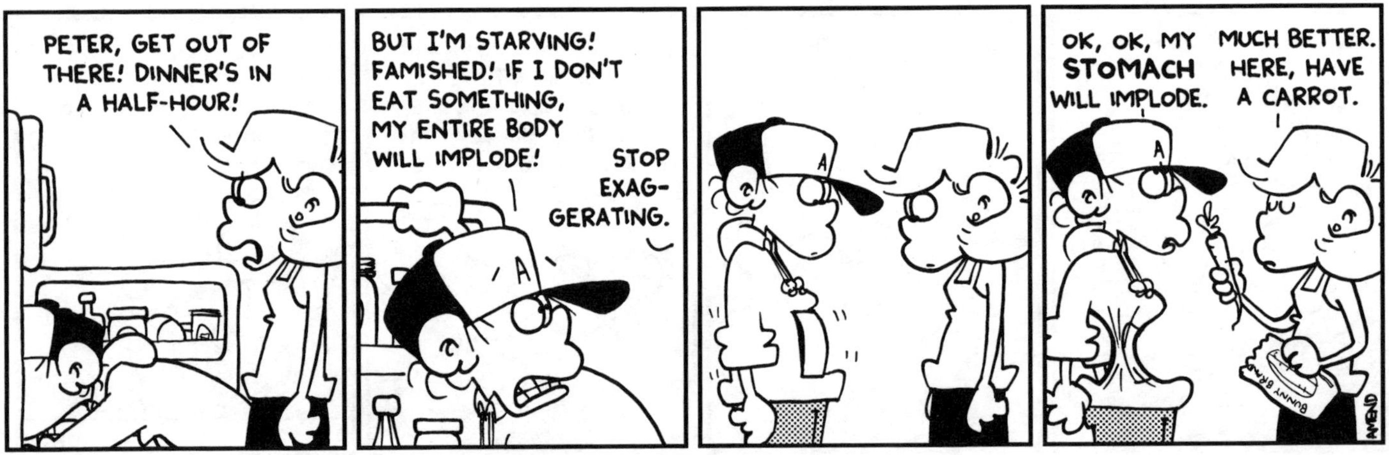
PETER, GET OUT OF THERE! DINNER'S IN A HALF-HOUR!
BUT I'M STARVING! FAMISHED! IF I DON'T EAT SOMETHING, MY ENTIRE BODY WILL IMPLODE!
STOP EXAGGERATING.
OK, OK, MY **STOMACH** WILL IMPLODE.
MUCH BETTER. HERE, HAVE A CARROT.
BUNNY BRAND
AMEND

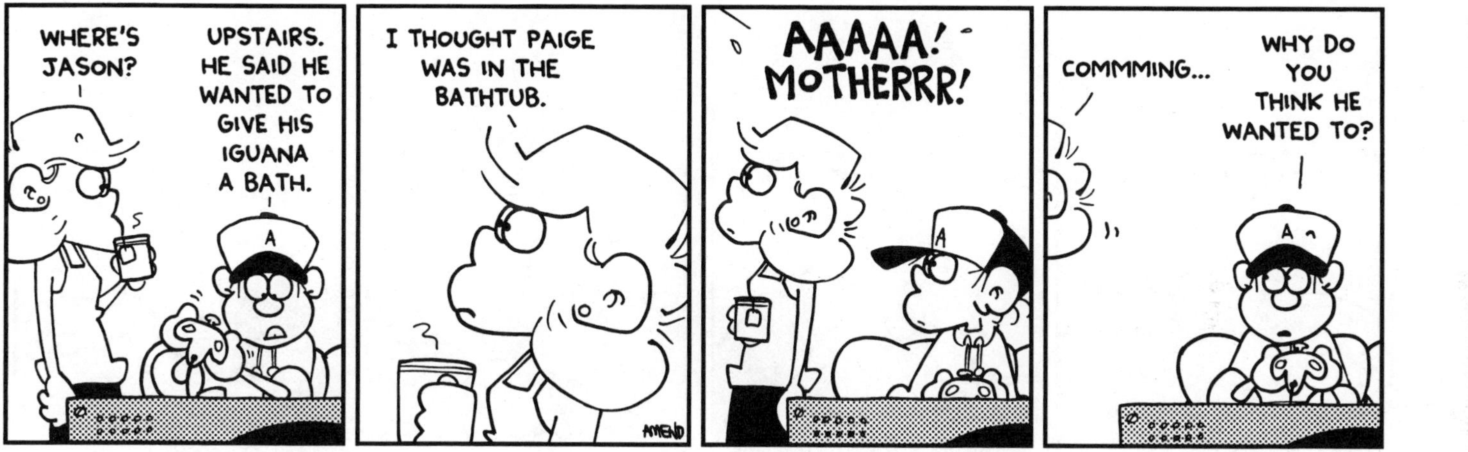
WHERE'S JASON?
UPSTAIRS. HE SAID HE WANTED TO GIVE HIS IGUANA A BATH.
I THOUGHT PAIGE WAS IN THE BATHTUB.
AAAAA! MOTHERRR!
COMMMING...
WHY DO YOU THINK HE WANTED TO?
AMEND

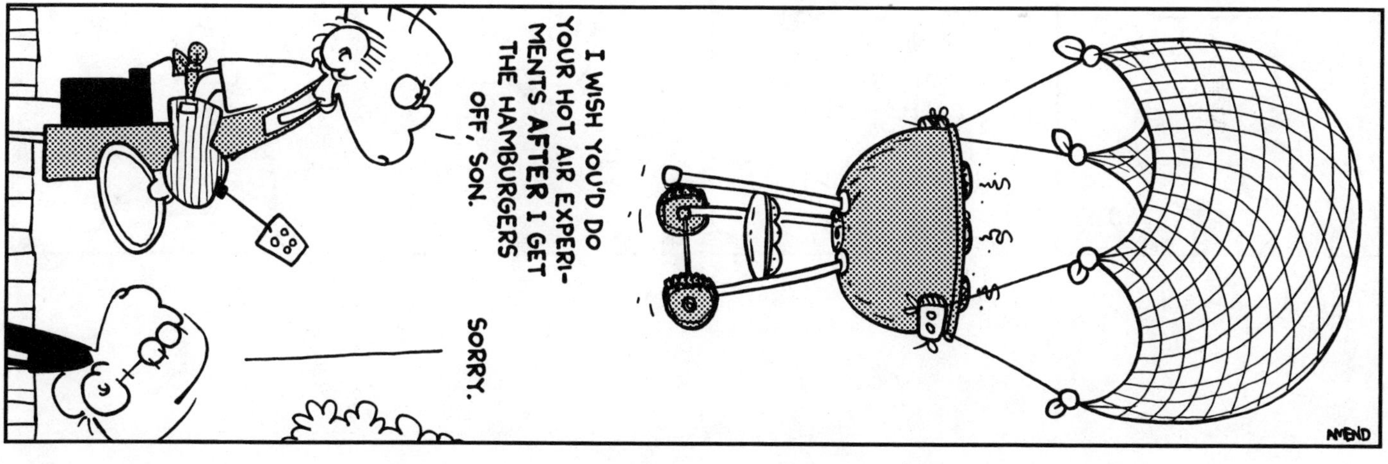
I WISH YOU'D DO YOUR HOT AIR EXPERI-MENTS AFTER I GET THE HAMBURGERS OFF, SON.
SORRY.
AMEND

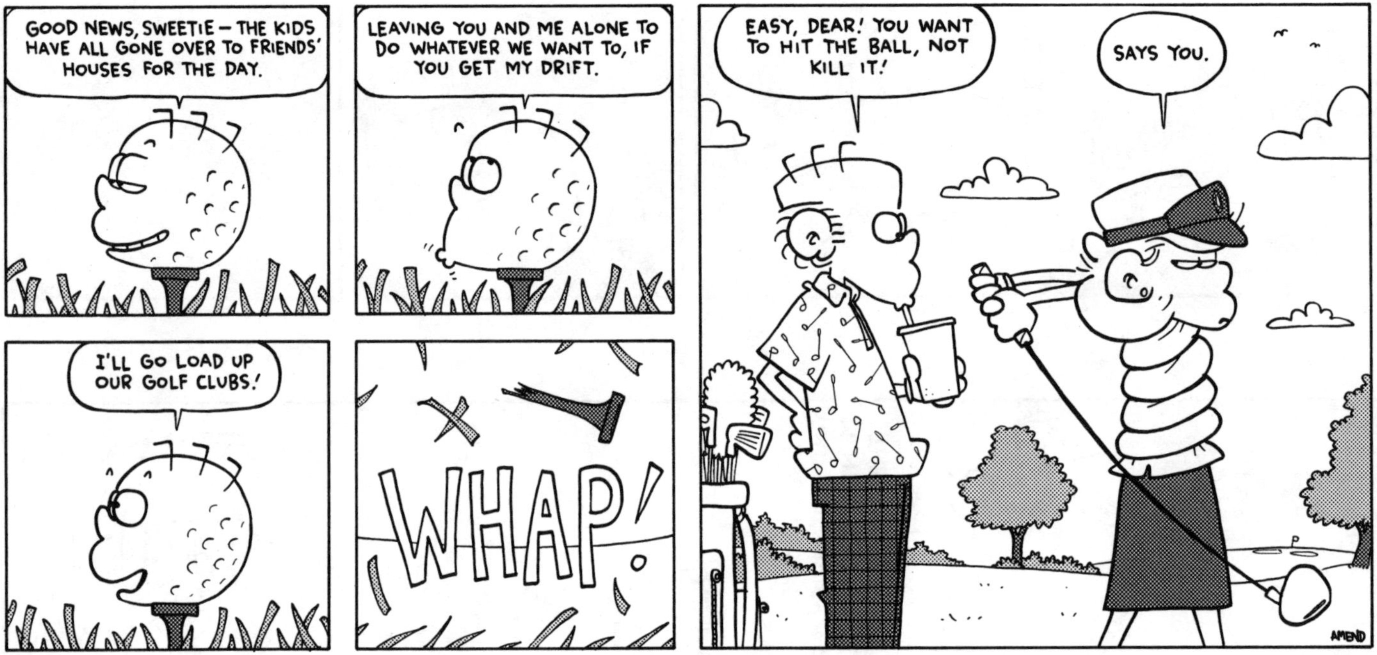
GOOD NEWS, SWEETIE – THE KIDS HAVE ALL GONE OVER TO FRIENDS' HOUSES FOR THE DAY.
LEAVING YOU AND ME ALONE TO DO WHATEVER WE WANT TO, IF YOU GET MY DRIFT.
I'LL GO LOAD UP OUR GOLF CLUBS!
WHAP!
EASY, DEAR! YOU WANT TO HIT THE BALL, NOT KILL IT!
SAYS YOU.
AMEND

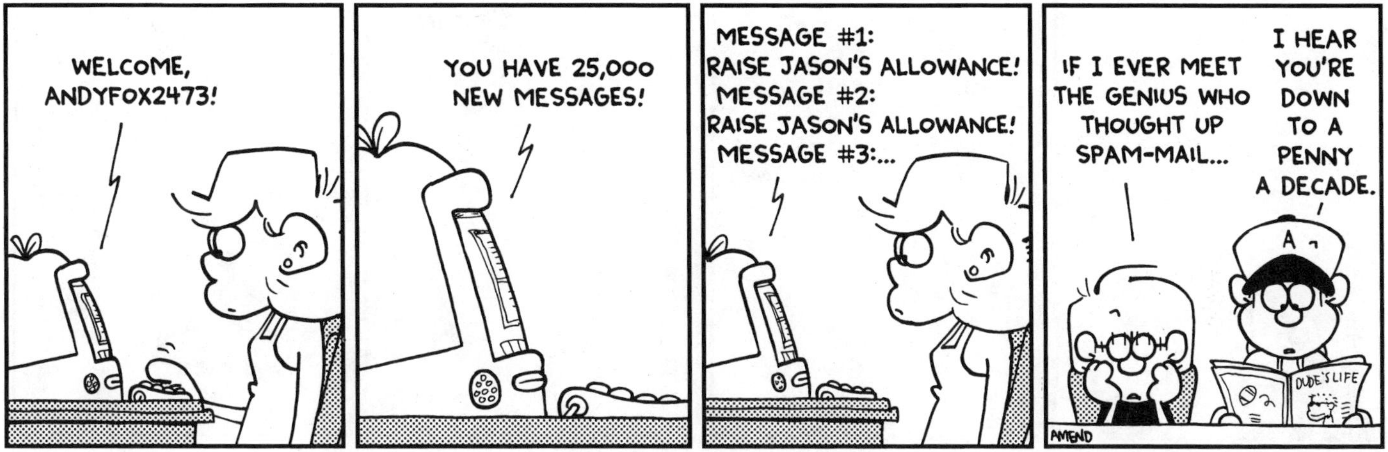
WELCOME, ANDYFOX2473!
YOU HAVE 25,000 NEW MESSAGES!
MESSAGE #1: RAISE JASON'S ALLOWANCE! MESSAGE #2: RAISE JASON'S ALLOWANCE! MESSAGE #3:...
IF I EVER MEET THE GENIUS WHO THOUGHT UP SPAM-MAIL...
I HEAR YOU'RE DOWN TO A PENNY A DECADE.
DUDE'S LIFE
AMEND

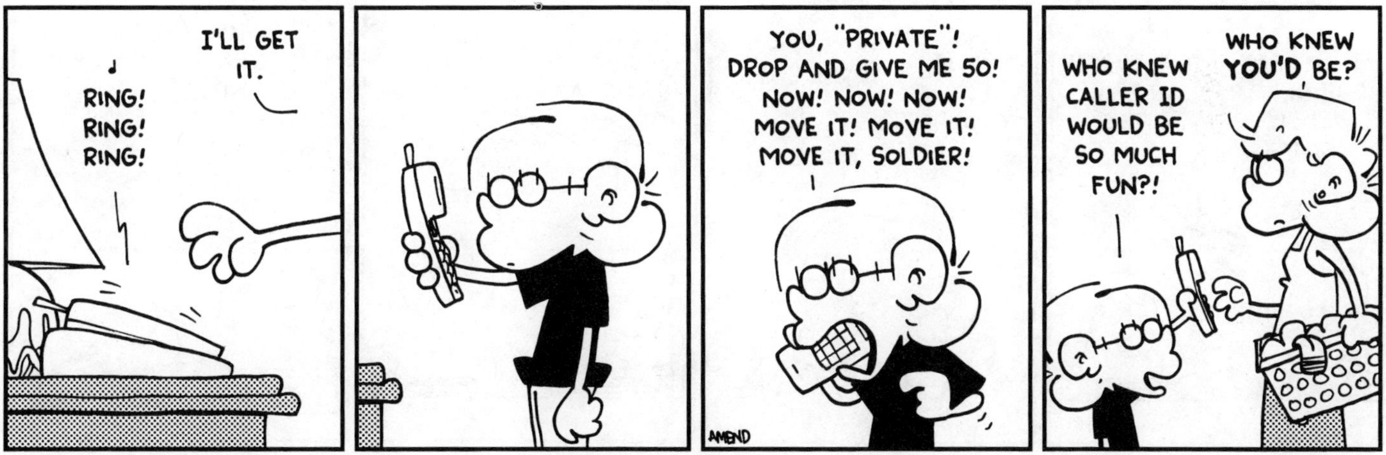
RING! RING! RING!
I'LL GET IT.
YOU, "PRIVATE"! DROP AND GIVE ME 50! NOW! NOW! NOW! MOVE IT! MOVE IT! MOVE IT, SOLDIER!
AMEND
WHO KNEW CALLER ID WOULD BE SO MUCH FUN?!
WHO KNEW YOU'D BE?

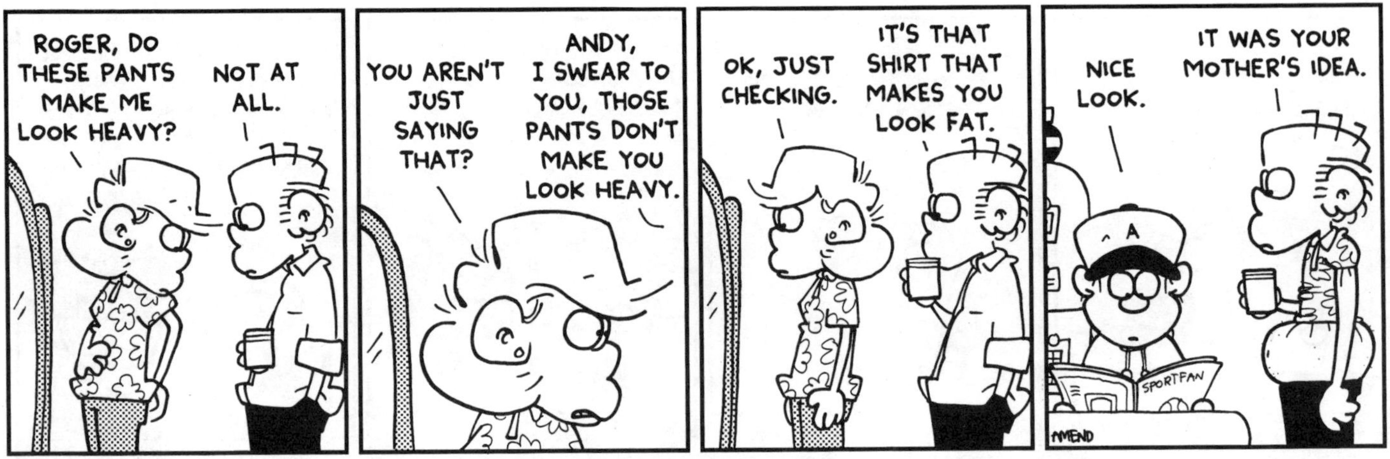
ROGER, DO THESE PANTS MAKE ME LOOK HEAVY?
NOT AT ALL.
YOU AREN'T JUST SAYING THAT?
ANDY, I SWEAR TO YOU, THOSE PANTS DON'T MAKE YOU LOOK HEAVY.
OK, JUST CHECKING.
IT'S THAT SHIRT THAT MAKES YOU LOOK FAT.
NICE LOOK.
IT WAS YOUR MOTHER'S IDEA.
SPORTFAN
AMEND

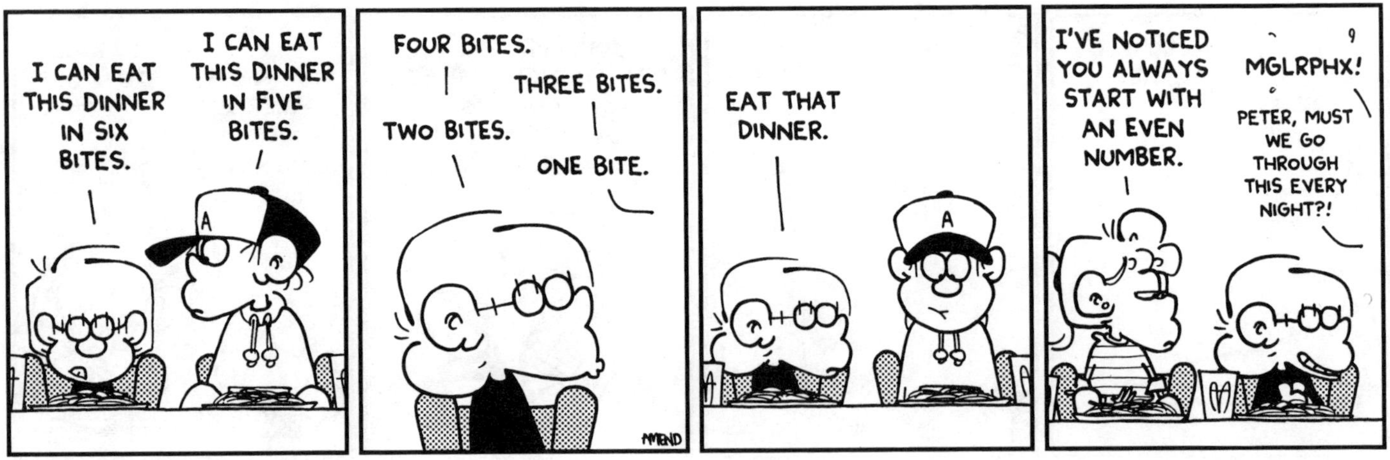
I CAN EAT THIS DINNER IN SIX BITES.
I CAN EAT THIS DINNER IN FIVE BITES.
FOUR BITES.
THREE BITES.
TWO BITES.
ONE BITE.
AMEND
EAT THAT DINNER.
I'VE NOTICED YOU ALWAYS START WITH AN EVEN NUMBER.
MGLRPHX!
PETER, MUST WE GO THROUGH THIS EVERY NIGHT?!

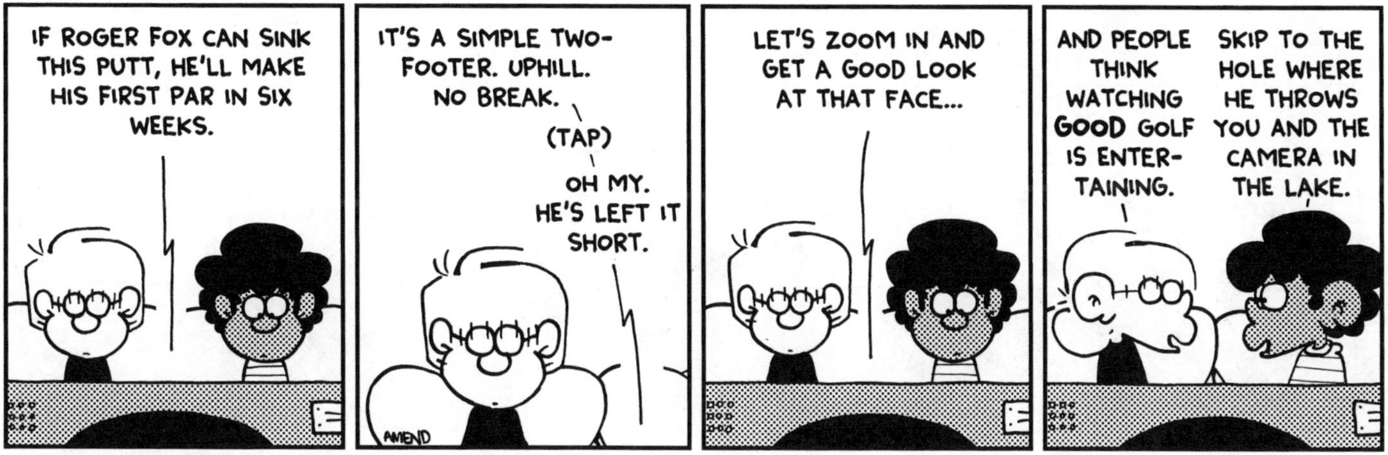
IF ROGER FOX CAN SINK THIS PUTT, HE'LL MAKE HIS FIRST PAR IN SIX WEEKS.
IT'S A SIMPLE TWO-FOOTER. UPHILL. NO BREAK.
(TAP)
OH MY. HE'S LEFT IT SHORT.
AMEND
LET'S ZOOM IN AND GET A GOOD LOOK AT THAT FACE...
AND PEOPLE THINK WATCHING **GOOD** GOLF IS ENTERTAINING.
SKIP TO THE HOLE WHERE HE THROWS YOU AND THE CAMERA IN THE LAKE.

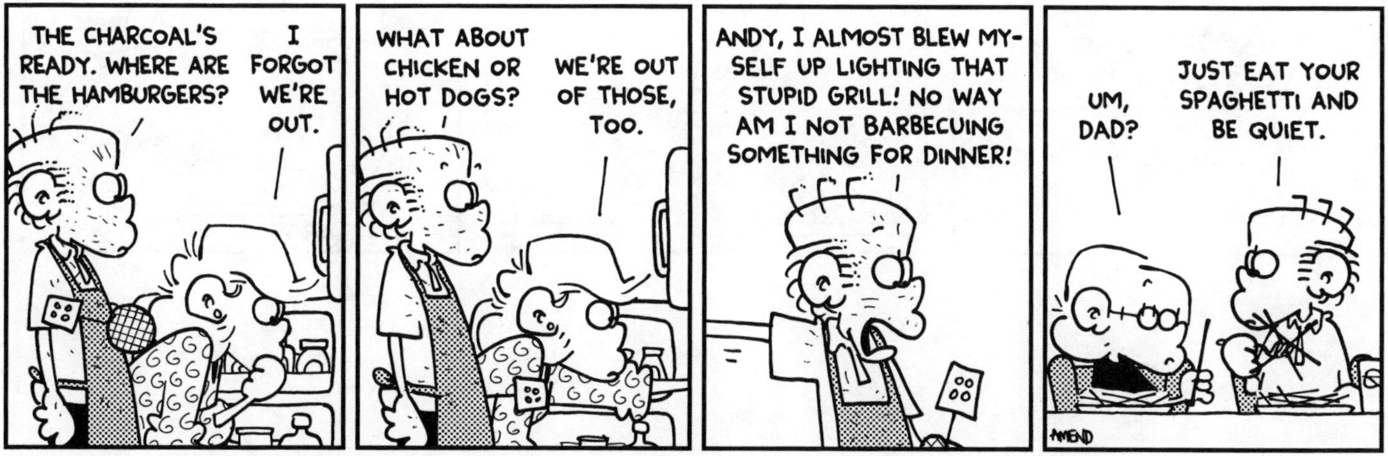
THE CHARCOAL'S READY. WHERE ARE THE HAMBURGERS?
I FORGOT WE'RE OUT.
WHAT ABOUT CHICKEN OR HOT DOGS?
WE'RE OUT OF THOSE, TOO.
ANDY, I ALMOST BLEW MYSELF UP LIGHTING THAT STUPID GRILL! NO WAY AM I NOT BARBECUING SOMETHING FOR DINNER!
UM, DAD?
JUST EAT YOUR SPAGHETTI AND BE QUIET.
AMEND

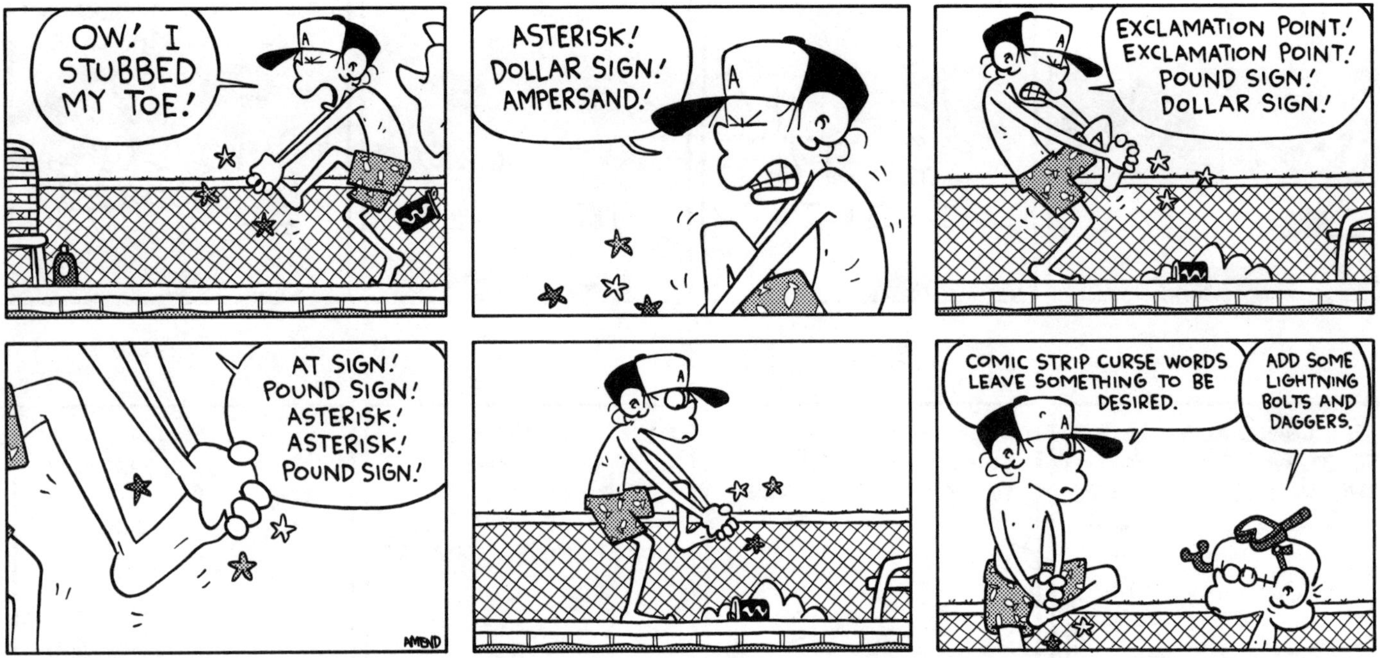
OW! I STUBBED MY TOE!
ASTERISK! DOLLAR SIGN! AMPERSAND!
EXCLAMATION POINT! EXCLAMATION POINT! POUND SIGN! DOLLAR SIGN!
AT SIGN! POUND SIGN! ASTERISK! ASTERISK! POUND SIGN!
AMEND
COMIC STRIP CURSE WORDS LEAVE SOMETHING TO BE DESIRED.
ADD SOME LIGHTNING BOLTS AND DAGGERS.

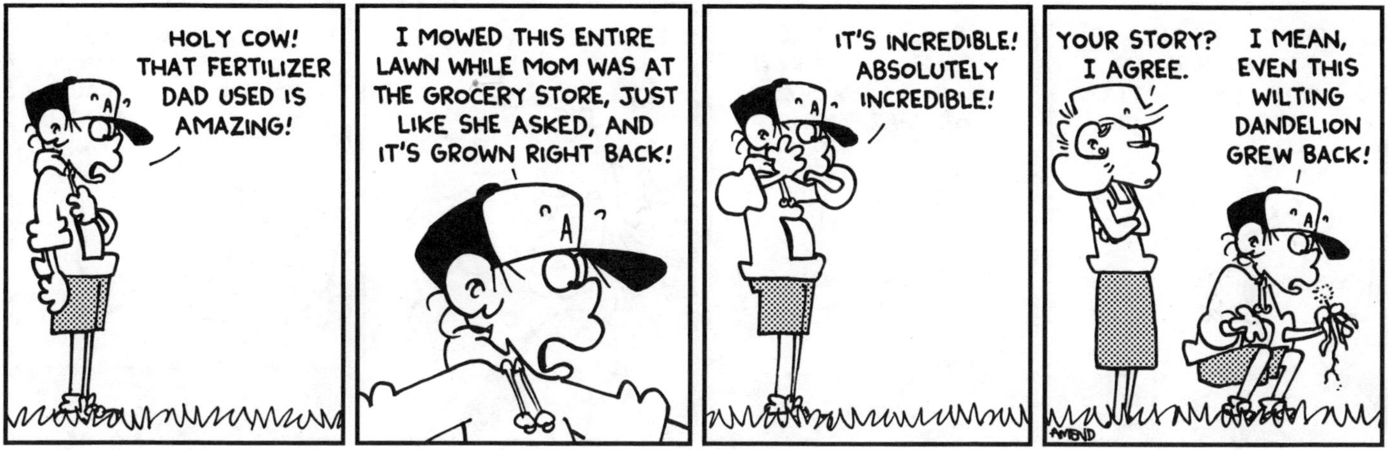
HOLY COW! THAT FERTILIZER DAD USED IS AMAZING!
I MOWED THIS ENTIRE LAWN WHILE MOM WAS AT THE GROCERY STORE, JUST LIKE SHE ASKED, AND IT'S GROWN RIGHT BACK!
IT'S INCREDIBLE! ABSOLUTELY INCREDIBLE!
YOUR STORY? I AGREE.
I MEAN, EVEN THIS WILTING DANDELION GREW BACK!
AMEND

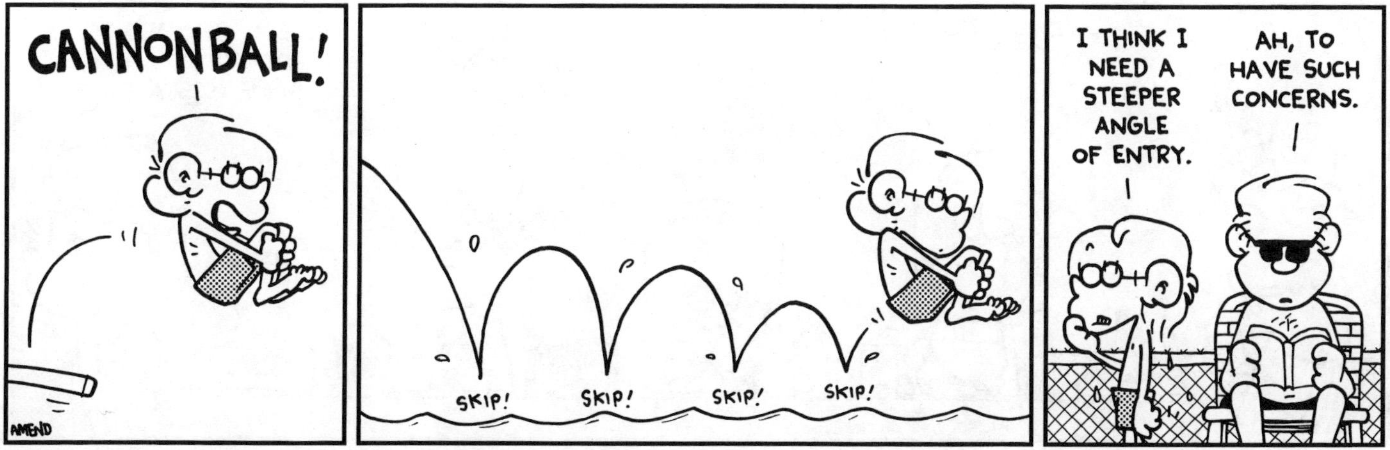
CANNONBALL!
AMEND
SKIP!
SKIP!
SKIP!
SKIP!
I THINK I NEED A STEEPER ANGLE OF ENTRY.
AH, TO HAVE SUCH CONCERNS.

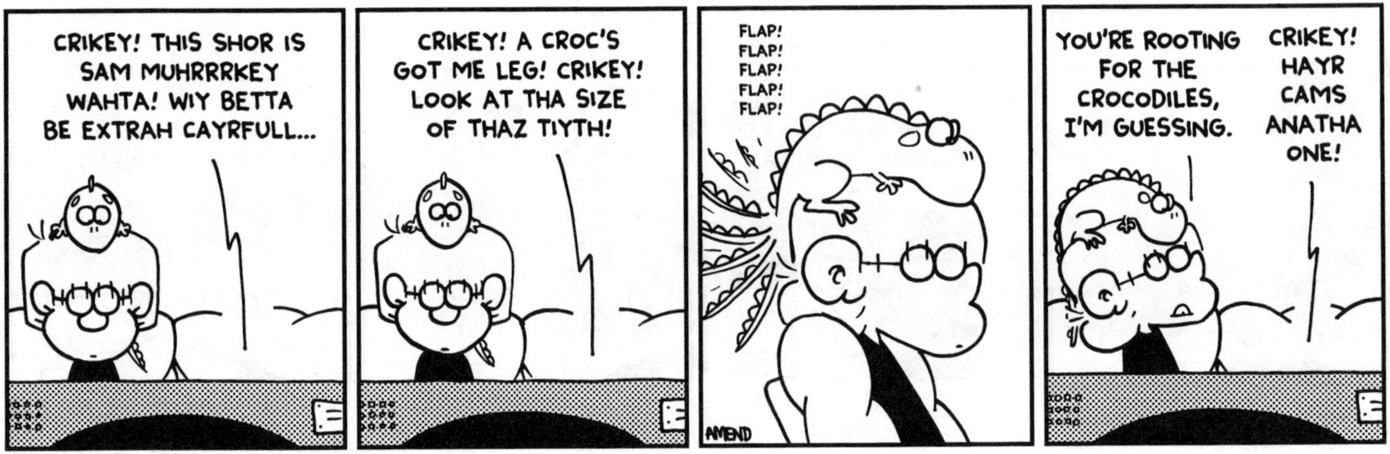
CRIKEY! THIS SHOR IS SAM MUHRRRKEY WAHTA! WIY BETTA BE EXTRAH CAYRFULL...
CRIKEY! A CROC'S GOT ME LEG! CRIKEY! LOOK AT THA SIZE OF THAZ TIYTH!
FLAP! FLAP! FLAP! FLAP! FLAP!
AMEND
YOU'RE ROOTING FOR THE CROCODILES, I'M GUESSING.
CRIKEY! HAYR CAMS ANATHA ONE!

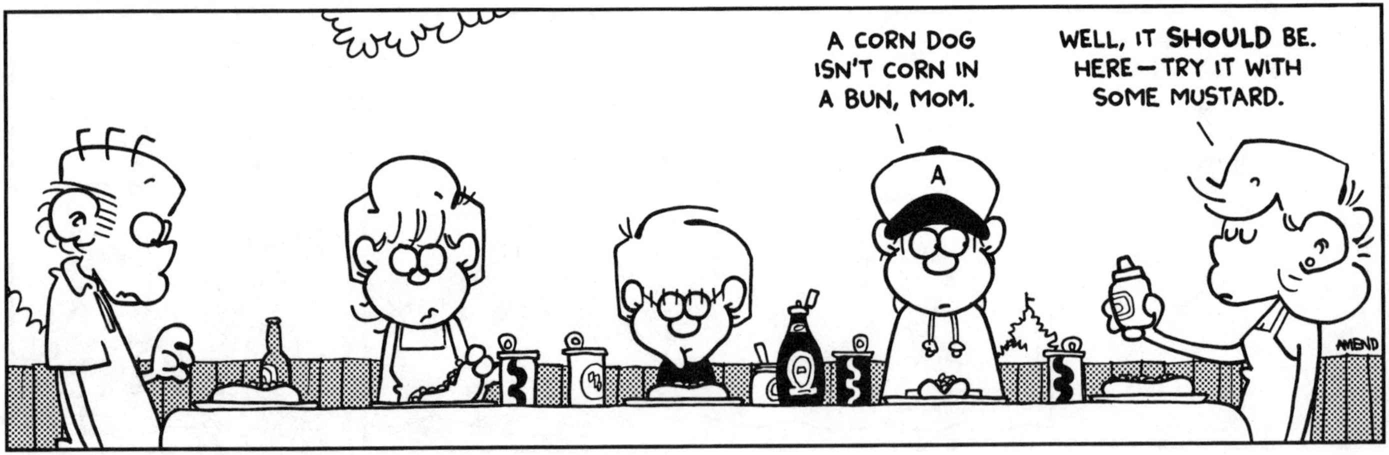
A CORN DOG ISN'T CORN IN A BUN, MOM.
WELL, IT **SHOULD** BE. HERE—TRY IT WITH SOME MUSTARD.
AMEND

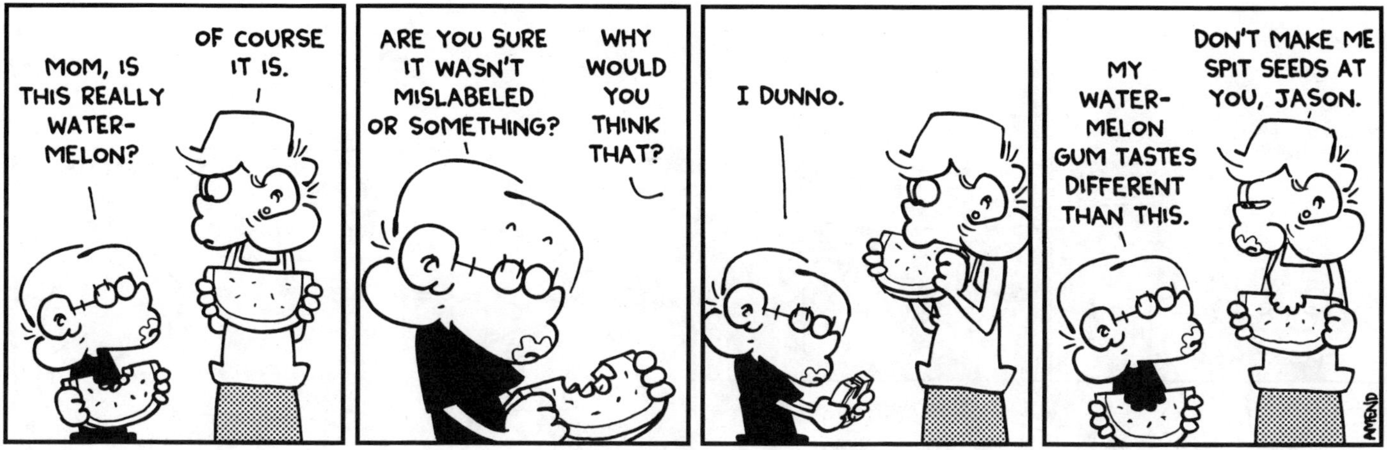
MOM, IS THIS REALLY WATER-MELON?
OF COURSE IT IS.
ARE YOU SURE IT WASN'T MISLABELED OR SOMETHING?
WHY WOULD YOU THINK THAT?
I DUNNO.
MY WATER-MELON GUM TASTES DIFFERENT THAN THIS.
DON'T MAKE ME SPIT SEEDS AT YOU, JASON.
AMEND

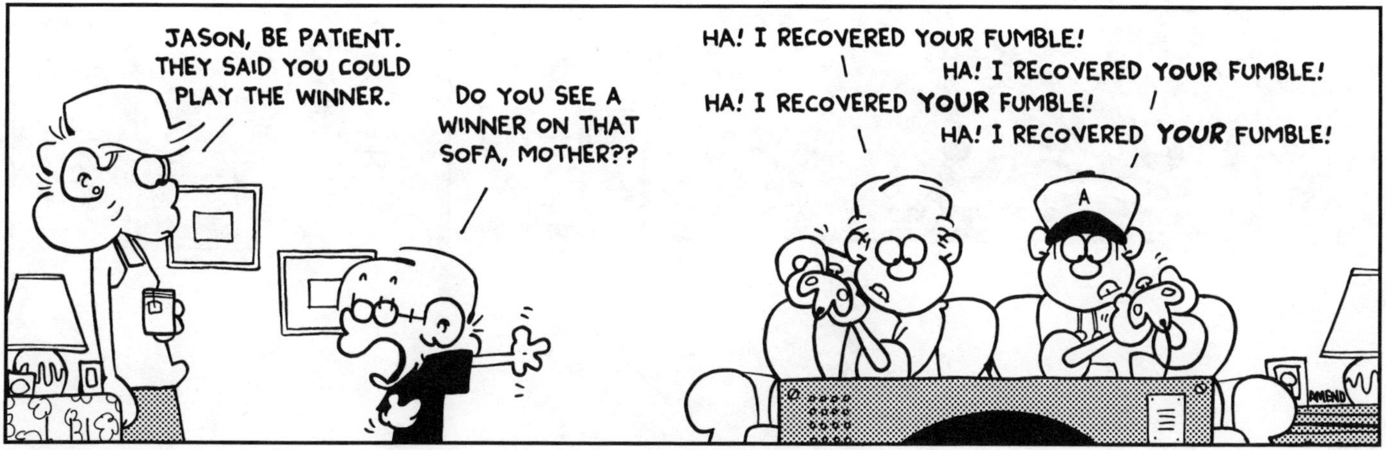
JASON, BE PATIENT. THEY SAID YOU COULD PLAY THE WINNER.
DO YOU SEE A WINNER ON THAT SOFA, MOTHER??
HA! I RECOVERED YOUR FUMBLE!
HA! I RECOVERED YOUR FUMBLE!
HA! I RECOVERED **YOUR** FUMBLE!
HA! I RECOVERED ***YOUR*** FUMBLE!
AMEND

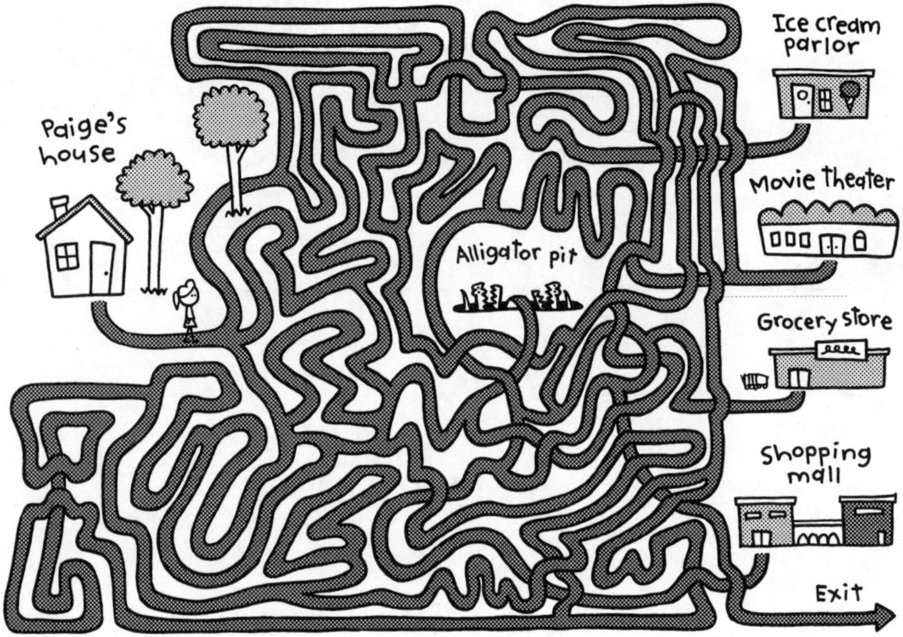
Paige's house
Ice cream parlor
Movie theater
Alligator pit
Grocery store
Shopping mall
Exit

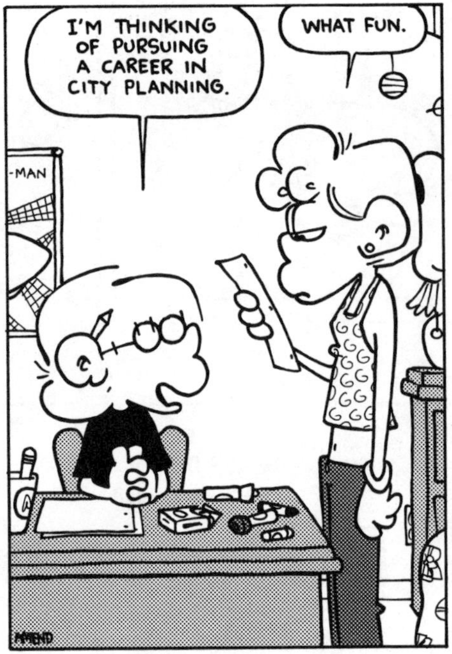
I'M THINKING OF PURSUING A CAREER IN CITY PLANNING.
WHAT FUN.
-MAN
AMEND

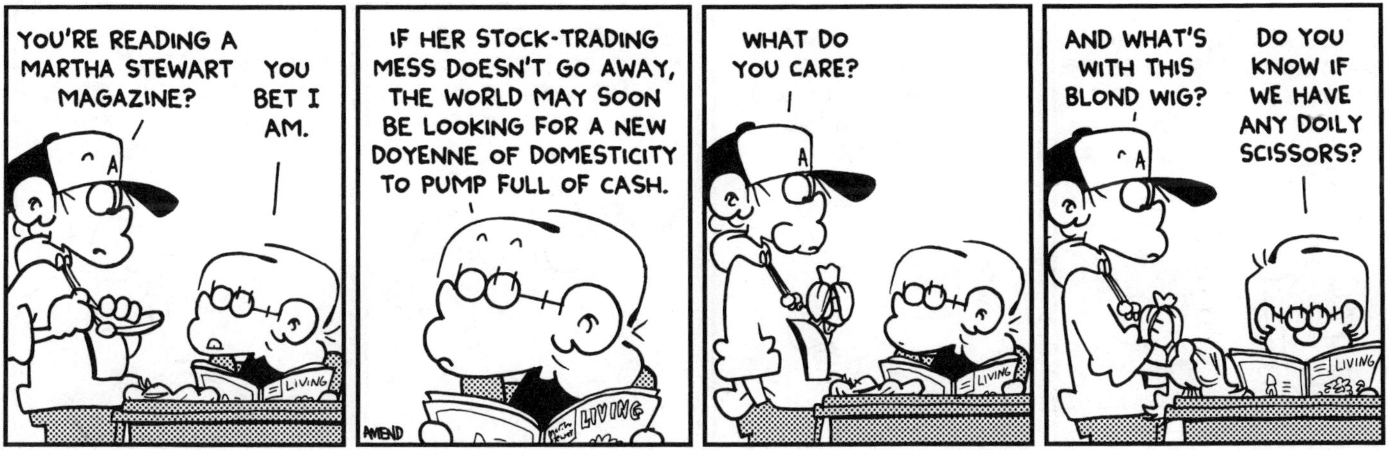
YOU'RE READING A MARTHA STEWART MAGAZINE?
YOU BET I AM.
IF HER STOCK-TRADING MESS DOESN'T GO AWAY, THE WORLD MAY SOON BE LOOKING FOR A NEW DOYENNE OF DOMESTICITY TO PUMP FULL OF CASH.
AMEND
WHAT DO YOU CARE?
AND WHAT'S WITH THIS BLOND WIG?
DO YOU KNOW IF WE HAVE ANY DOILY SCISSORS?

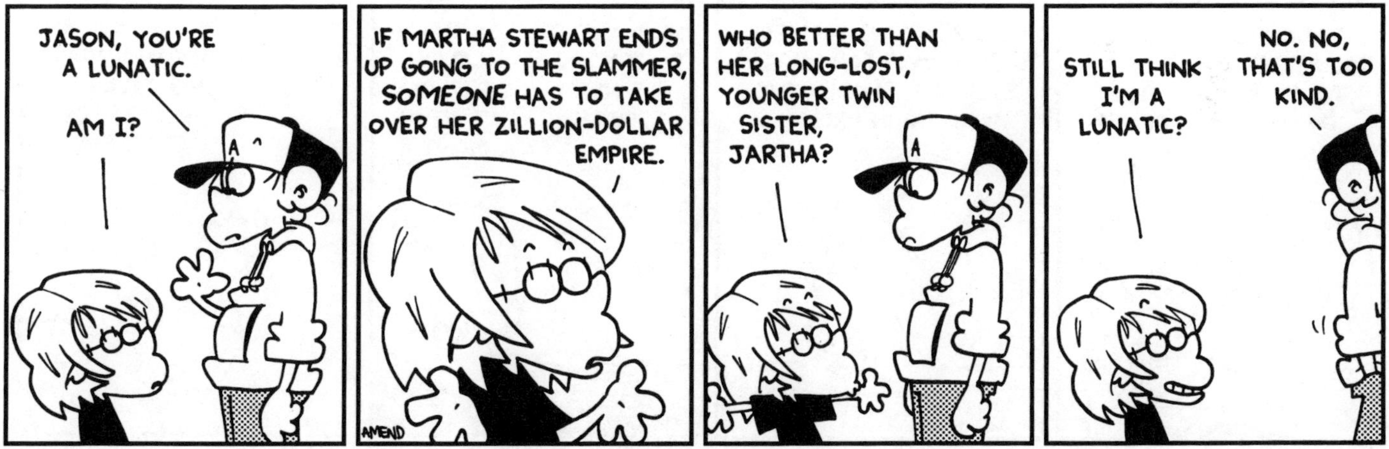
JASON, YOU'RE A LUNATIC.
AM I?
IF MARTHA STEWART ENDS UP GOING TO THE SLAMMER, SOMEONE HAS TO TAKE OVER HER ZILLION-DOLLAR EMPIRE.
AMEND
WHO BETTER THAN HER LONG-LOST, YOUNGER TWIN SISTER, JARTHA?
STILL THINK I'M A LUNATIC?
NO. NO, THAT'S TOO KIND.

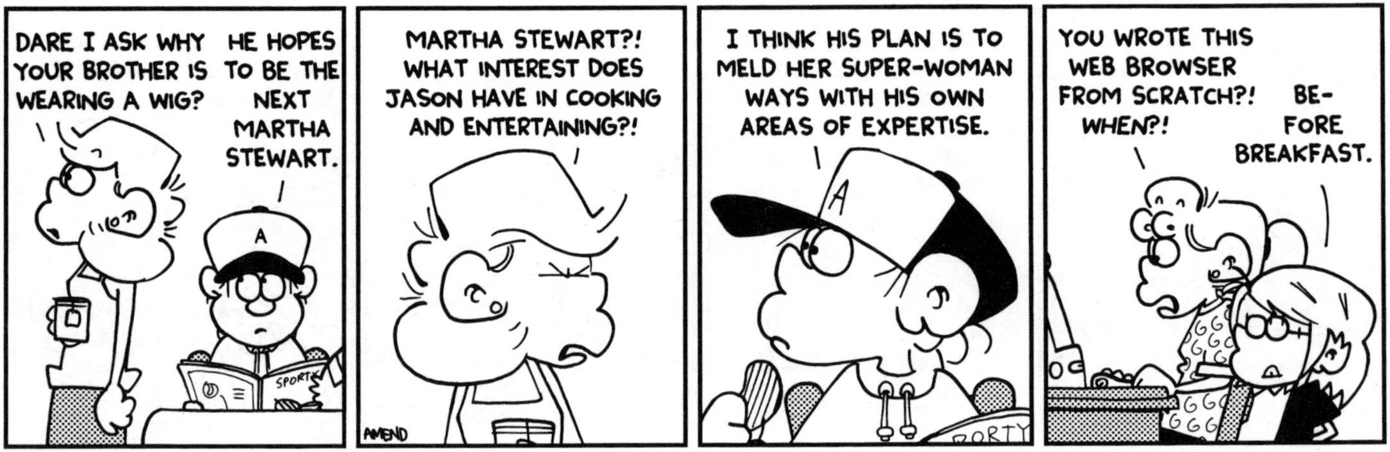
DARE I ASK WHY YOUR BROTHER IS WEARING A WIG?
HE HOPES TO BE THE NEXT MARTHA STEWART.
MARTHA STEWART?! WHAT INTEREST DOES JASON HAVE IN COOKING AND ENTERTAINING?!
AMEND
I THINK HIS PLAN IS TO MELD HER SUPER-WOMAN WAYS WITH HIS OWN AREAS OF EXPERTISE.
YOU WROTE THIS WEB BROWSER FROM SCRATCH?! WHEN?!
BE-FORE BREAKFAST.

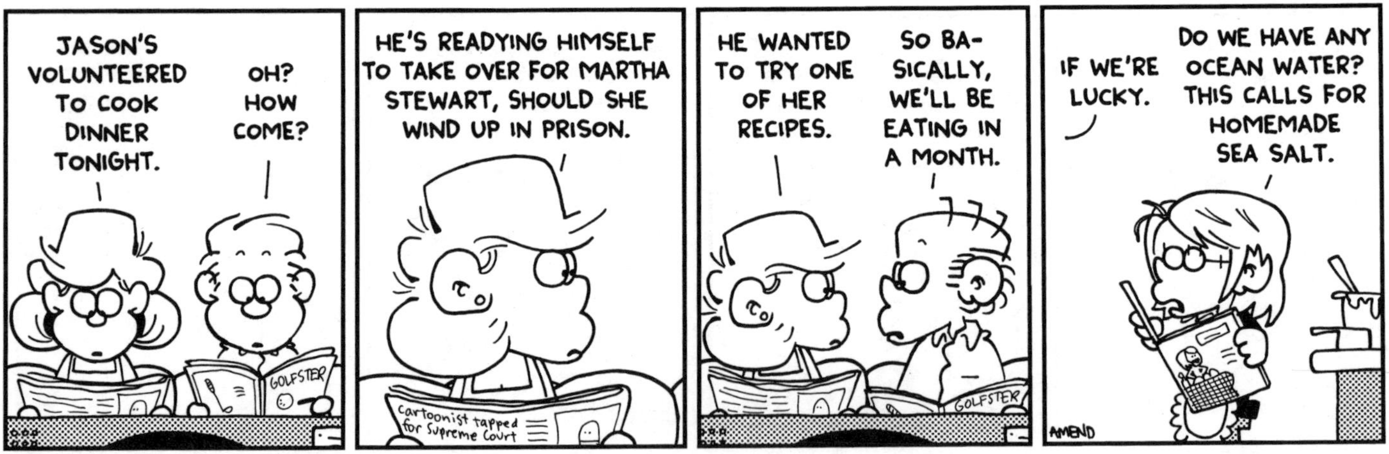
JASON'S VOLUNTEERED TO COOK DINNER TONIGHT.
OH? HOW COME?
GOLFSTER
HE'S READYING HIMSELF TO TAKE OVER FOR MARTHA STEWART, SHOULD SHE WIND UP IN PRISON.
Cartoonist tapped for Supreme Court
HE WANTED TO TRY ONE OF HER RECIPES.
SO BA-SICALLY, WE'LL BE EATING IN A MONTH.
GOLFSTER
IF WE'RE LUCKY.
DO WE HAVE ANY OCEAN WATER? THIS CALLS FOR HOMEMADE SEA SALT.
AMEND

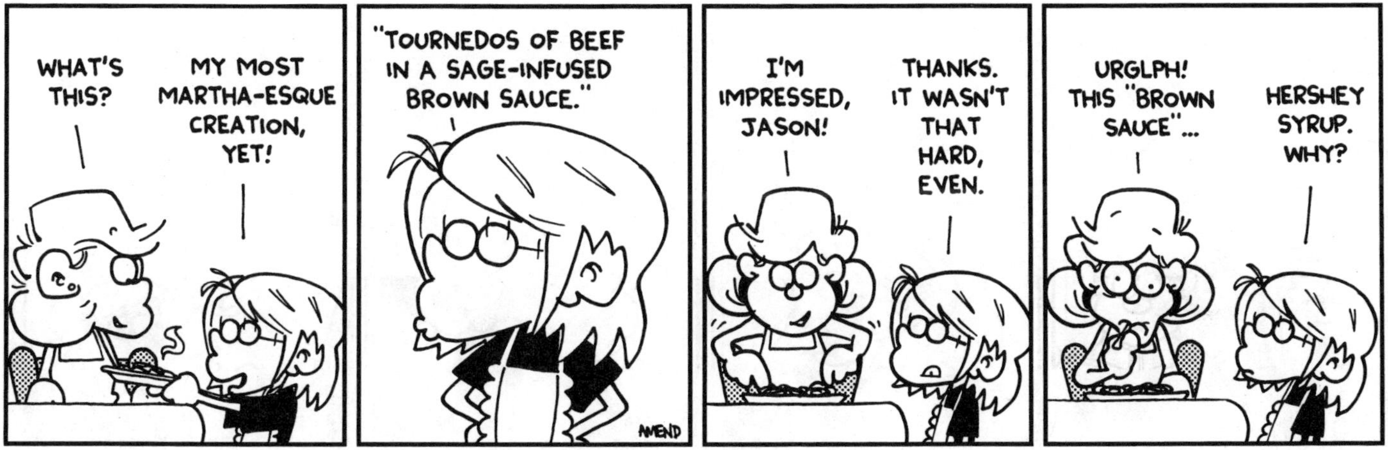
WHAT'S THIS?
MY MOST MARTHA-ESQUE CREATION, YET!
"TOURNEDOS OF BEEF IN A SAGE-INFUSED BROWN SAUCE."
I'M IMPRESSED, JASON!
THANKS. IT WASN'T THAT HARD, EVEN.
URGLPH! THIS "BROWN SAUCE"...
HERSHEY SYRUP. WHY?
AMEND

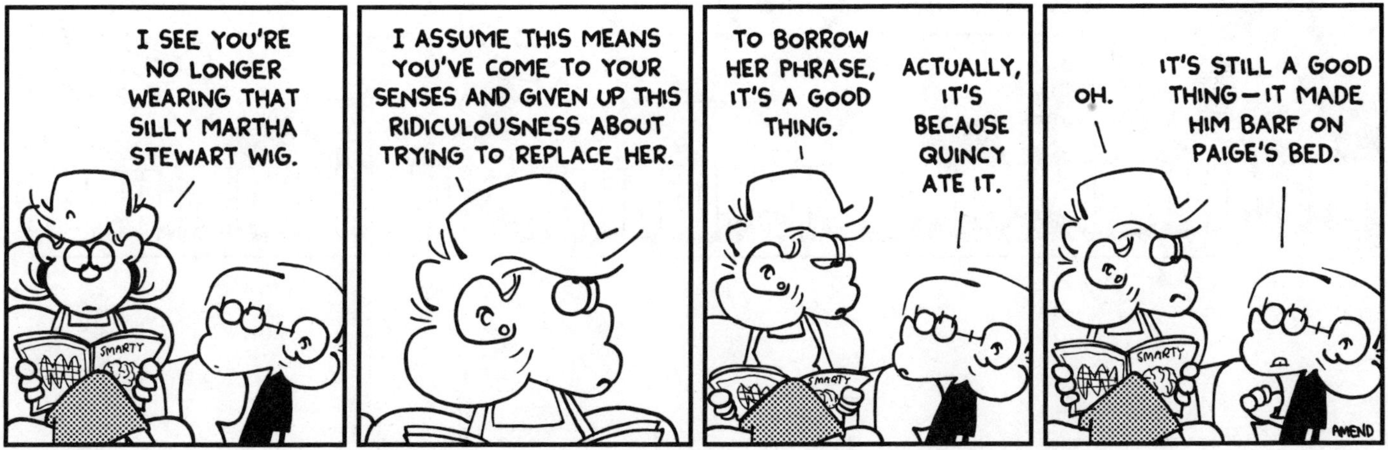
I SEE YOU'RE NO LONGER WEARING THAT SILLY MARTHA STEWART WIG.
SMARTY
I ASSUME THIS MEANS YOU'VE COME TO YOUR SENSES AND GIVEN UP THIS RIDICULOUSNESS ABOUT TRYING TO REPLACE HER.
TO BORROW HER PHRASE, IT'S A GOOD THING.
ACTUALLY, IT'S BECAUSE QUINCY ATE IT.
SMARTY
OH.
IT'S STILL A GOOD THING—IT MADE HIM BARF ON PAIGE'S BED.
SMARTY
AMEND

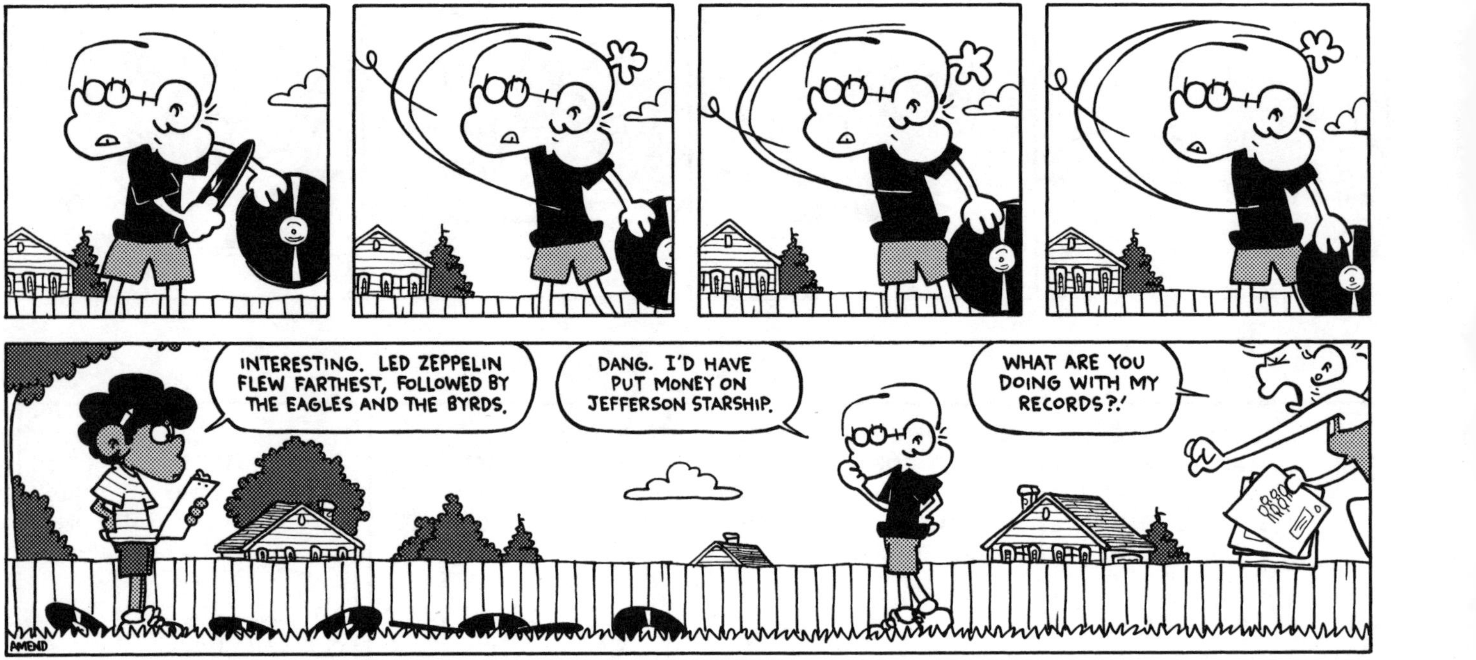
INTERESTING. LED ZEPPELIN FLEW FARTHEST, FOLLOWED BY THE EAGLES AND THE BYRDS.
DANG. I'D HAVE PUT MONEY ON JEFFERSON STARSHIP.
WHAT ARE YOU DOING WITH MY RECORDS?!
AMEND

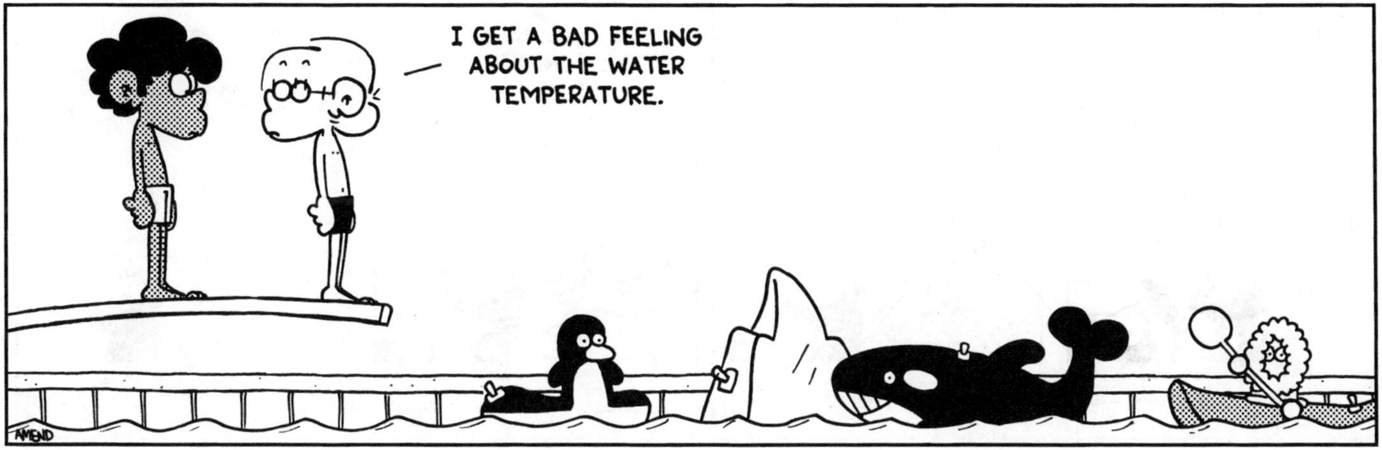
I GET A BAD FEELING ABOUT THE WATER TEMPERATURE.
AMEND

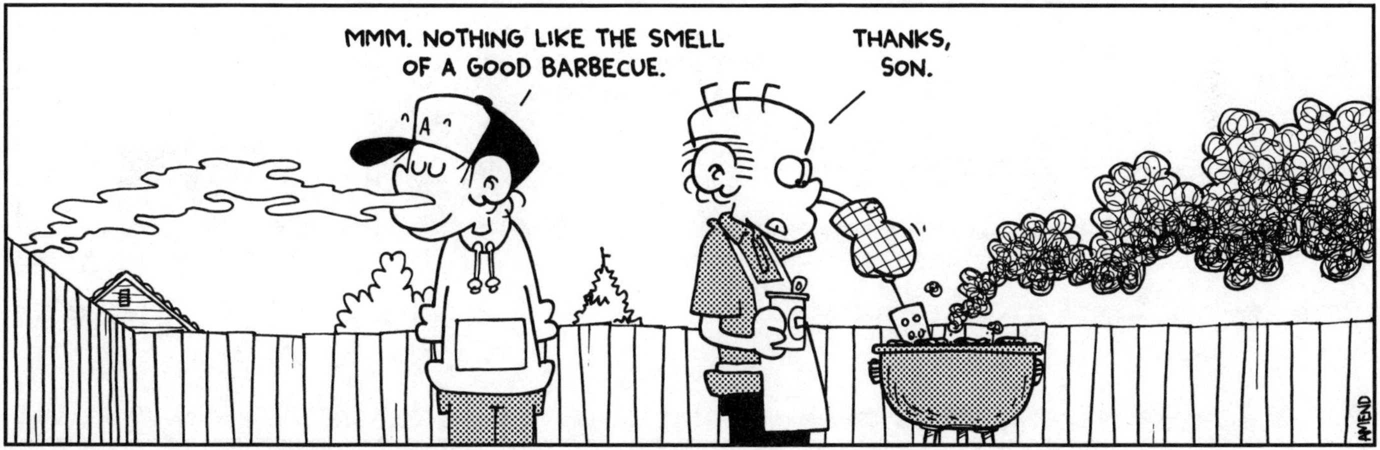
MMM. NOTHING LIKE THE SMELL OF A GOOD BARBECUE.
THANKS, SON.
AMEND

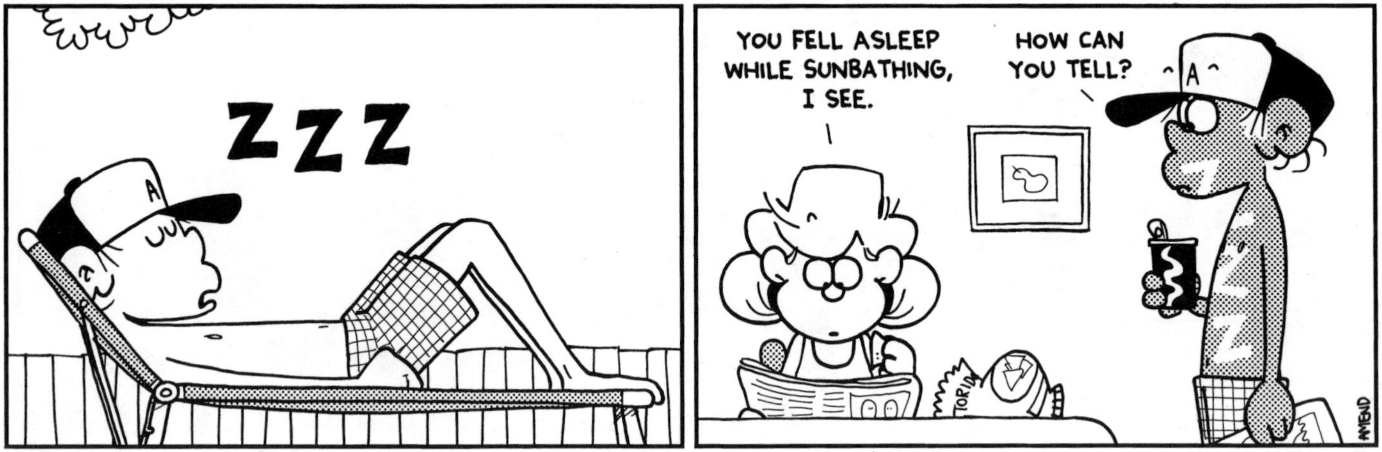
ZZZ
YOU FELL ASLEEP WHILE SUNBATHING, I SEE.
HOW CAN YOU TELL?
AMEND

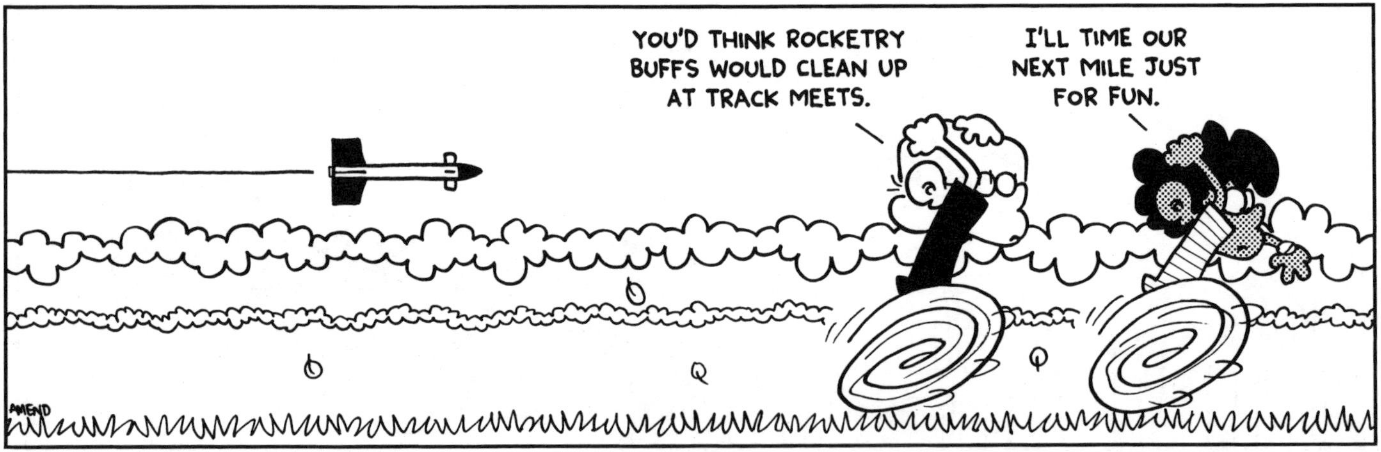
YOU'D THINK ROCKETRY BUFFS WOULD CLEAN UP AT TRACK MEETS.
I'LL TIME OUR NEXT MILE JUST FOR FUN.
AMEND

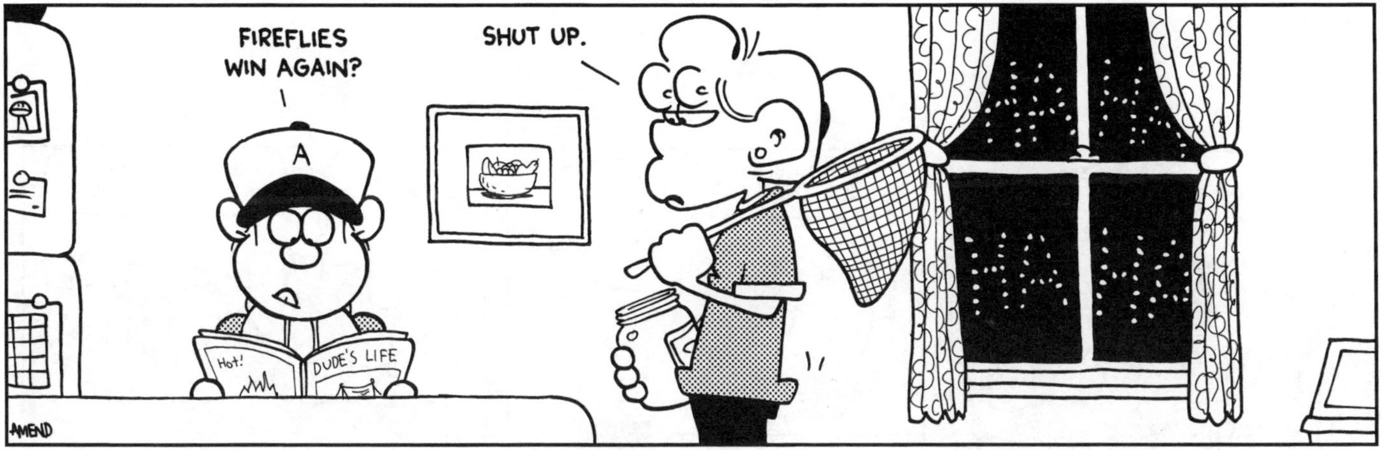
FIREFLIES WIN AGAIN?
SHUT UP.
HA HA
Hot!
DUDE'S LIFE
AMEND

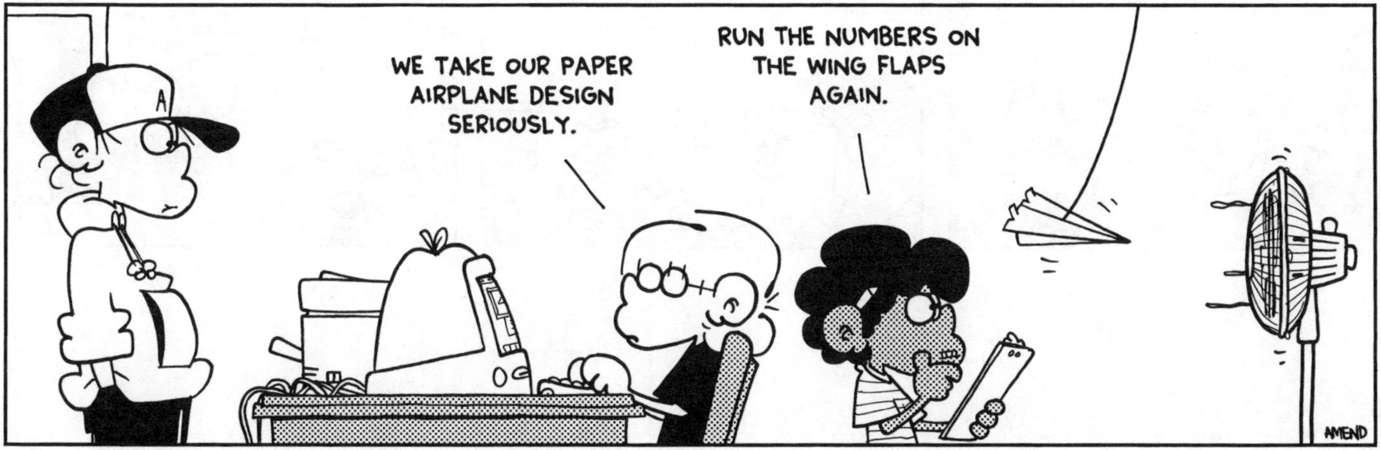
WE TAKE OUR PAPER AIRPLANE DESIGN SERIOUSLY.
RUN THE NUMBERS ON THE WING FLAPS AGAIN.
AMEND

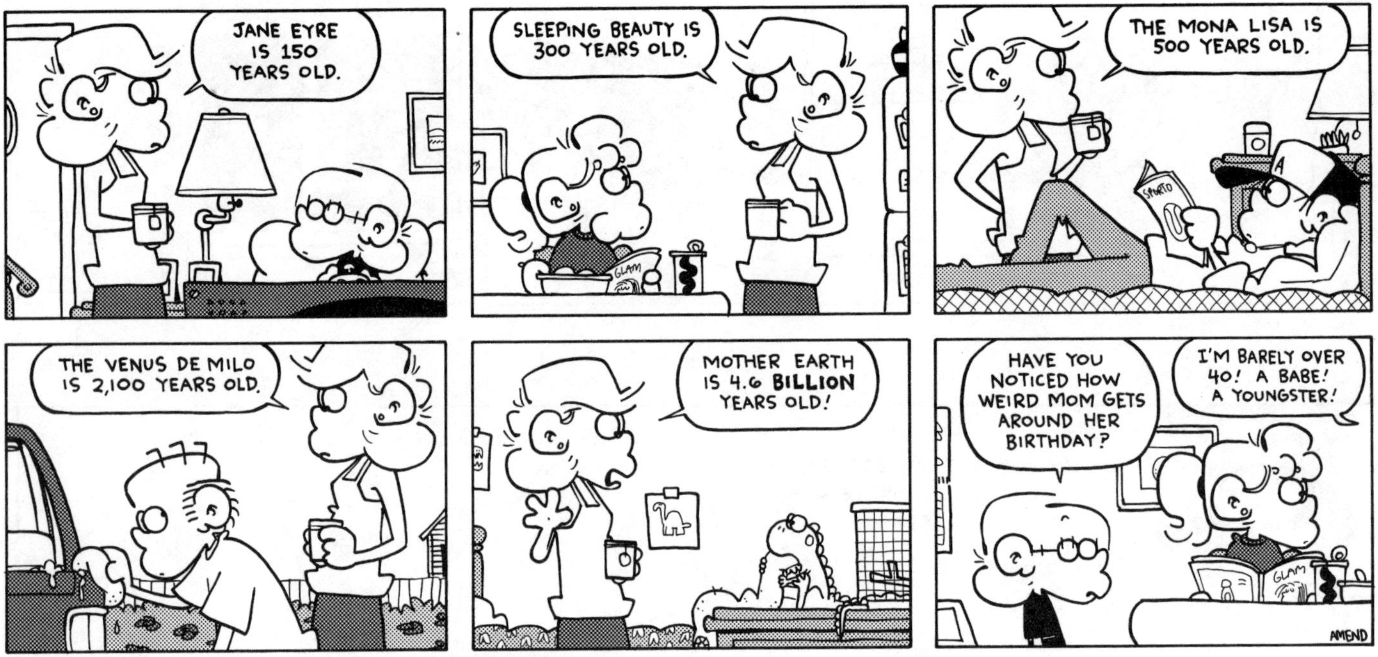

JANE EYRE IS 150 YEARS OLD.
SLEEPING BEAUTY IS 300 YEARS OLD.
GLAM
THE MONA LISA IS 500 YEARS OLD.
SPORTO
THE VENUS DE MILO IS 2,100 YEARS OLD.
MOTHER EARTH IS 4.6 **BILLION** YEARS OLD!
HAVE YOU NOTICED HOW WEIRD MOM GETS AROUND HER BIRTHDAY?
I'M BARELY OVER 40! A BABE! A YOUNGSTER!
GLAM
AMEND

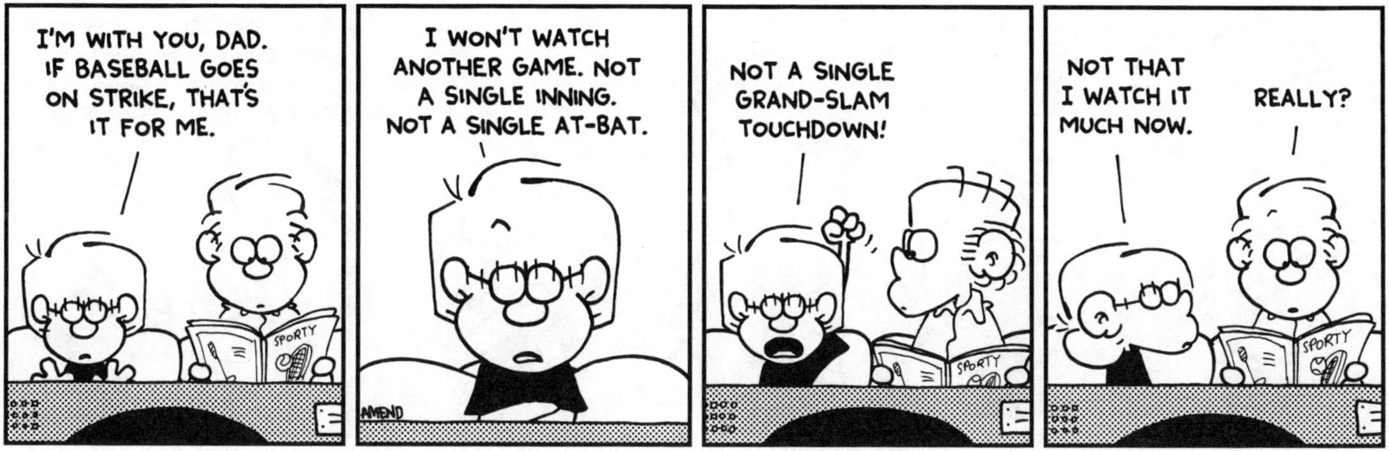
I'M WITH YOU, DAD. IF BASEBALL GOES ON STRIKE, THAT'S IT FOR ME.
SPORTY
I WON'T WATCH ANOTHER GAME. NOT A SINGLE INNING. NOT A SINGLE AT-BAT.
AMEND
NOT A SINGLE GRAND-SLAM TOUCHDOWN!
SPORTY
NOT THAT I WATCH IT MUCH NOW.
REALLY?
SPORTY

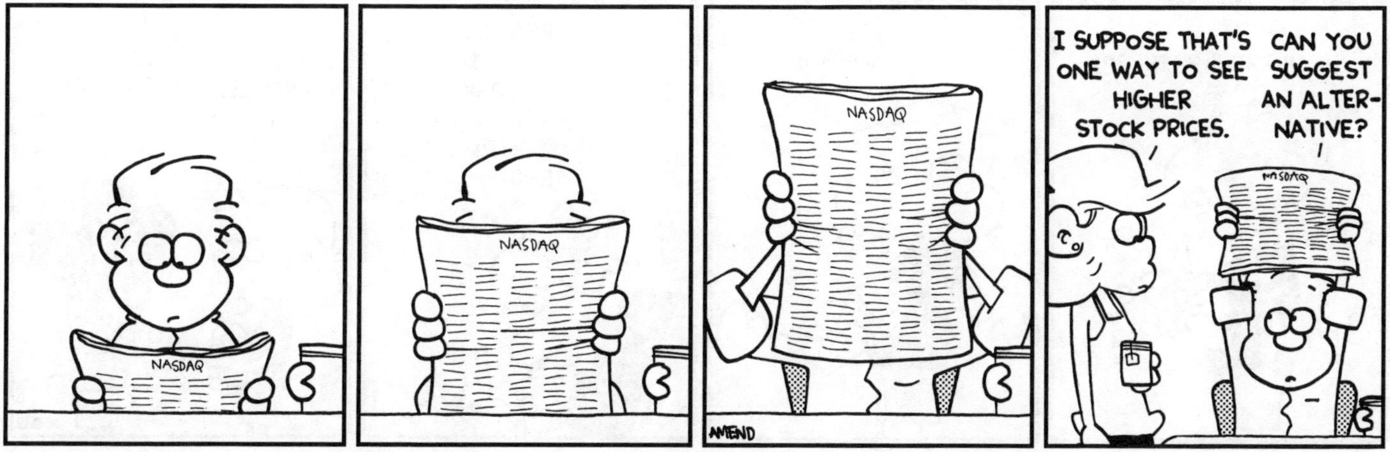
NASDAQ
NASDAQ
NASDAQ
AMEND
I SUPPOSE THAT'S ONE WAY TO SEE HIGHER STOCK PRICES.
CAN YOU SUGGEST AN ALTER-NATIVE?
NASDAQ

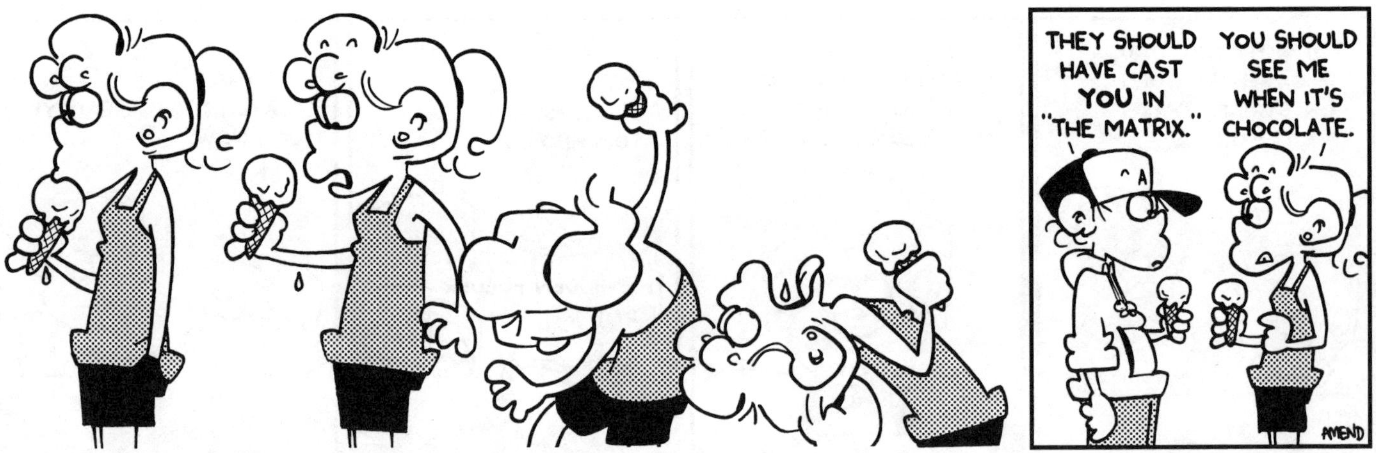
THEY SHOULD HAVE CAST YOU IN "THE MATRIX."
YOU SHOULD SEE ME WHEN IT'S CHOCOLATE.
AMEND

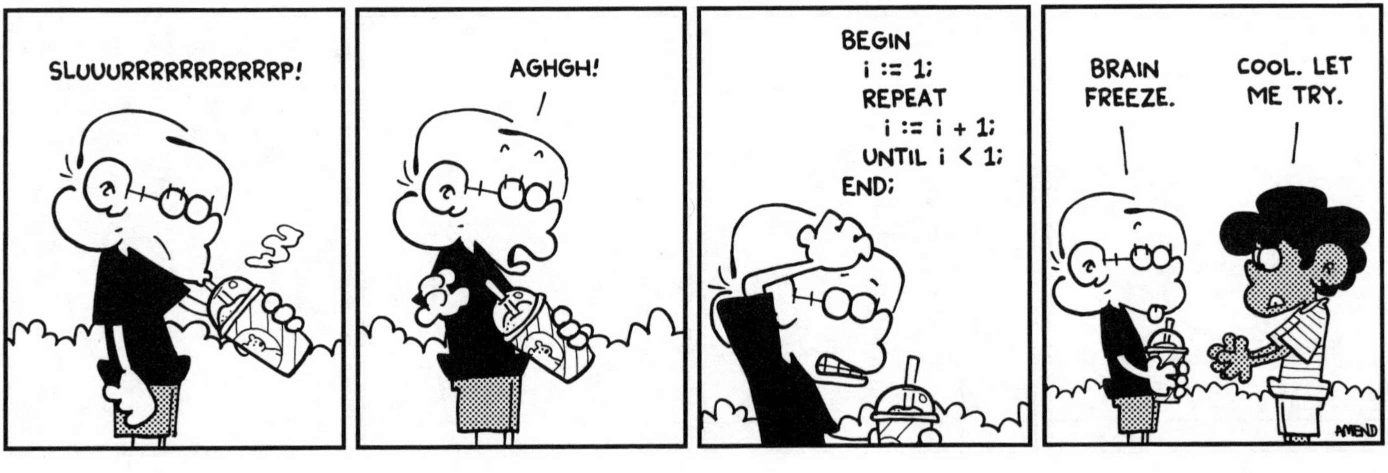
SLUUURRRRRRRRRRP!
AGHGH!
BEGIN
i := 1;
REPEAT
i := i + 1;
UNTIL i < 1;
END;
BRAIN FREEZE.
COOL. LET ME TRY.
AMEND

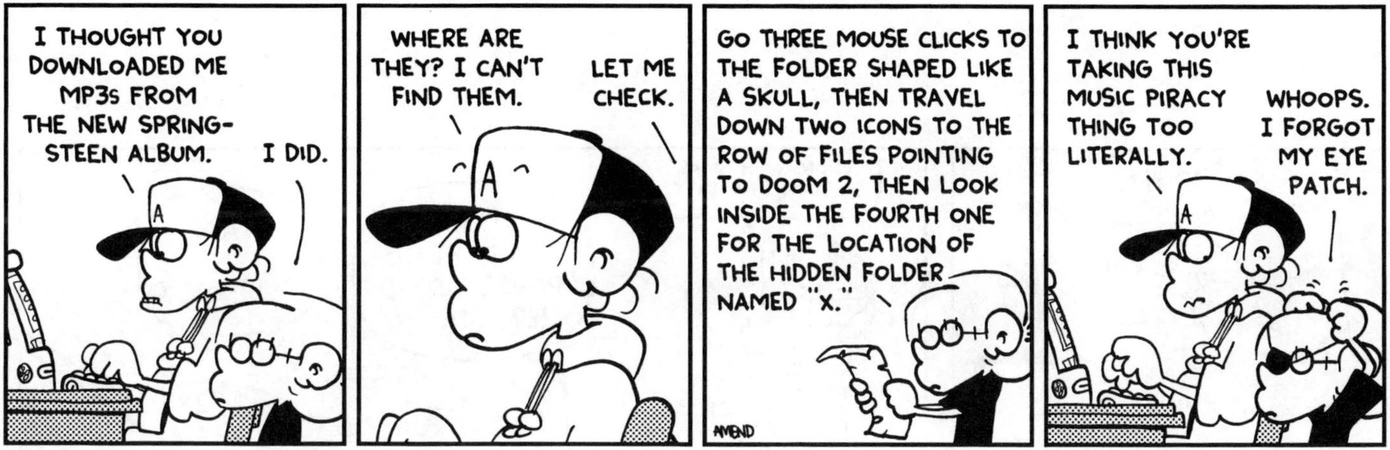
I THOUGHT YOU DOWNLOADED ME MP3s FROM THE NEW SPRING-STEEN ALBUM.
I DID.
WHERE ARE THEY? I CAN'T FIND THEM.
LET ME CHECK.
GO THREE MOUSE CLICKS TO THE FOLDER SHAPED LIKE A SKULL, THEN TRAVEL DOWN TWO ICONS TO THE ROW OF FILES POINTING TO DOOM 2, THEN LOOK INSIDE THE FOURTH ONE FOR THE LOCATION OF THE HIDDEN FOLDER NAMED "X."
AMEND
I THINK YOU'RE TAKING THIS MUSIC PIRACY THING TOO LITERALLY.
WHOOPS. I FORGOT MY EYE PATCH.

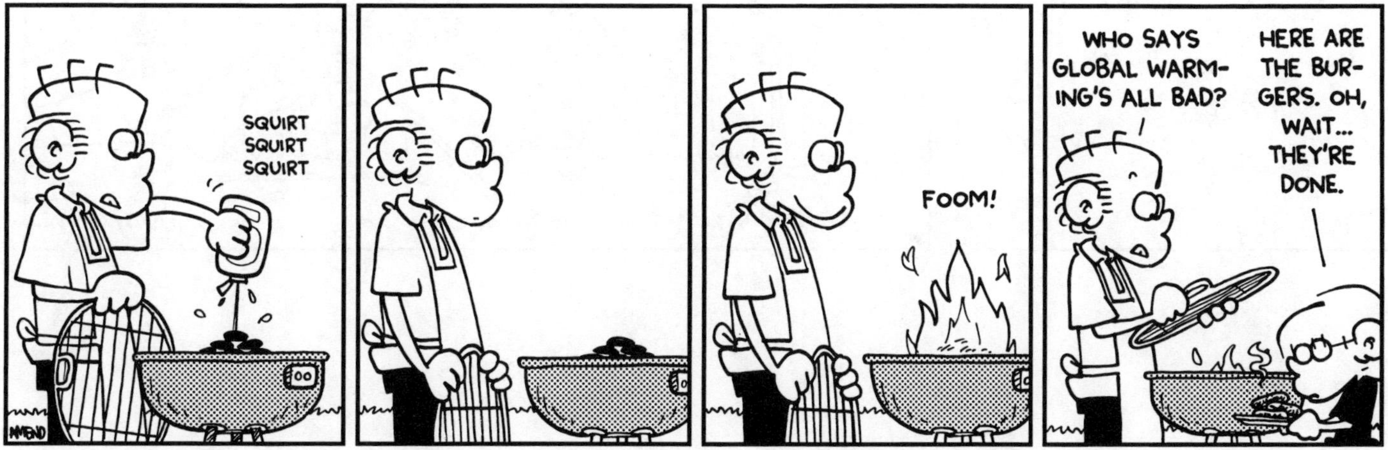
SQUIRT SQUIRT SQUIRT
AMEND
FOOM!
WHO SAYS GLOBAL WARM-ING'S ALL BAD?
HERE ARE THE BUR-GERS. OH, WAIT... THEY'RE DONE.

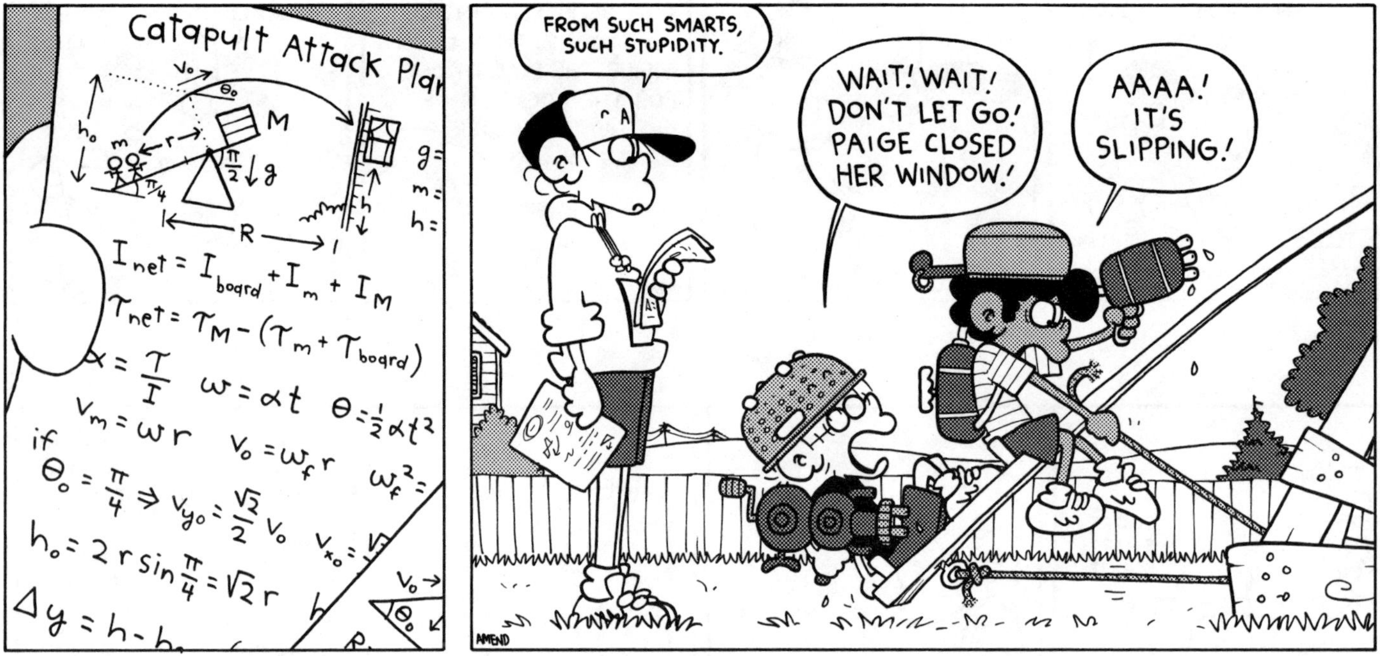
Catapult Attack
I net = I board + I m + I M
FROM SUCH SMARTS, SUCH STUPIDITY.
WAIT! WAIT! DON'T LET GO! PAIGE CLOSED HER WINDOW!
AAAA! IT'S SLIPPING!
AMEND

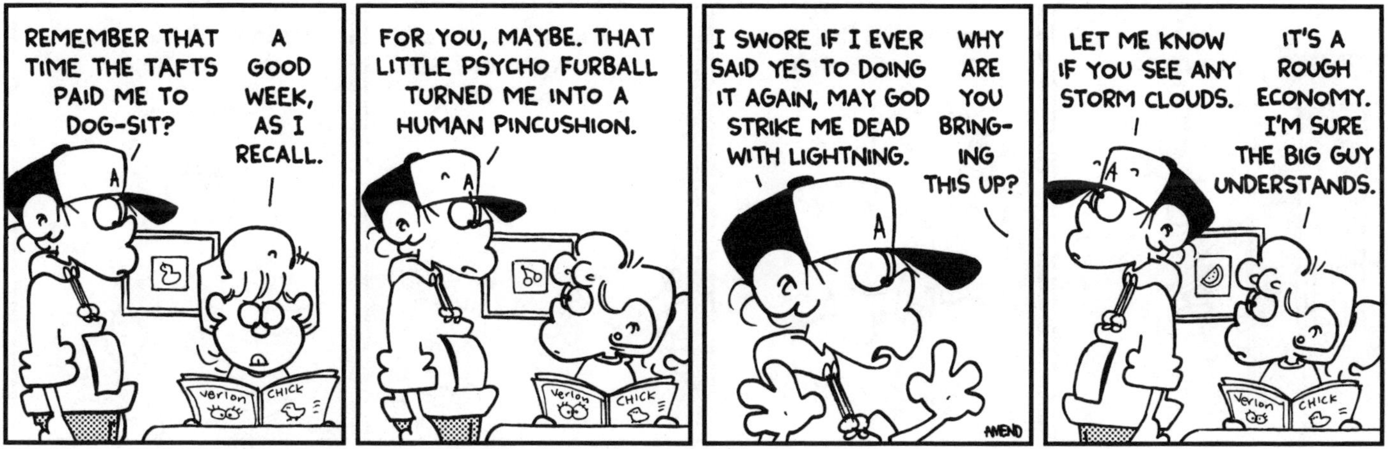
REMEMBER THAT TIME THE TAFTS PAID ME TO DOG-SIT?
A GOOD WEEK, AS I RECALL.
FOR YOU, MAYBE. THAT LITTLE PSYCHO FURBALL TURNED ME INTO A HUMAN PINCUSHION.
I SWORE IF I EVER SAID YES TO DOING IT AGAIN, MAY GOD STRIKE ME DEAD WITH LIGHTNING.
WHY ARE YOU BRING-ING THIS UP?
LET ME KNOW IF YOU SEE ANY STORM CLOUDS.
IT'S A ROUGH ECONOMY. I'M SURE THE BIG GUY UNDERSTANDS.
AMEND

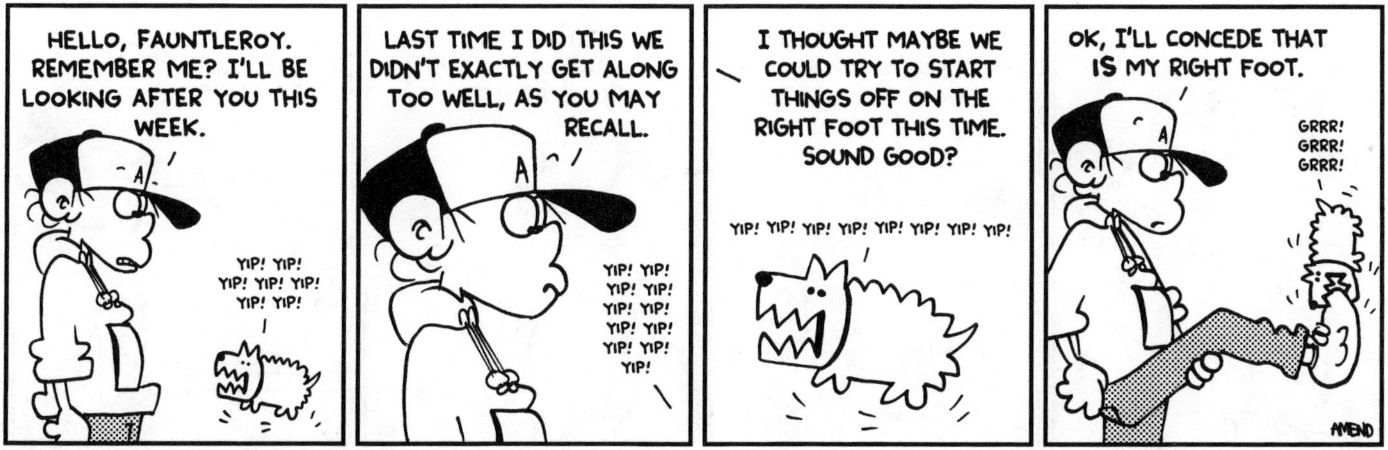
HELLO, FAUNTLEROY. REMEMBER ME? I'LL BE LOOKING AFTER YOU THIS WEEK.
YIP! YIP! YIP! YIP! YIP! YIP! YIP!
LAST TIME I DID THIS WE DIDN'T EXACTLY GET ALONG TOO WELL, AS YOU MAY RECALL.
YIP! YIP! YIP! YIP! YIP! YIP! YIP! YIP! YIP! YIP! YIP!
I THOUGHT MAYBE WE COULD TRY TO START THINGS OFF ON THE RIGHT FOOT THIS TIME. SOUND GOOD?
YIP! YIP! YIP! YIP! YIP! YIP! YIP! YIP!
OK, I'LL CONCEDE THAT IS MY RIGHT FOOT.
GRRR! GRRR! GRRR!
AMEND

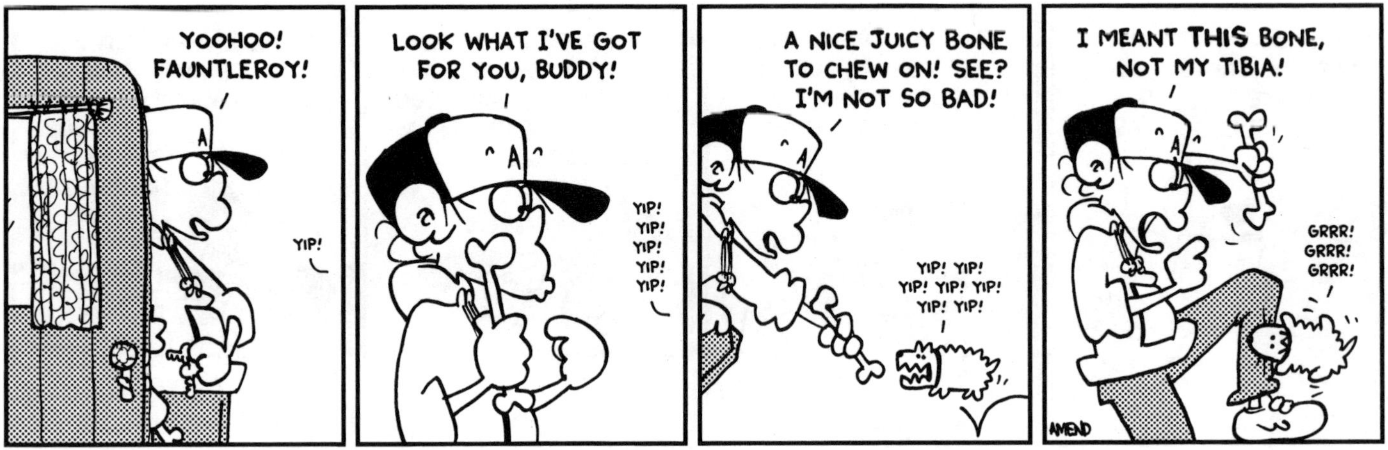
YOOHOO! FAUNTLEROY!
YIP!
LOOK WHAT I'VE GOT FOR YOU, BUDDY!
YIP! YIP! YIP! YIP! YIP!
A NICE JUICY BONE TO CHEW ON! SEE? I'M NOT SO BAD!
YIP! YIP! YIP! YIP! YIP! YIP! YIP!
I MEANT THIS BONE, NOT MY TIBIA!
GRRR! GRRR! GRRR!
AMEND

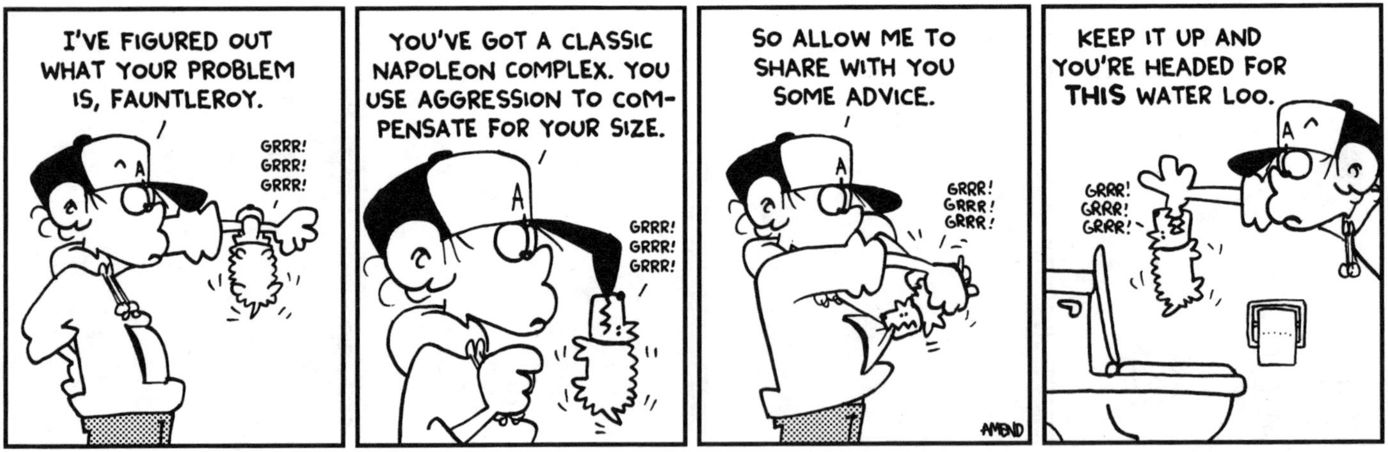
I'VE FIGURED OUT WHAT YOUR PROBLEM IS, FAUNTLEROY.
GRRR! GRRR! GRRR!
YOU'VE GOT A CLASSIC NAPOLEON COMPLEX. YOU USE AGGRESSION TO COMPENSATE FOR YOUR SIZE.
GRRR! GRRR! GRRR!
SO ALLOW ME TO SHARE WITH YOU SOME ADVICE.
GRRR! GRRR! GRRR!
AMEND
KEEP IT UP AND YOU'RE HEADED FOR THIS WATER LOO.
GRRR! GRRR! GRRR!

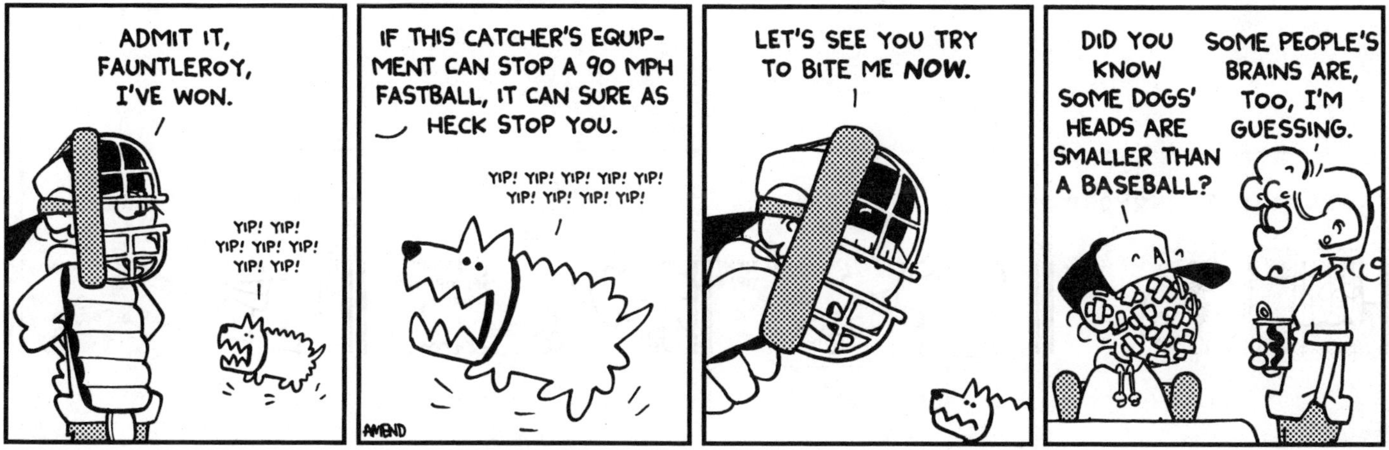
ADMIT IT, FAUNTLEROY, I'VE WON.
YIP! YIP! YIP! YIP! YIP! YIP! YIP!
IF THIS CATCHER'S EQUIPMENT CAN STOP A 90 MPH FASTBALL, IT CAN SURE AS HECK STOP YOU.
YIP! YIP! YIP! YIP! YIP! YIP! YIP! YIP! YIP!
AMEND
LET'S SEE YOU TRY TO BITE ME NOW.
DID YOU KNOW SOME DOGS' HEADS ARE SMALLER THAN A BASEBALL?
SOME PEOPLE'S BRAINS ARE, TOO, I'M GUESSING.

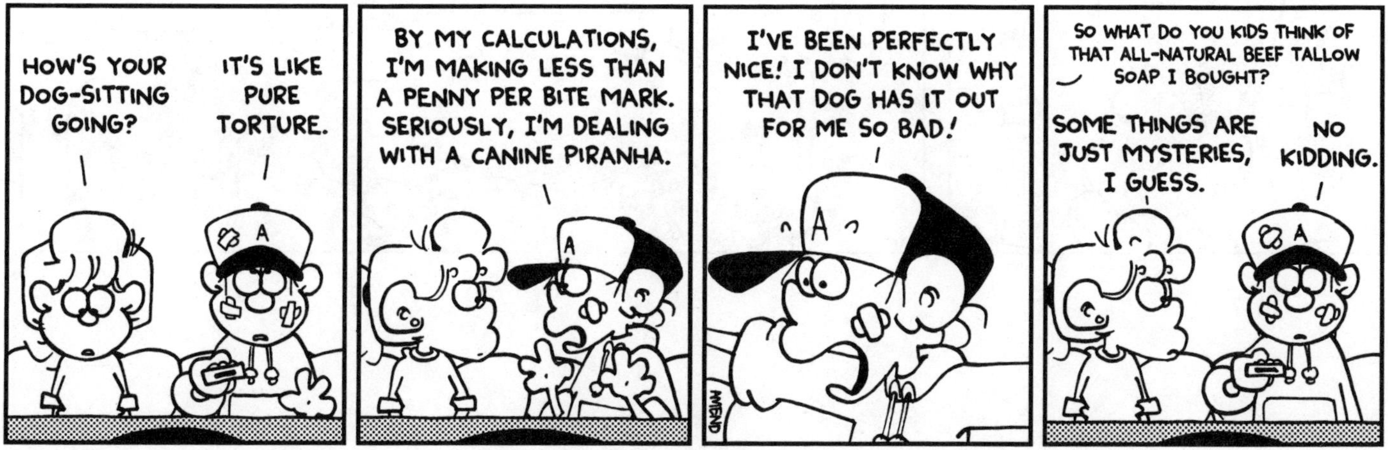
HOW'S YOUR DOG-SITTING GOING?
IT'S LIKE PURE TORTURE.
BY MY CALCULATIONS, I'M MAKING LESS THAN A PENNY PER BITE MARK. SERIOUSLY, I'M DEALING WITH A CANINE PIRANHA.
AMEND
I'VE BEEN PERFECTLY NICE! I DON'T KNOW WHY THAT DOG HAS IT OUT FOR ME SO BAD!
SO WHAT DO YOU KIDS THINK OF THAT ALL-NATURAL BEEF TALLOW SOAP I BOUGHT?
SOME THINGS ARE JUST MYSTERIES, I GUESS.
NO KIDDING.

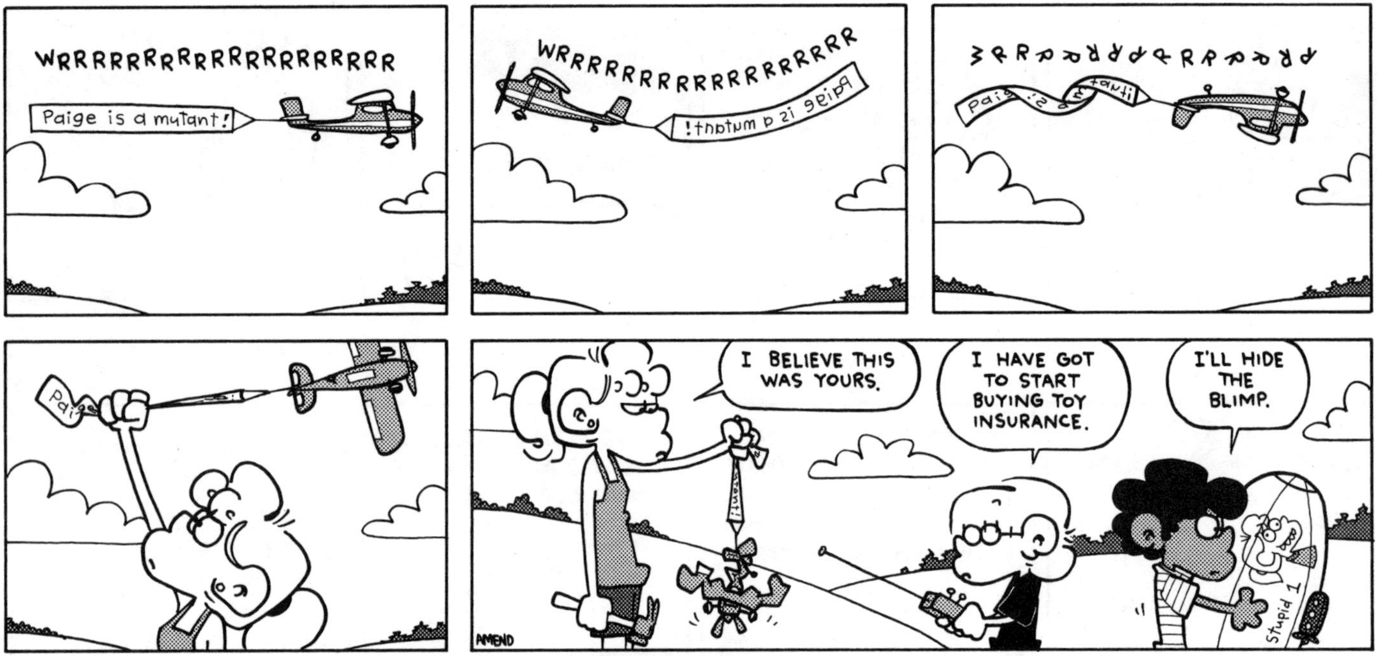
WRRRRRRRRRRRRRRRRRRR
Paige is a mutant!
I BELIEVE THIS WAS YOURS.
I HAVE GOT TO START BUYING TOY INSURANCE.
I'LL HIDE THE BLIMP.
Stupid 1
AMEND

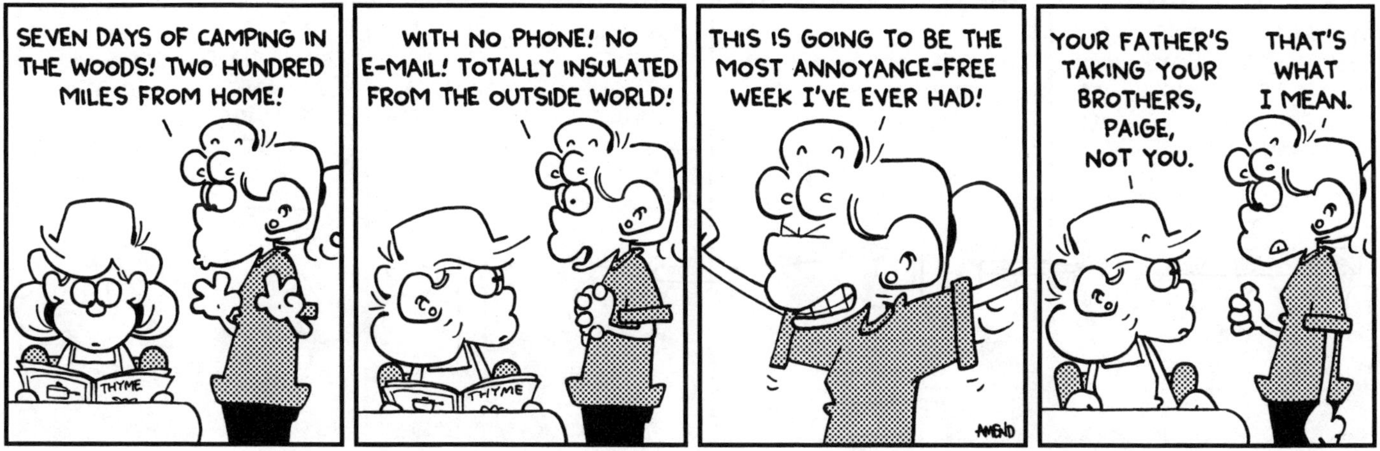
SEVEN DAYS OF CAMPING IN THE WOODS! TWO HUNDRED MILES FROM HOME!
WITH NO PHONE! NO E-MAIL! TOTALLY INSULATED FROM THE OUTSIDE WORLD!
THIS IS GOING TO BE THE MOST ANNOYANCE-FREE WEEK I'VE EVER HAD!
YOUR FATHER'S TAKING YOUR BROTHERS, PAIGE, NOT YOU.
THAT'S WHAT I MEAN.

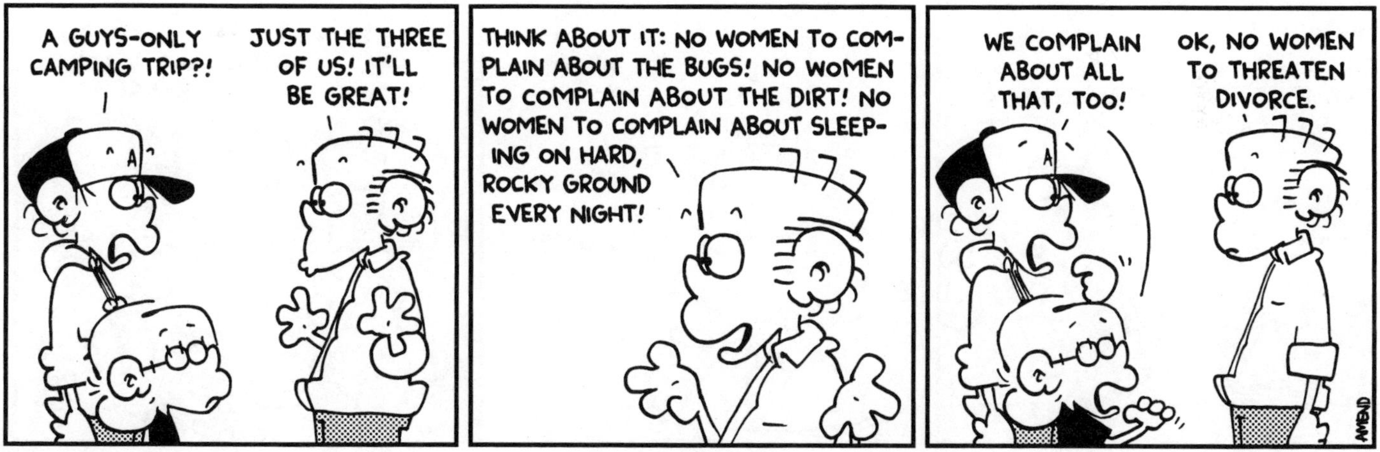
A GUYS-ONLY CAMPING TRIP?!
JUST THE THREE OF US! IT'LL BE GREAT!
THINK ABOUT IT: NO WOMEN TO COMPLAIN ABOUT THE BUGS! NO WOMEN TO COMPLAIN ABOUT THE DIRT! NO WOMEN TO COMPLAIN ABOUT SLEEPING ON HARD, ROCKY GROUND EVERY NIGHT!
WE COMPLAIN ABOUT ALL THAT, TOO!
OK, NO WOMEN TO THREATEN DIVORCE.

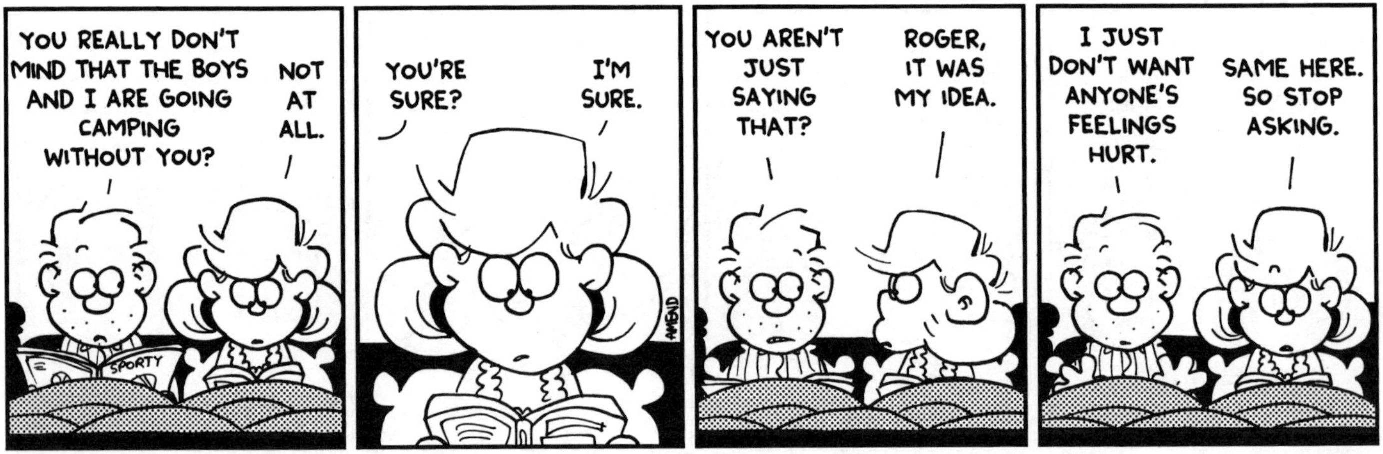
YOU REALLY DON'T MIND THAT THE BOYS AND I ARE GOING CAMPING WITHOUT YOU?
NOT AT ALL.
SPORTY
YOU'RE SURE?
I'M SURE.
AMEND
YOU AREN'T JUST SAYING THAT?
ROGER, IT WAS MY IDEA.
I JUST DON'T WANT ANYONE'S FEELINGS HURT.
SAME HERE. SO STOP ASKING.

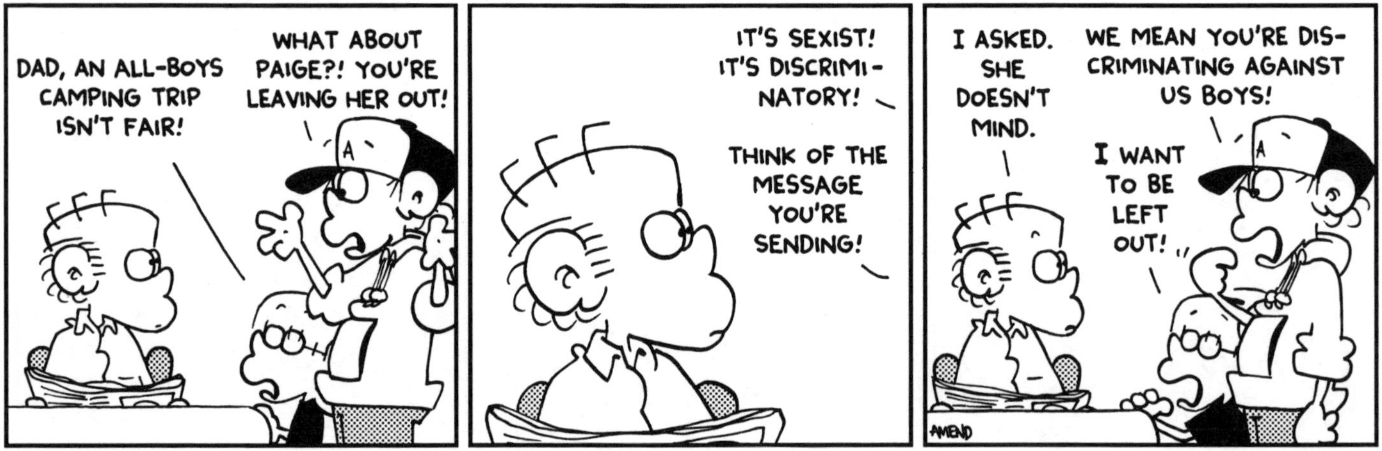
DAD, AN ALL-BOYS CAMPING TRIP ISN'T FAIR!
WHAT ABOUT PAIGE?! YOU'RE LEAVING HER OUT!
IT'S SEXIST! IT'S DISCRIMI-NATORY!
THINK OF THE MESSAGE YOU'RE SENDING!
I ASKED. SHE DOESN'T MIND.
WE MEAN YOU'RE DIS-CRIMINATING AGAINST US BOYS!
I WANT TO BE LEFT OUT!
AMEND

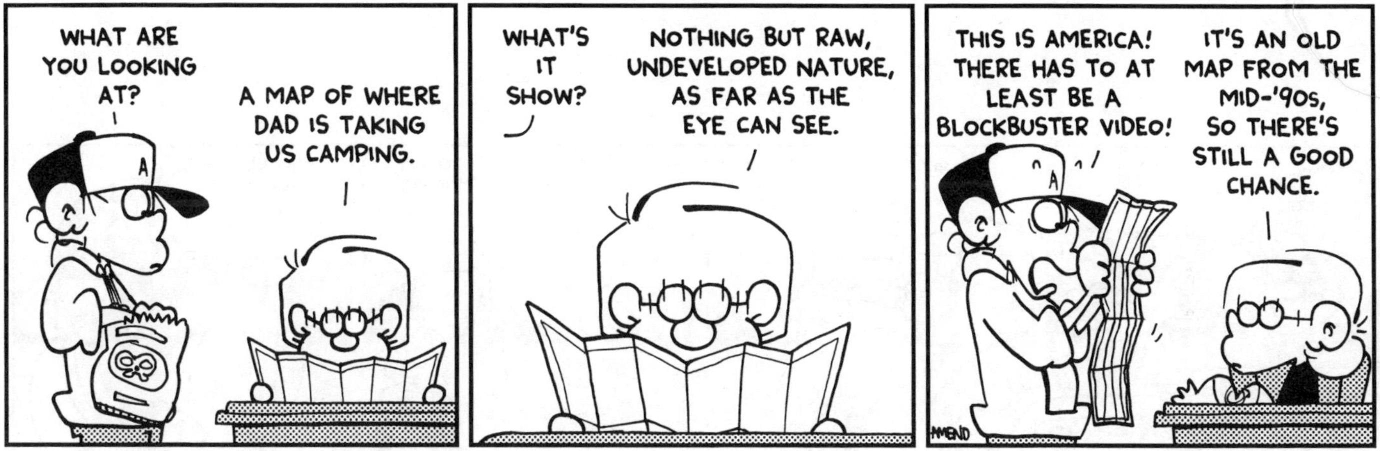
WHAT ARE YOU LOOKING AT?
A MAP OF WHERE DAD IS TAKING US CAMPING.
WHAT'S IT SHOW?
NOTHING BUT RAW, UNDEVELOPED NATURE, AS FAR AS THE EYE CAN SEE.
THIS IS AMERICA! THERE HAS TO AT LEAST BE A BLOCKBUSTER VIDEO!
IT'S AN OLD MAP FROM THE MID-'90s, SO THERE'S STILL A GOOD CHANCE.
AMEND

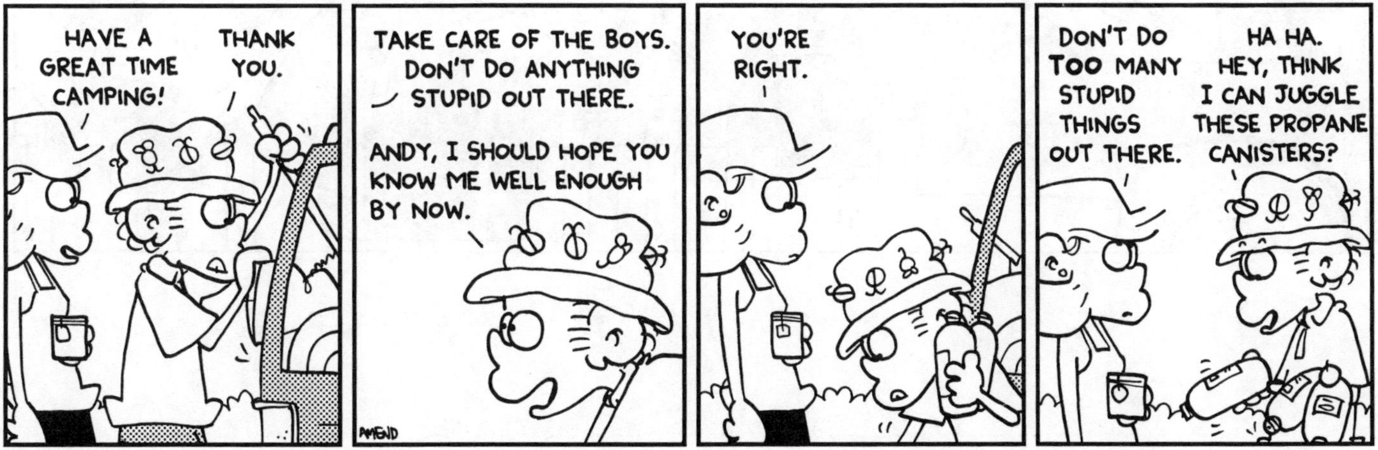
HAVE A GREAT TIME CAMPING!
THANK YOU.
TAKE CARE OF THE BOYS. DON'T DO ANYTHING STUPID OUT THERE.
ANDY, I SHOULD HOPE YOU KNOW ME WELL ENOUGH BY NOW.
AMEND
YOU'RE RIGHT.
DON'T DO **TOO** MANY STUPID THINGS OUT THERE.
HA HA. HEY, THINK I CAN JUGGLE THESE PROPANE CANISTERS?

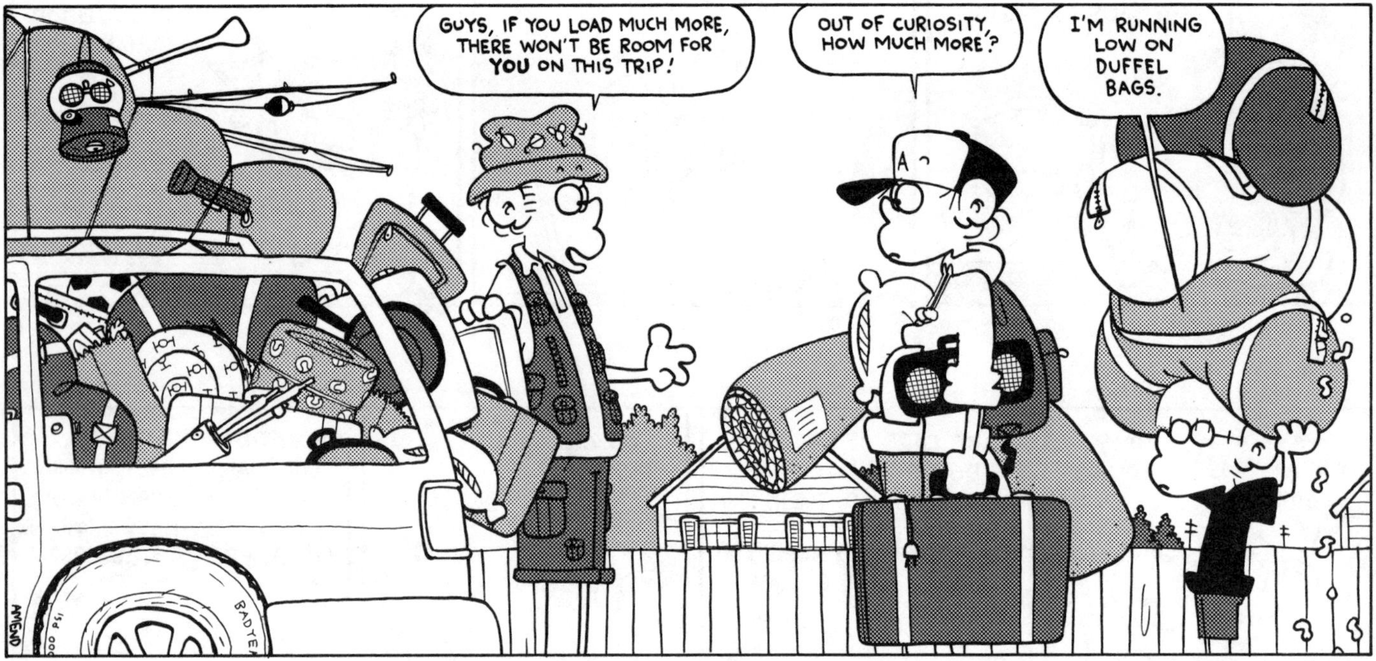
GUYS, IF YOU LOAD MUCH MORE, THERE WON'T BE ROOM FOR **YOU** ON THIS TRIP!
OUT OF CURIOSITY, HOW MUCH MORE?
I'M RUNNING LOW ON DUFFEL BAGS.

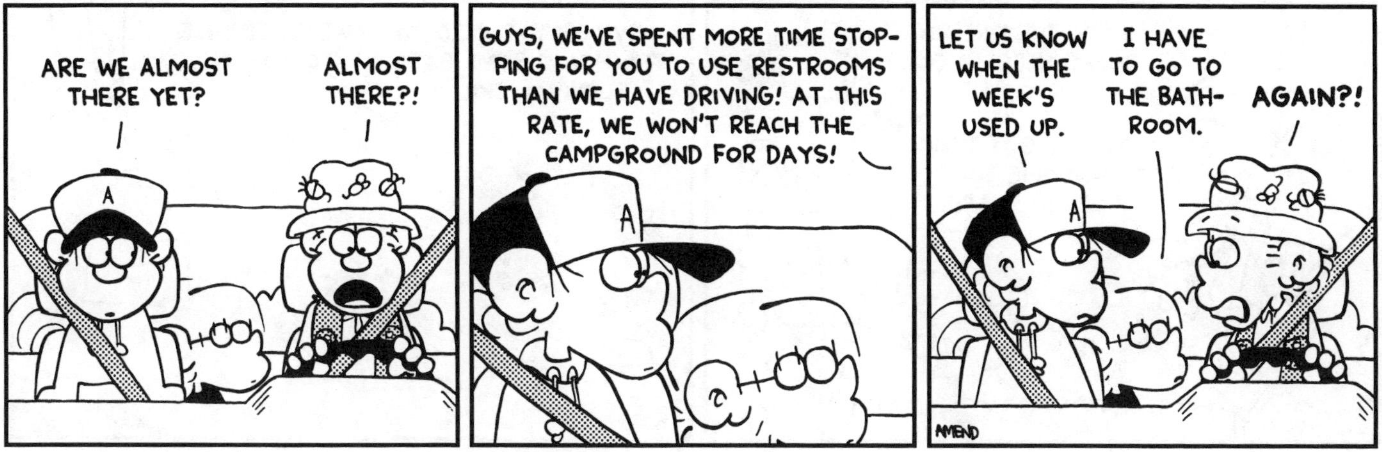
ARE WE ALMOST THERE YET?
ALMOST THERE?!
GUYS, WE'VE SPENT MORE TIME STOPPING FOR YOU TO USE RESTROOMS THAN WE HAVE DRIVING! AT THIS RATE, WE WON'T REACH THE CAMPGROUND FOR DAYS!
LET US KNOW WHEN THE WEEK'S USED UP.
I HAVE TO GO TO THE BATHROOM.
AGAIN?!
AMEND

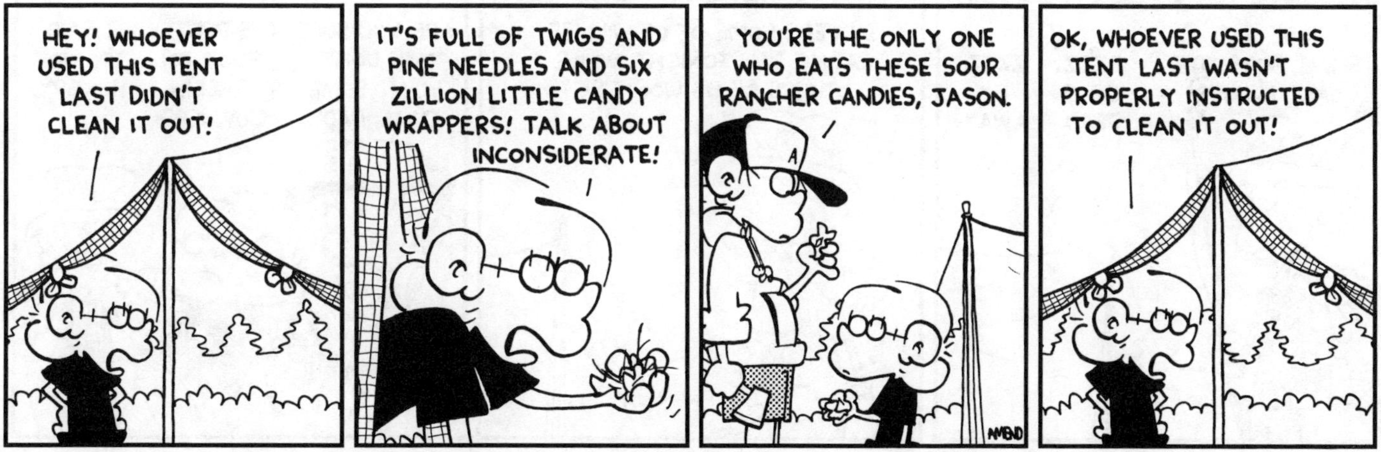
HEY! WHOEVER USED THIS TENT LAST DIDN'T CLEAN IT OUT!
IT'S FULL OF TWIGS AND PINE NEEDLES AND SIX ZILLION LITTLE CANDY WRAPPERS! TALK ABOUT INCONSIDERATE!
YOU'RE THE ONLY ONE WHO EATS THESE SOUR RANCHER CANDIES, JASON.
AMEND
OK, WHOEVER USED THIS TENT LAST WASN'T PROPERLY INSTRUCTED TO CLEAN IT OUT!

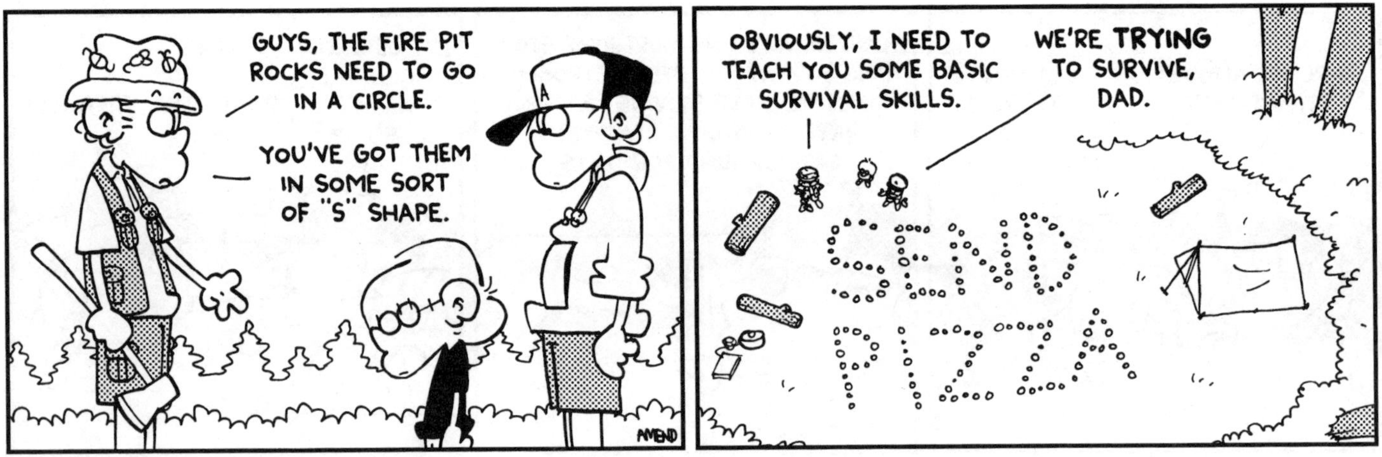
GUYS, THE FIRE PIT ROCKS NEED TO GO IN A CIRCLE.
YOU'VE GOT THEM IN SOME SORT OF "S" SHAPE.
AMEND
OBVIOUSLY, I NEED TO TEACH YOU SOME BASIC SURVIVAL SKILLS.
WE'RE TRYING TO SURVIVE, DAD.
SEND PIZZA

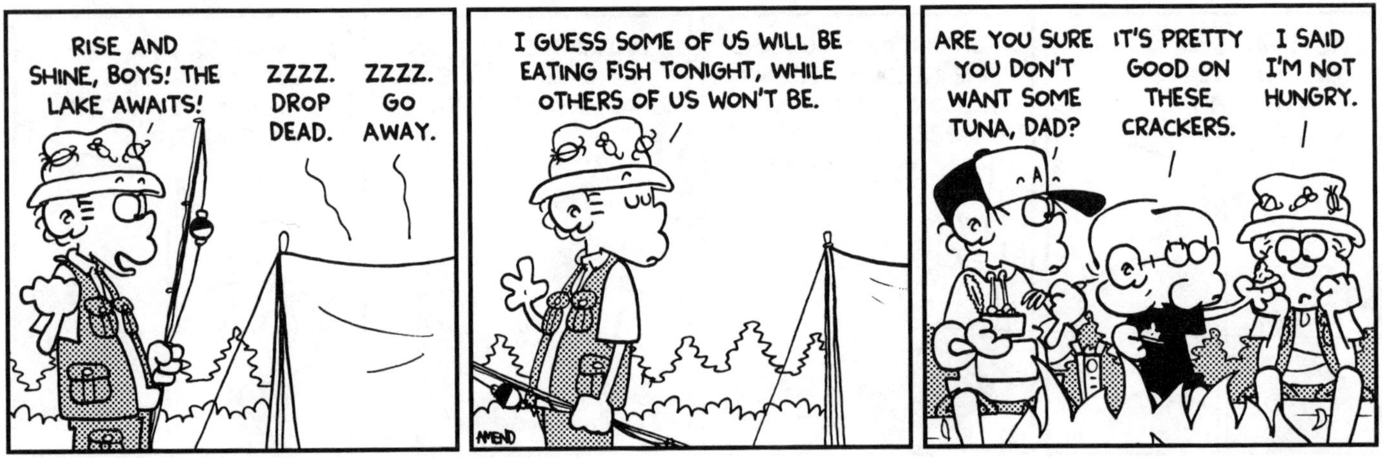
RISE AND SHINE, BOYS! THE LAKE AWAITS!
ZZZZ. DROP DEAD.
ZZZZ. GO AWAY.
I GUESS SOME OF US WILL BE EATING FISH TONIGHT, WHILE OTHERS OF US WON'T BE.
AMEND
ARE YOU SURE YOU DON'T WANT SOME TUNA, DAD?
IT'S PRETTY GOOD ON THESE CRACKERS.
I SAID I'M NOT HUNGRY.

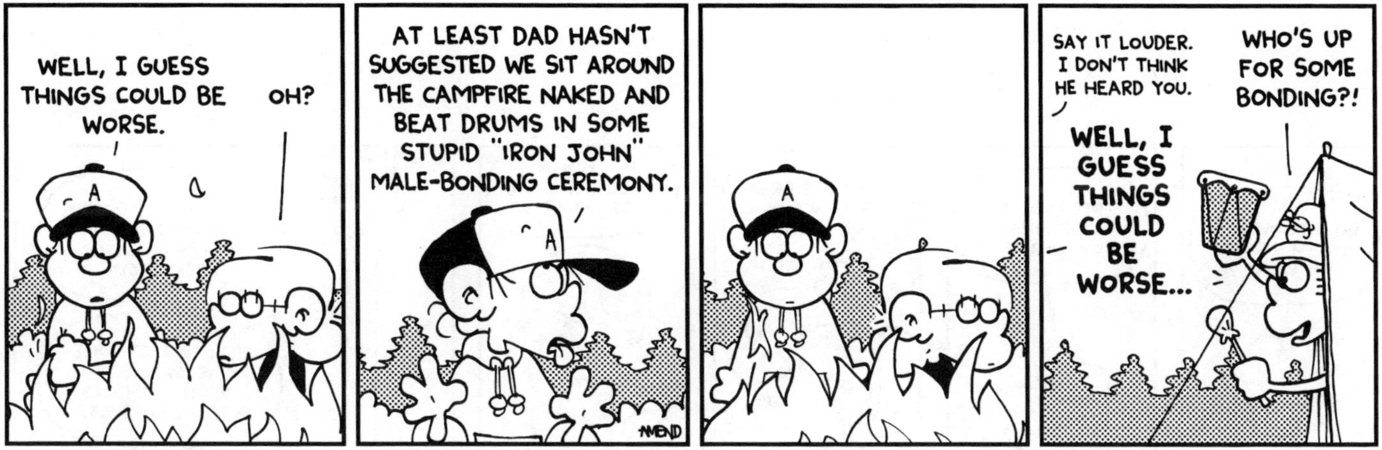
WELL, I GUESS THINGS COULD BE WORSE.
OH?
AT LEAST DAD HASN'T SUGGESTED WE SIT AROUND THE CAMPFIRE NAKED AND BEAT DRUMS IN SOME STUPID "IRON JOHN" MALE-BONDING CEREMONY.
AMEND
SAY IT LOUDER. I DON'T THINK HE HEARD YOU.
WELL, I GUESS THINGS COULD BE WORSE...
WHO'S UP FOR SOME BONDING?!

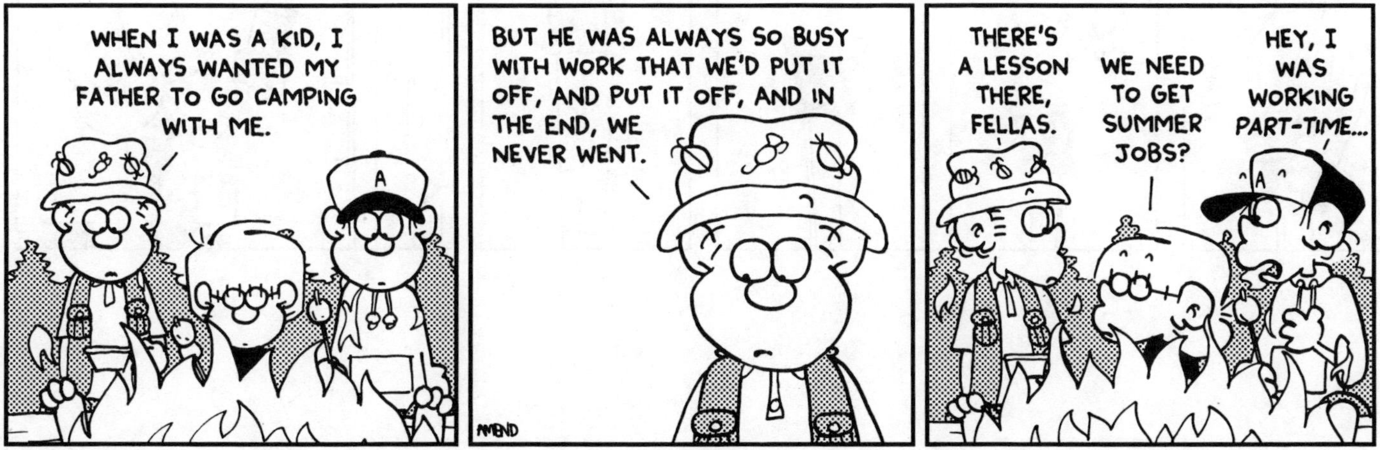
WHEN I WAS A KID, I ALWAYS WANTED MY FATHER TO GO CAMPING WITH ME.
BUT HE WAS ALWAYS SO BUSY WITH WORK THAT WE'D PUT IT OFF, AND PUT IT OFF, AND IN THE END, WE NEVER WENT.
AMEND
THERE'S A LESSON THERE, FELLAS.
WE NEED TO GET SUMMER JOBS?
HEY, I WAS WORKING PART-TIME...

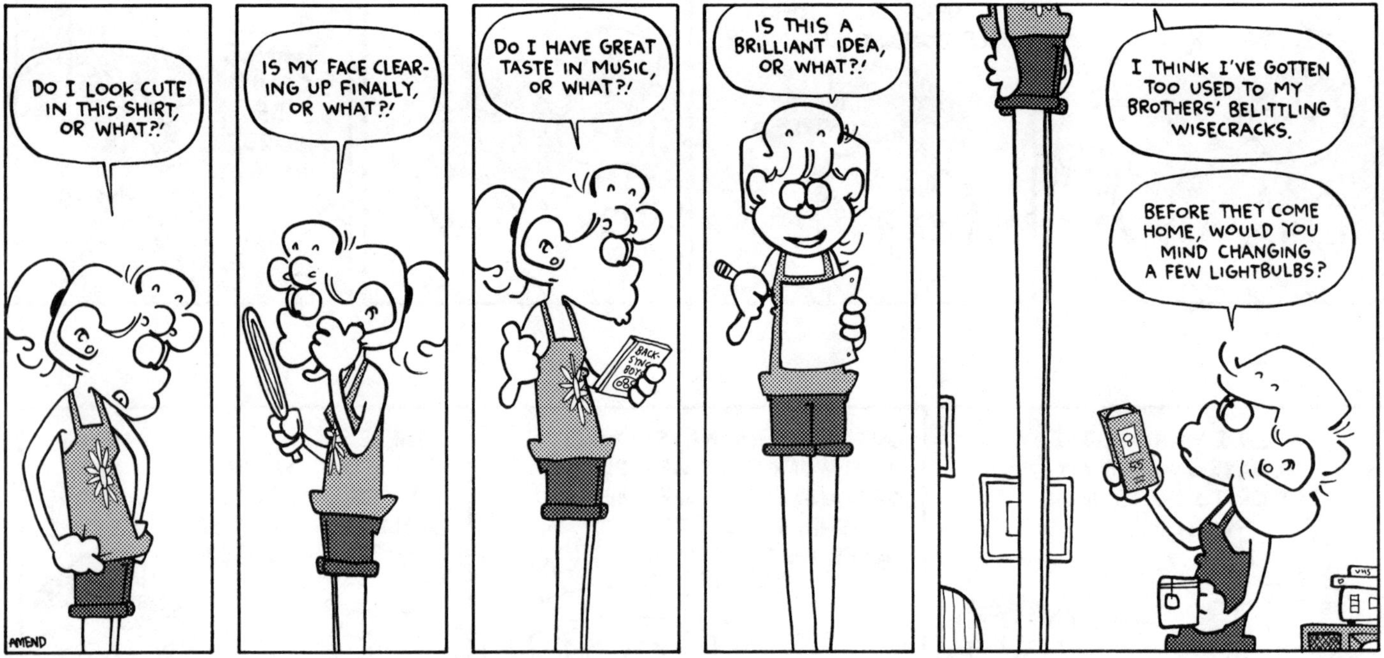
DO I LOOK CUTE IN THIS SHIRT, OR WHAT?!
IS MY FACE CLEAR-ING UP FINALLY, OR WHAT?!
DO I HAVE GREAT TASTE IN MUSIC, OR WHAT?!
BACK-SYNC BOY
IS THIS A BRILLIANT IDEA, OR WHAT?!
I THINK I'VE GOTTEN TOO USED TO MY BROTHERS' BELITTLING WISECRACKS.
BEFORE THEY COME HOME, WOULD YOU MIND CHANGING A FEW LIGHTBULBS?
AMEND

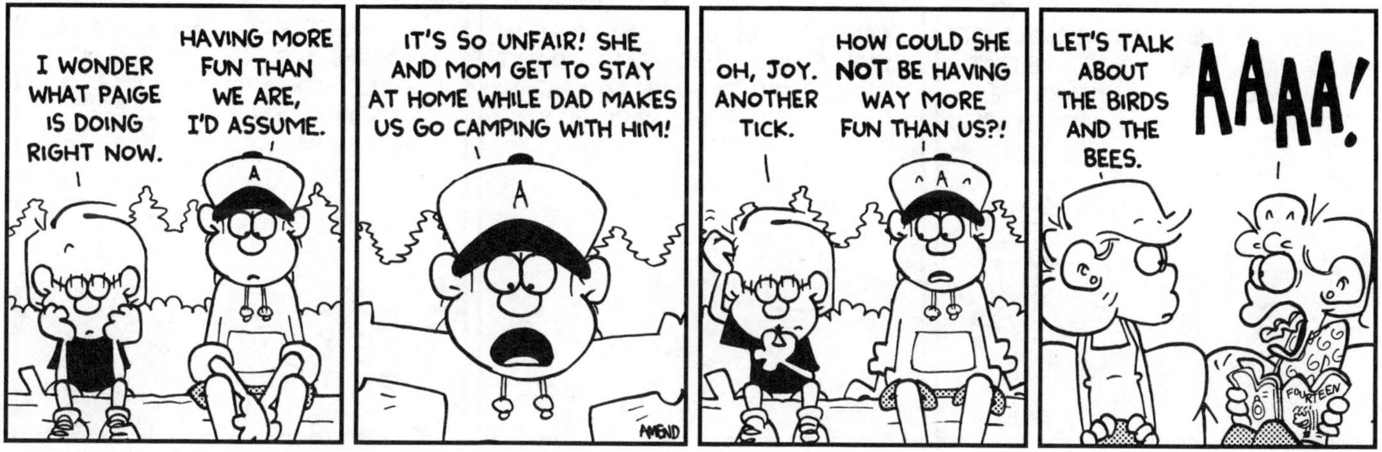
I WONDER WHAT PAIGE IS DOING RIGHT NOW.
HAVING MORE FUN THAN WE ARE, I'D ASSUME.
IT'S SO UNFAIR! SHE AND MOM GET TO STAY AT HOME WHILE DAD MAKES US GO CAMPING WITH HIM!
AMEND
OH, JOY. ANOTHER TICK.
HOW COULD SHE NOT BE HAVING WAY MORE FUN THAN US?!
LET'S TALK ABOUT THE BIRDS AND THE BEES.
AAAA!
FOURTEEN

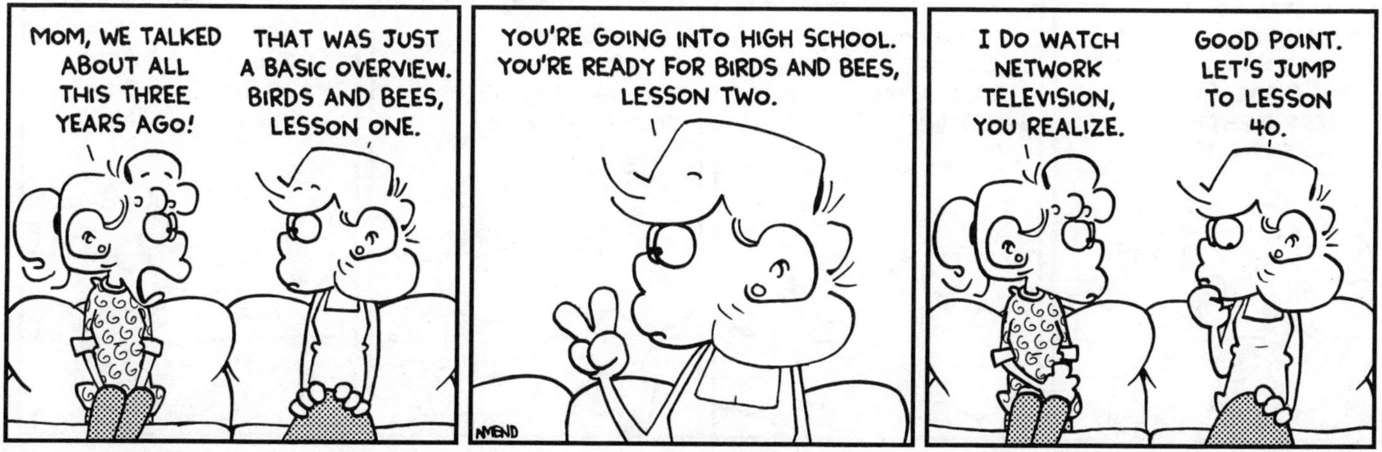
MOM, WE TALKED ABOUT ALL THIS THREE YEARS AGO!
THAT WAS JUST A BASIC OVERVIEW. BIRDS AND BEES, LESSON ONE.
YOU'RE GOING INTO HIGH SCHOOL. YOU'RE READY FOR BIRDS AND BEES, LESSON TWO.
AMEND
I DO WATCH NETWORK TELEVISION, YOU REALIZE.
GOOD POINT. LET'S JUMP TO LESSON 40.

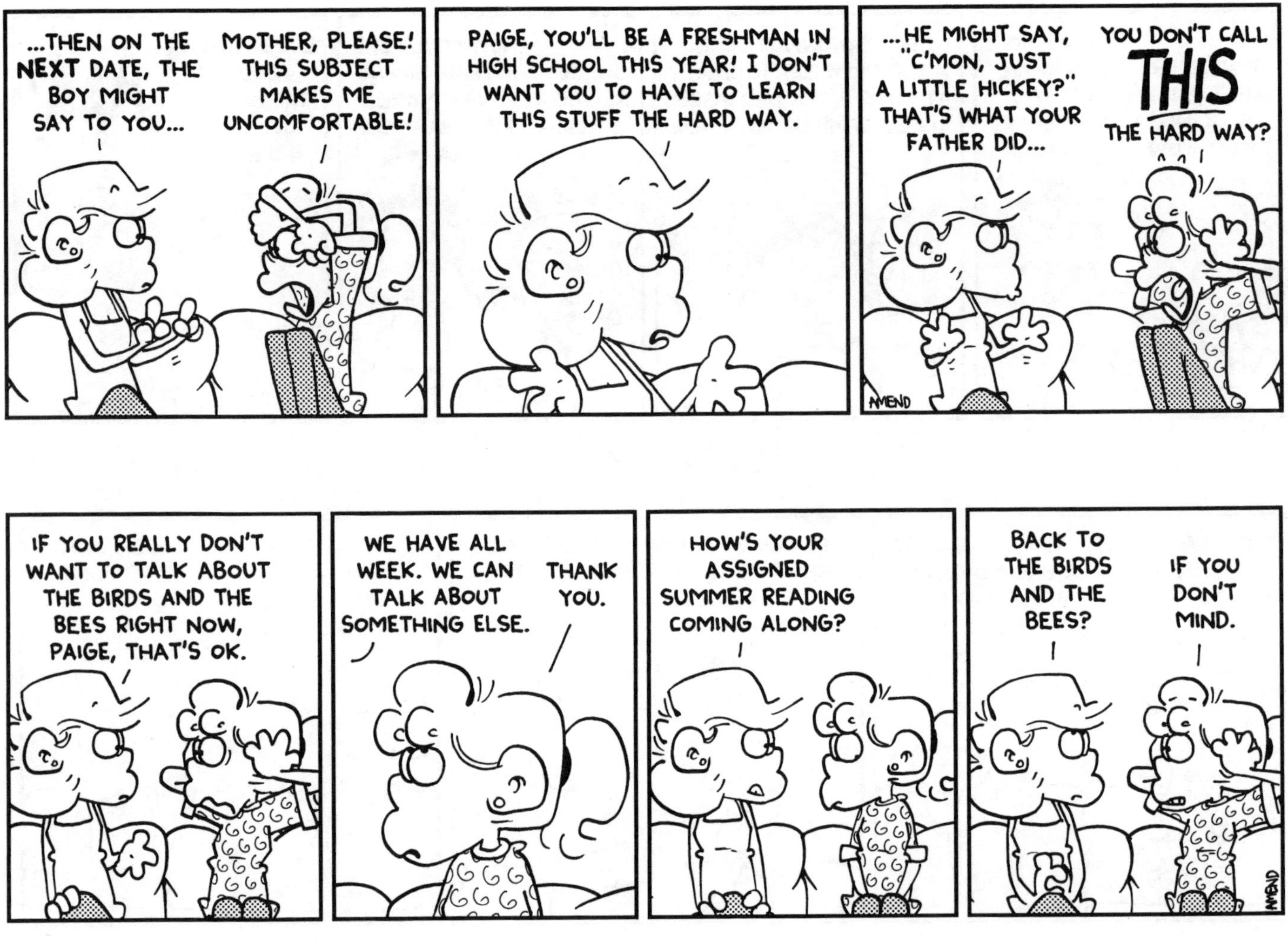
...THEN ON THE **NEXT** DATE, THE BOY MIGHT SAY TO YOU...
MOTHER, PLEASE! THIS SUBJECT MAKES ME UNCOMFORTABLE!
PAIGE, YOU'LL BE A FRESHMAN IN HIGH SCHOOL THIS YEAR! I DON'T WANT YOU TO HAVE TO LEARN THIS STUFF THE HARD WAY.
...HE MIGHT SAY, "C'MON, JUST A LITTLE HICKEY?" THAT'S WHAT YOUR FATHER DID...
YOU DON'T CALL **THIS** THE HARD WAY?
AMEND
IF YOU REALLY DON'T WANT TO TALK ABOUT THE BIRDS AND THE BEES RIGHT NOW, PAIGE, THAT'S OK.
WE HAVE ALL WEEK. WE CAN TALK ABOUT SOMETHING ELSE.
THANK YOU.
HOW'S YOUR ASSIGNED SUMMER READING COMING ALONG?
BACK TO THE BIRDS AND THE BEES?
IF YOU DON'T MIND.
AMEND

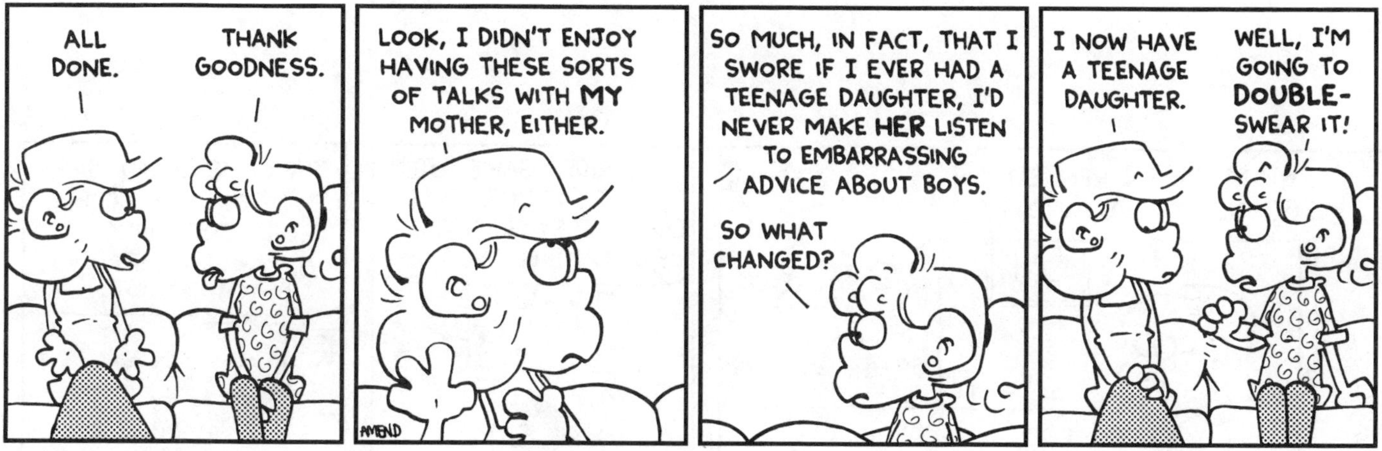
ALL DONE.
THANK GOODNESS.
LOOK, I DIDN'T ENJOY HAVING THESE SORTS OF TALKS WITH MY MOTHER, EITHER.
SO MUCH, IN FACT, THAT I SWORE IF I EVER HAD A TEENAGE DAUGHTER, I'D NEVER MAKE HER LISTEN TO EMBARRASSING ADVICE ABOUT BOYS.
SO WHAT CHANGED?
I NOW HAVE A TEENAGE DAUGHTER.
WELL, I'M GOING TO DOUBLE-SWEAR IT!
AMEND

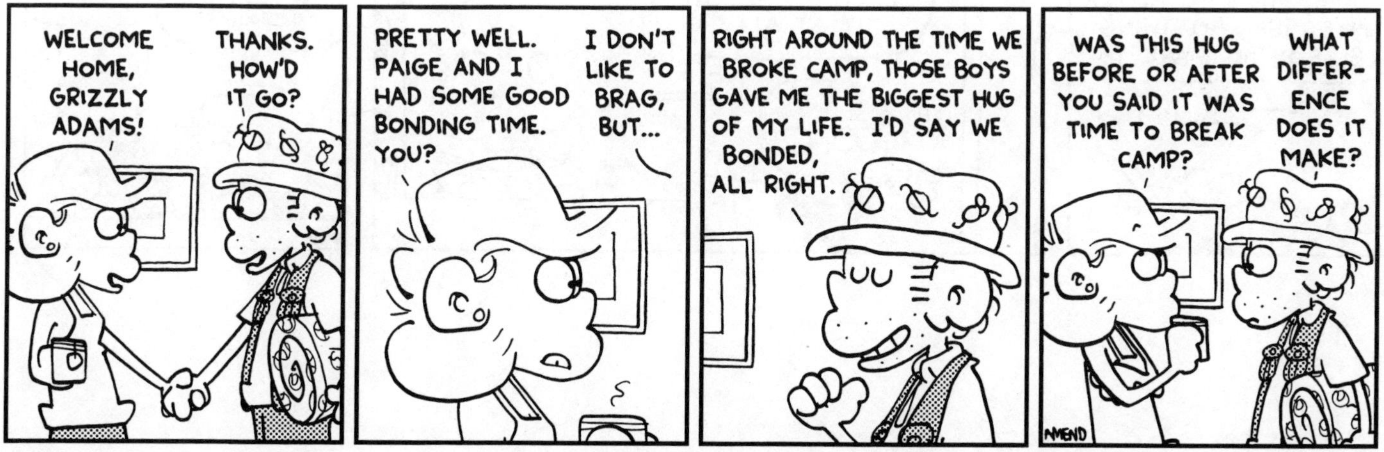
WELCOME HOME, GRIZZLY ADAMS!
THANKS. HOW'D IT GO?
PRETTY WELL. PAIGE AND I HAD SOME GOOD BONDING TIME. YOU?
I DON'T LIKE TO BRAG, BUT...
RIGHT AROUND THE TIME WE BROKE CAMP, THOSE BOYS GAVE ME THE BIGGEST HUG OF MY LIFE. I'D SAY WE BONDED, ALL RIGHT.
WAS THIS HUG BEFORE OR AFTER YOU SAID IT WAS TIME TO BREAK CAMP?
WHAT DIFFERENCE DOES IT MAKE?
AMEND

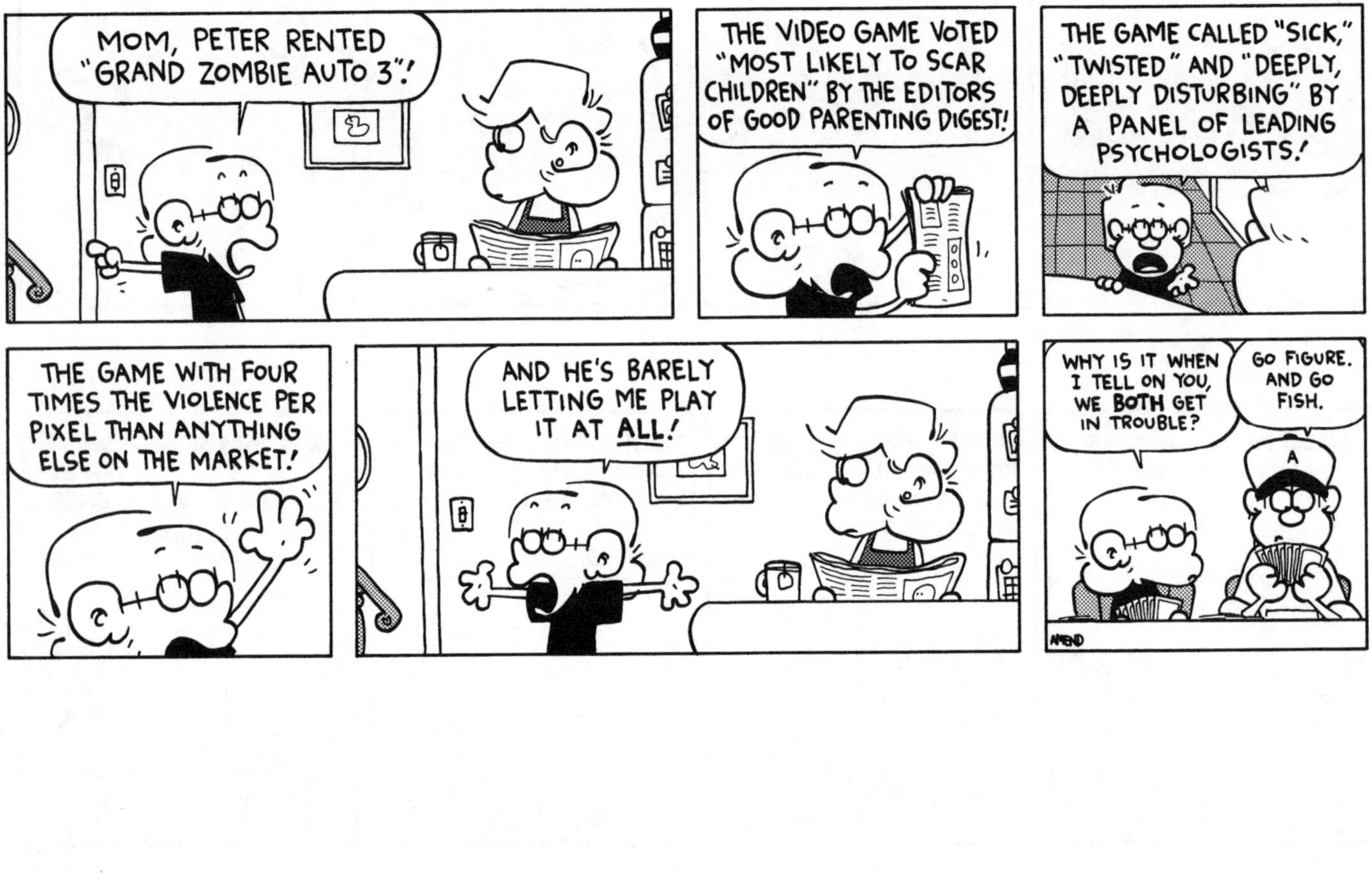
MOM, PETER RENTED "GRAND ZOMBIE AUTO 3"!
THE VIDEO GAME VOTED "MOST LIKELY TO SCAR CHILDREN" BY THE EDITORS OF GOOD PARENTING DIGEST!
THE GAME CALLED "SICK," "TWISTED" AND "DEEPLY, DEEPLY DISTURBING" BY A PANEL OF LEADING PSYCHOLOGISTS!
THE GAME WITH FOUR TIMES THE VIOLENCE PER PIXEL THAN ANYTHING ELSE ON THE MARKET!
AND HE'S BARELY LETTING ME PLAY IT AT ALL!
WHY IS IT WHEN I TELL ON YOU, WE BOTH GET IN TROUBLE?
GO FIGURE. AND GO FISH.
A
AMEND

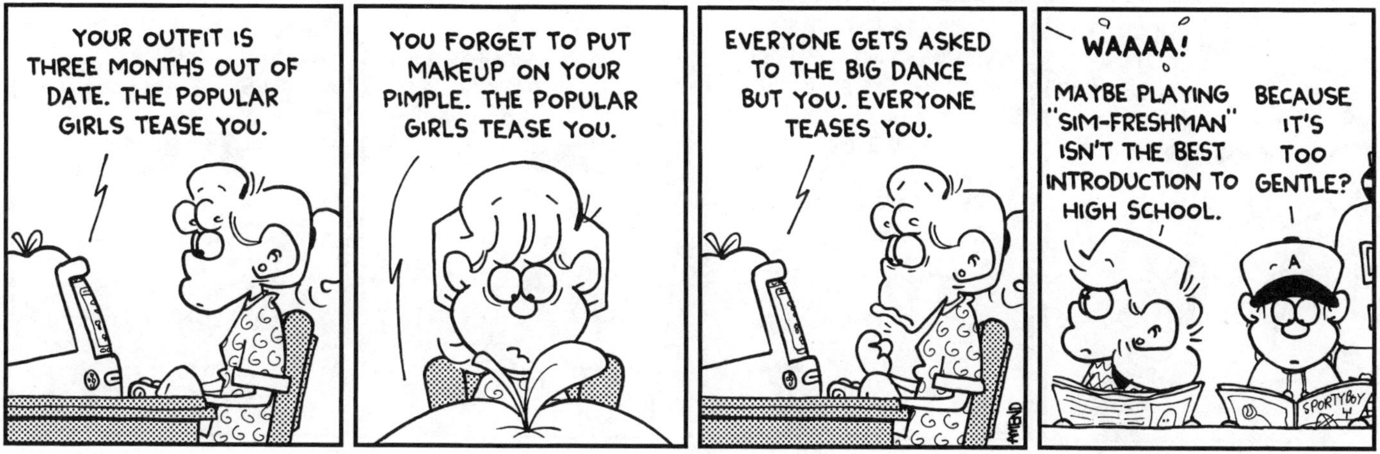
YOUR OUTFIT IS THREE MONTHS OUT OF DATE. THE POPULAR GIRLS TEASE YOU.
YOU FORGET TO PUT MAKEUP ON YOUR PIMPLE. THE POPULAR GIRLS TEASE YOU.
EVERYONE GETS ASKED TO THE BIG DANCE BUT YOU. EVERYONE TEASES YOU.
WAAAA!
MAYBE PLAYING "SIM-FRESHMAN" ISN'T THE BEST INTRODUCTION TO HIGH SCHOOL.
BECAUSE IT'S TOO GENTLE?
SPORTYBOY 4
AMEND

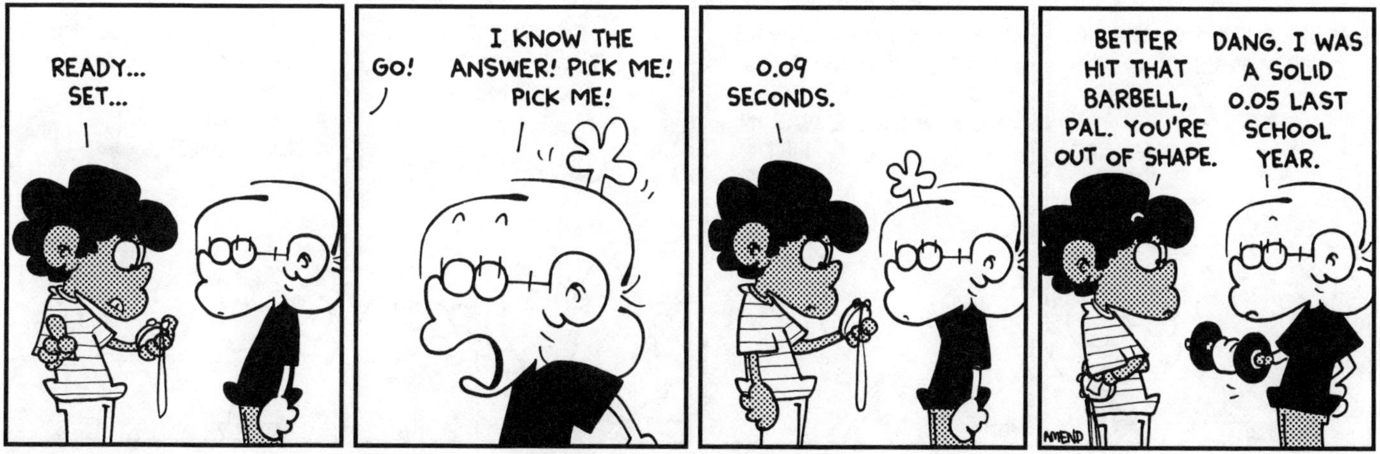
READY... SET...
GO!
I KNOW THE ANSWER! PICK ME! PICK ME!
0.09 SECONDS.
BETTER HIT THAT BARBELL, PAL. YOU'RE OUT OF SHAPE.
DANG. I WAS A SOLID 0.05 LAST SCHOOL YEAR.
AMEND

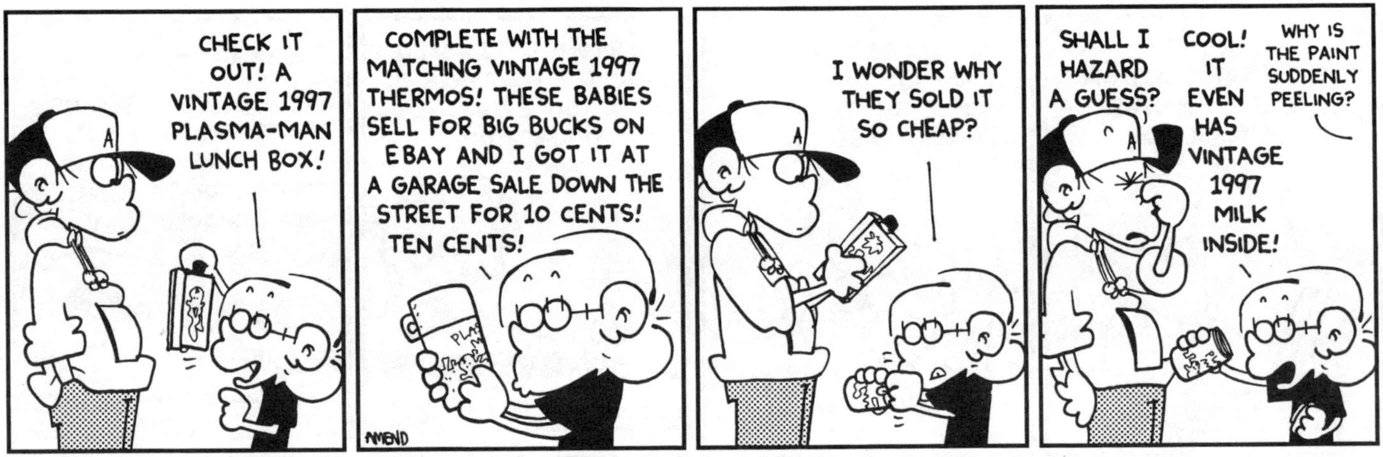
CHECK IT OUT! A VINTAGE 1997 PLASMA-MAN LUNCH BOX!
COMPLETE WITH THE MATCHING VINTAGE 1997 THERMOS! THESE BABIES SELL FOR BIG BUCKS ON EBAY AND I GOT IT AT A GARAGE SALE DOWN THE STREET FOR 10 CENTS! TEN CENTS!
AMEND
I WONDER WHY THEY SOLD IT SO CHEAP?
SHALL I HAZARD A GUESS?
COOL! IT EVEN HAS VINTAGE 1997 MILK INSIDE!
WHY IS THE PAINT SUDDENLY PEELING?

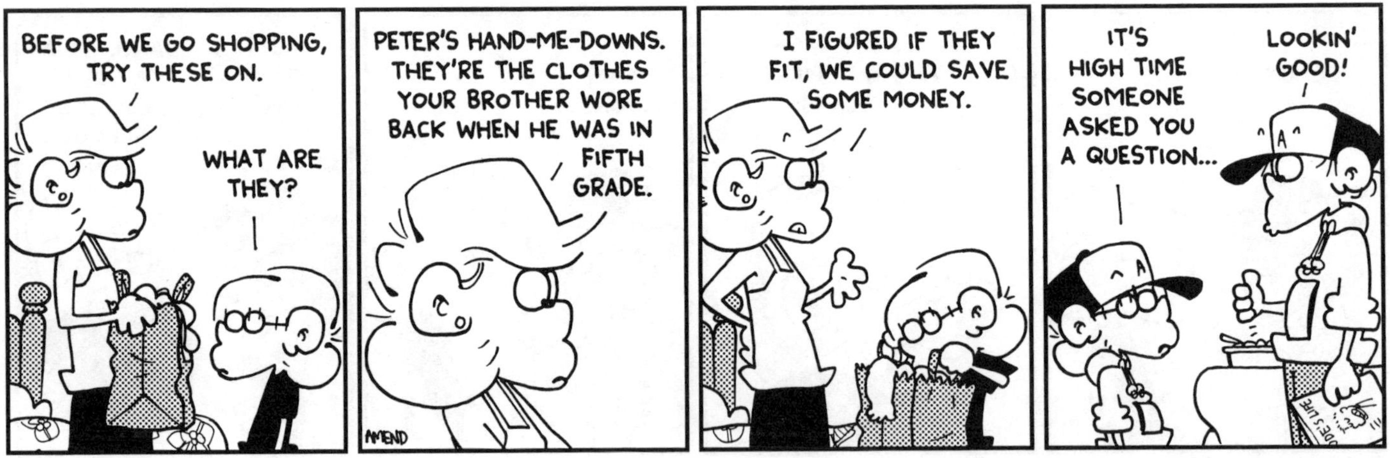
BEFORE WE GO SHOPPING, TRY THESE ON.
WHAT ARE THEY?
PETER'S HAND-ME-DOWNS. THEY'RE THE CLOTHES YOUR BROTHER WORE BACK WHEN HE WAS IN FIFTH GRADE.
AMEND
I FIGURED IF THEY FIT, WE COULD SAVE SOME MONEY.
IT'S HIGH TIME SOMEONE ASKED YOU A QUESTION...
LOOKIN' GOOD!

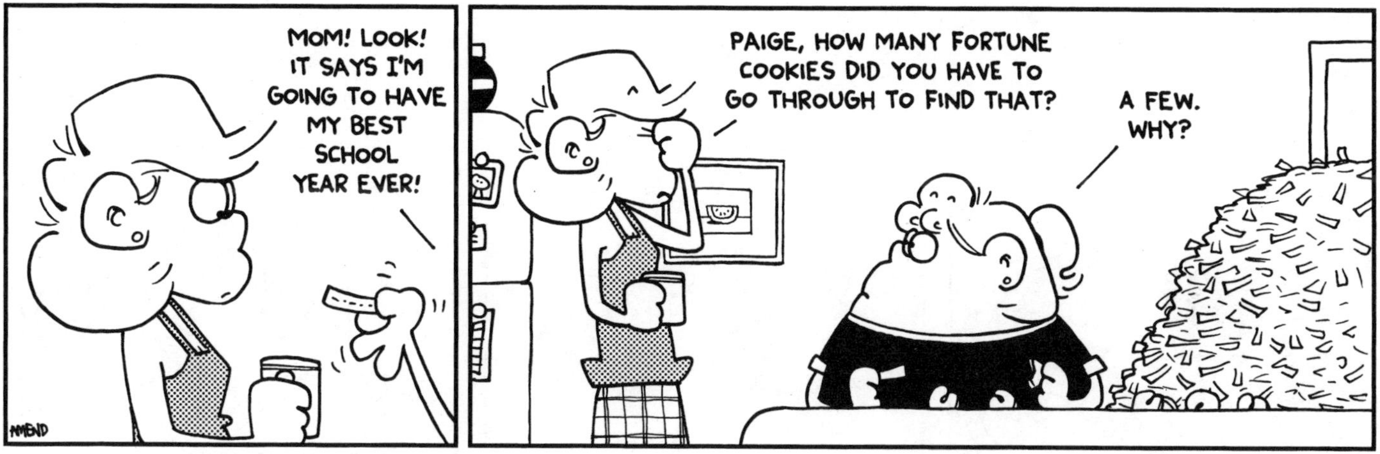
MOM! LOOK! IT SAYS I'M GOING TO HAVE MY BEST SCHOOL YEAR EVER!
PAIGE, HOW MANY FORTUNE COOKIES DID YOU HAVE TO GO THROUGH TO FIND THAT?
A FEW. WHY?
AMEND

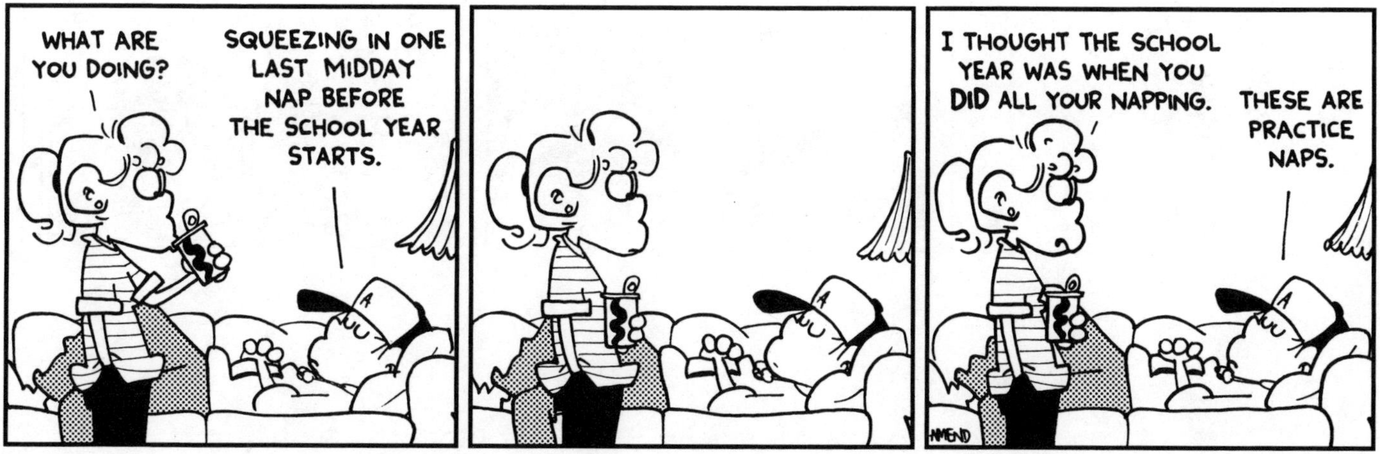
WHAT ARE YOU DOING?
SQUEEZING IN ONE LAST MIDDAY NAP BEFORE THE SCHOOL YEAR STARTS.
I THOUGHT THE SCHOOL YEAR WAS WHEN YOU DID ALL YOUR NAPPING.
THESE ARE PRACTICE NAPS.
AMEND

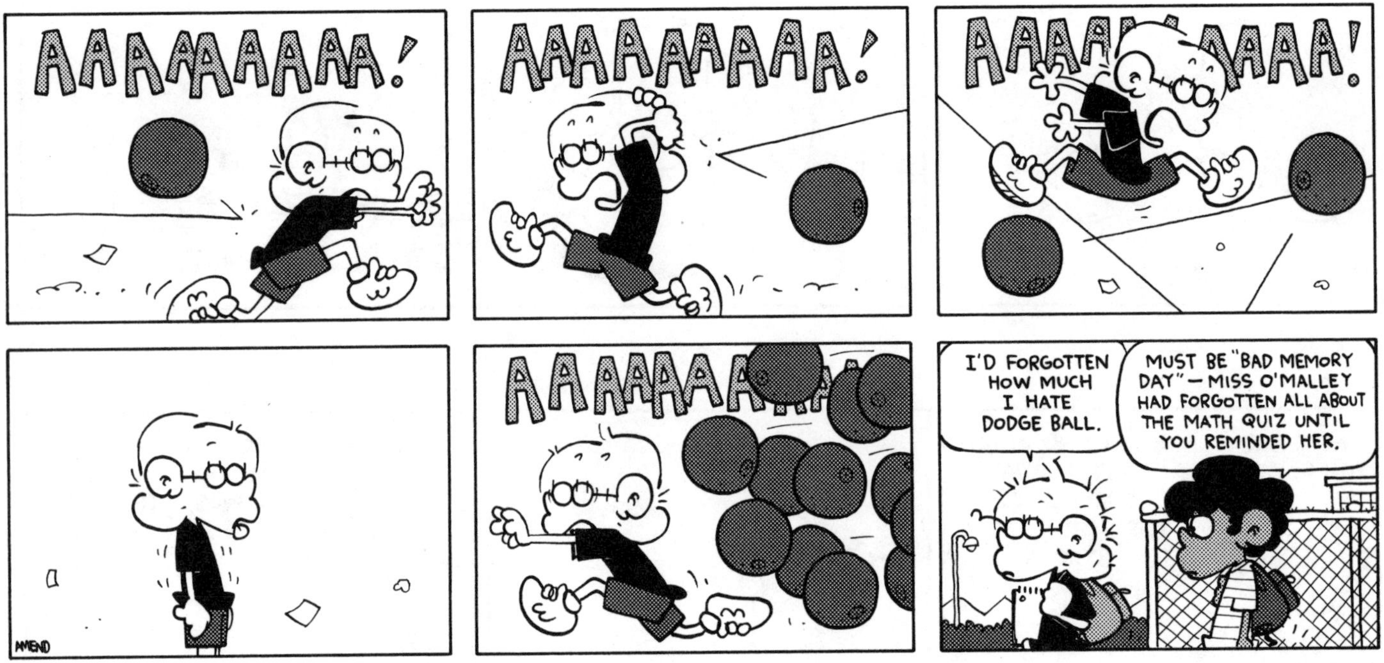
AAAAAAAAA!
AAAAAAAAAA!
AAAAAAAA!
AAAAAA
I'D FORGOTTEN HOW MUCH I HATE DODGE BALL.
MUST BE "BAD MEMORY DAY" — MISS O'MALLEY HAD FORGOTTEN ALL ABOUT THE MATH QUIZ UNTIL YOU REMINDED HER.
AMEND

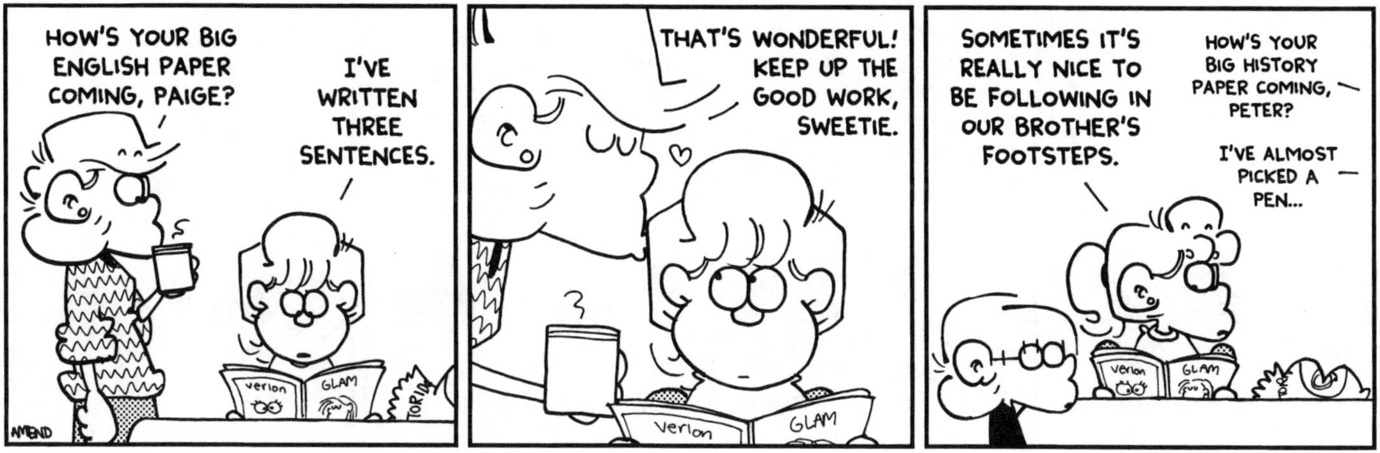
HOW'S YOUR BIG ENGLISH PAPER COMING, PAIGE?
I'VE WRITTEN THREE SENTENCES.
THAT'S WONDERFUL! KEEP UP THE GOOD WORK, SWEETIE.
SOMETIMES IT'S REALLY NICE TO BE FOLLOWING IN OUR BROTHER'S FOOTSTEPS.
HOW'S YOUR BIG HISTORY PAPER COMING, PETER?
I'VE ALMOST PICKED A PEN...

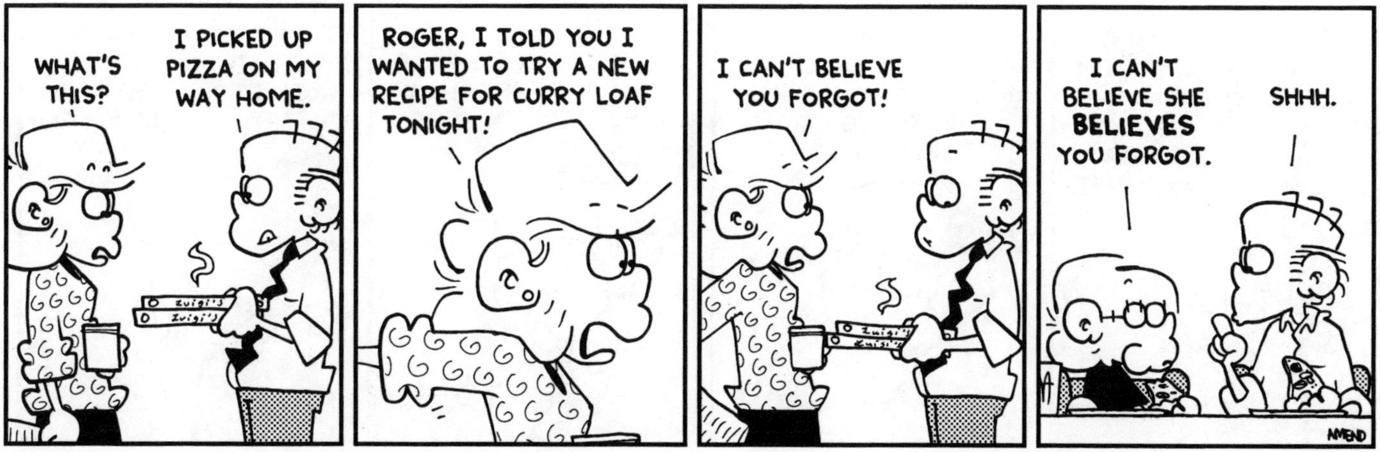
WHAT'S THIS?
I PICKED UP PIZZA ON MY WAY HOME.
ROGER, I TOLD YOU I WANTED TO TRY A NEW RECIPE FOR CURRY LOAF TONIGHT!
I CAN'T BELIEVE YOU FORGOT!
I CAN'T BELIEVE SHE **BELIEVES** YOU FORGOT.
SHHH.

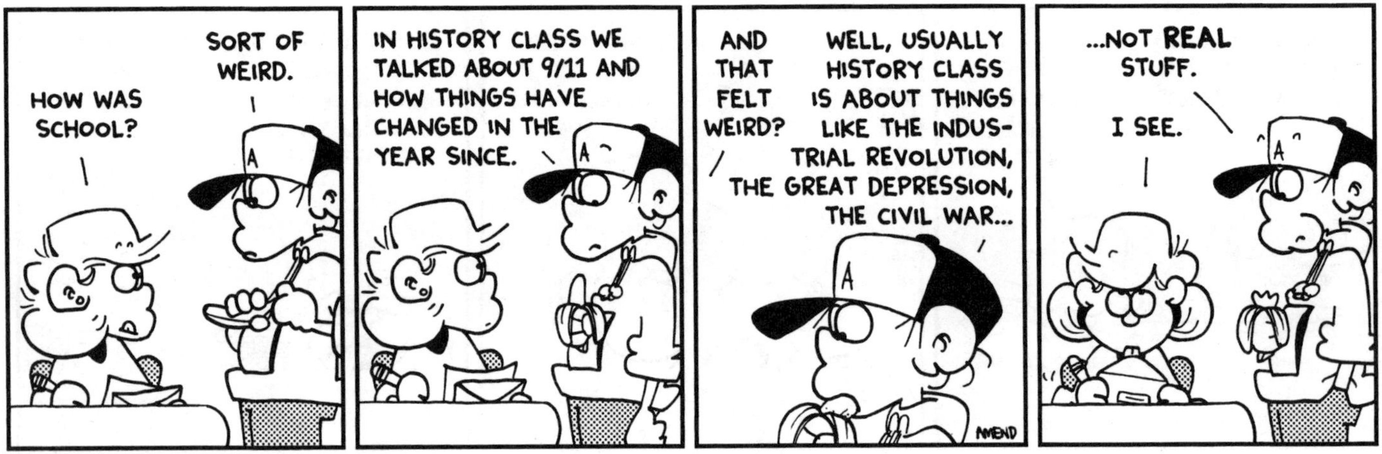
HOW WAS SCHOOL?
SORT OF WEIRD.
IN HISTORY CLASS WE TALKED ABOUT 9/11 AND HOW THINGS HAVE CHANGED IN THE YEAR SINCE.
AND THAT FELT WEIRD?
WELL, USUALLY HISTORY CLASS IS ABOUT THINGS LIKE THE INDUSTRIAL REVOLUTION, THE GREAT DEPRESSION, THE CIVIL WAR...
AMEND
...NOT REAL STUFF.
I SEE.

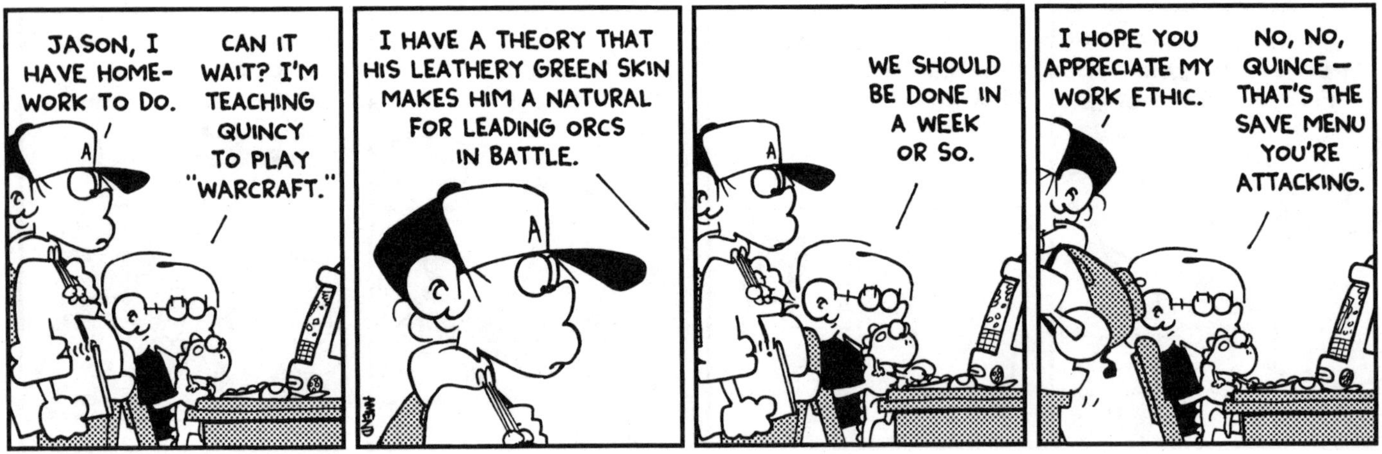
JASON, I HAVE HOMEWORK TO DO.
CAN IT WAIT? I'M TEACHING QUINCY TO PLAY "WARCRAFT."
I HAVE A THEORY THAT HIS LEATHERY GREEN SKIN MAKES HIM A NATURAL FOR LEADING ORCS IN BATTLE.
WE SHOULD BE DONE IN A WEEK OR SO.
I HOPE YOU APPRECIATE MY WORK ETHIC.
NO, NO, QUINCE— THAT'S THE SAVE MENU YOU'RE ATTACKING.

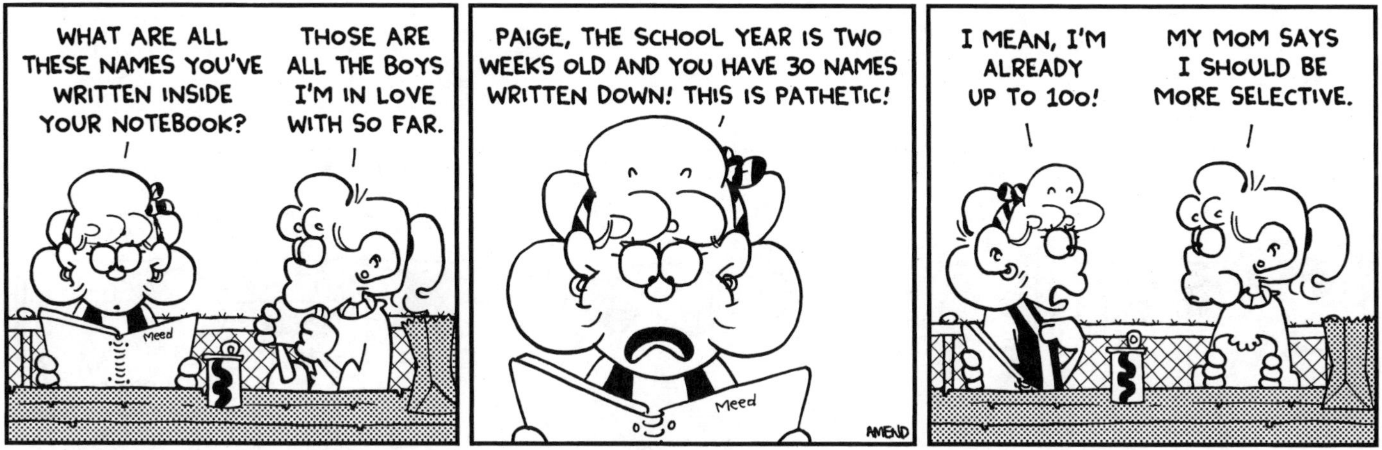
WHAT ARE ALL THESE NAMES YOU'VE WRITTEN INSIDE YOUR NOTEBOOK?
THOSE ARE ALL THE BOYS I'M IN LOVE WITH SO FAR.
Meed
PAIGE, THE SCHOOL YEAR IS TWO WEEKS OLD AND YOU HAVE 30 NAMES WRITTEN DOWN! THIS IS PATHETIC!
Meed
AMEND
I MEAN, I'M ALREADY UP TO 100!
MY MOM SAYS I SHOULD BE MORE SELECTIVE.

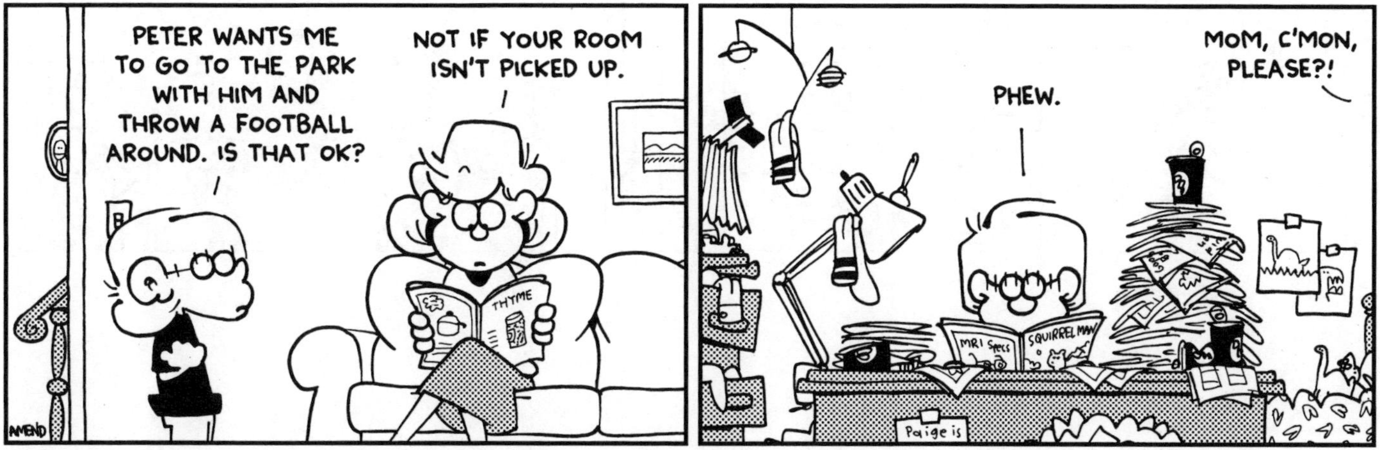
PETER WANTS ME TO GO TO THE PARK WITH HIM AND THROW A FOOTBALL AROUND. IS THAT OK?
NOT IF YOUR ROOM ISN'T PICKED UP.
THYME
AMEND
PHEW.
MOM, C'MON, PLEASE?!
MRI Specs
SQUIRREL MAN
Paige is

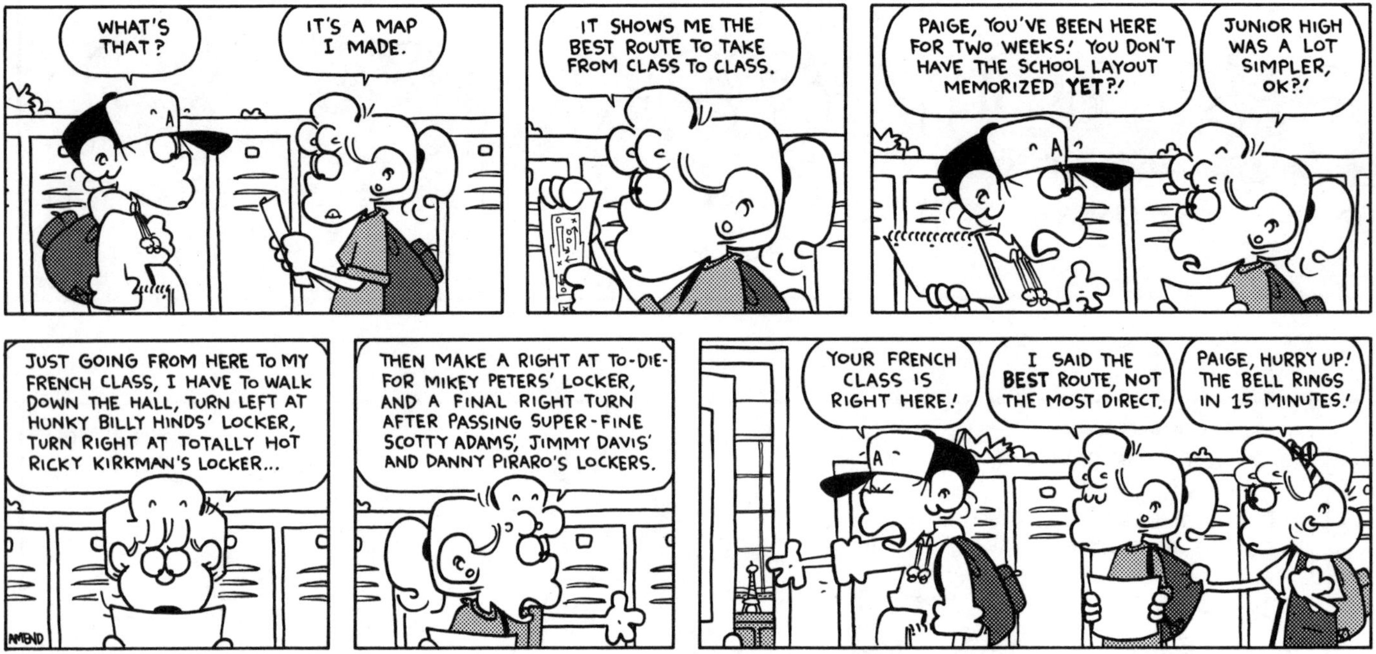
WHAT'S THAT?
IT'S A MAP I MADE.
IT SHOWS ME THE BEST ROUTE TO TAKE FROM CLASS TO CLASS.
PAIGE, YOU'VE BEEN HERE FOR TWO WEEKS! YOU DON'T HAVE THE SCHOOL LAYOUT MEMORIZED **YET**?!
JUNIOR HIGH WAS A LOT SIMPLER, OK?!
JUST GOING FROM HERE TO MY FRENCH CLASS, I HAVE TO WALK DOWN THE HALL, TURN LEFT AT HUNKY BILLY HINDS' LOCKER, TURN RIGHT AT TOTALLY HOT RICKY KIRKMAN'S LOCKER...
AMEND
THEN MAKE A RIGHT AT TO-DIE-FOR MIKEY PETERS' LOCKER, AND A FINAL RIGHT TURN AFTER PASSING SUPER-FINE SCOTTY ADAMS', JIMMY DAVIS' AND DANNY PIRARO'S LOCKERS.
YOUR FRENCH CLASS IS RIGHT HERE!
I SAID THE **BEST** ROUTE, NOT THE MOST DIRECT.
PAIGE, HURRY UP! THE BELL RINGS IN 15 MINUTES!

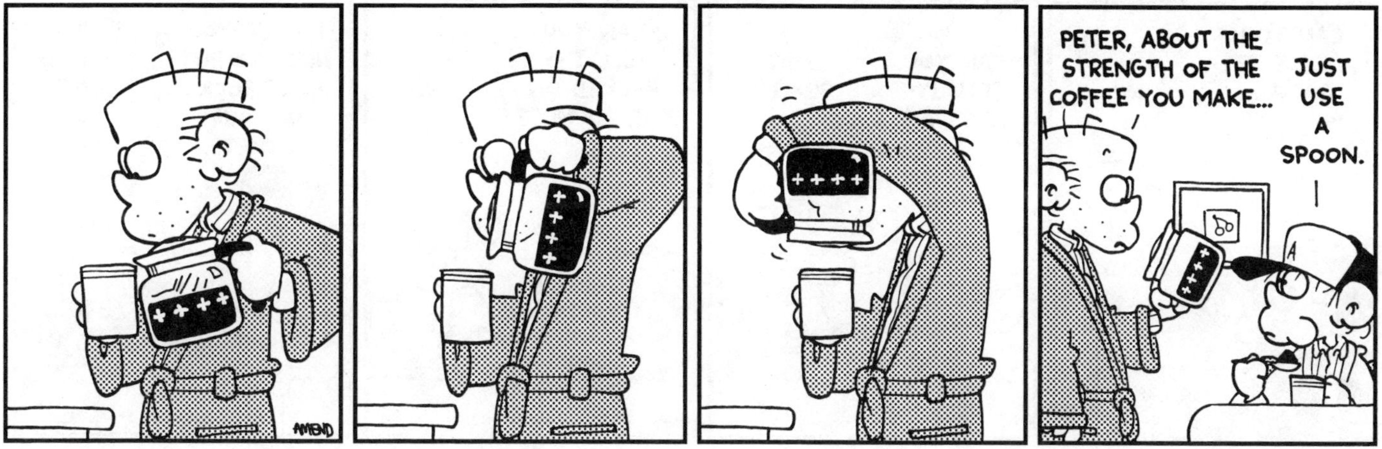
AMEND
PETER, ABOUT THE STRENGTH OF THE COFFEE YOU MAKE...
JUST USE A SPOON.

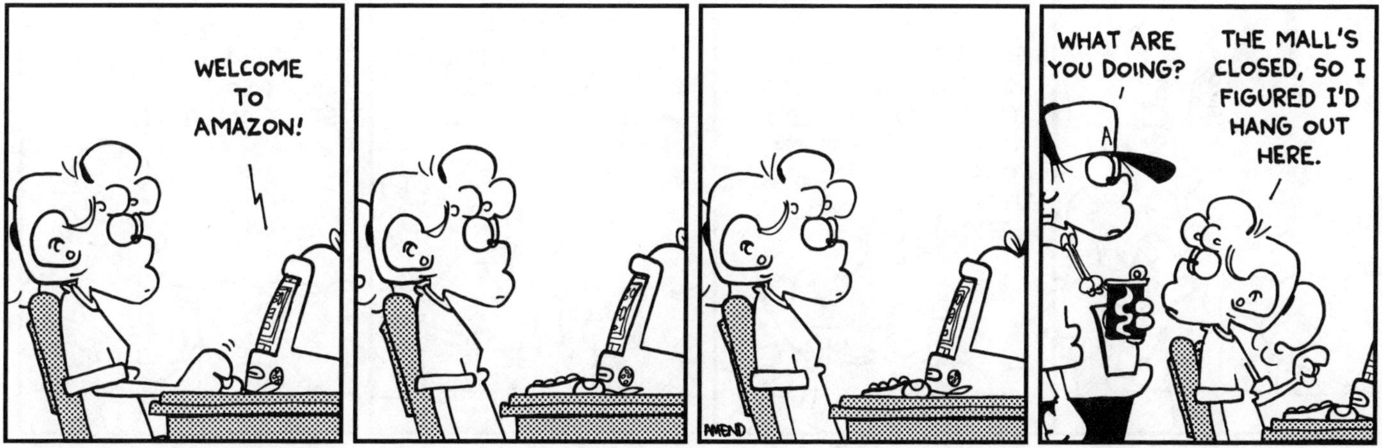
WELCOME TO AMAZON!
AMEND
WHAT ARE YOU DOING?
THE MALL'S CLOSED, SO I FIGURED I'D HANG OUT HERE.

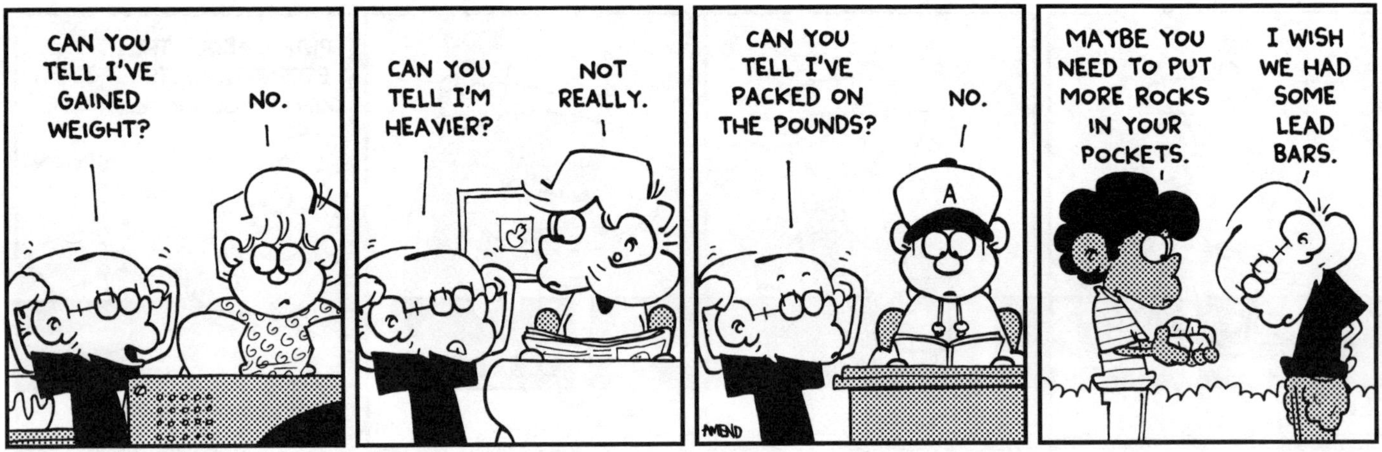
CAN YOU TELL I'VE GAINED WEIGHT?
NO.
CAN YOU TELL I'M HEAVIER?
NOT REALLY.
CAN YOU TELL I'VE PACKED ON THE POUNDS?
NO.
A
AMEND
MAYBE YOU NEED TO PUT MORE ROCKS IN YOUR POCKETS.
I WISH WE HAD SOME LEAD BARS.

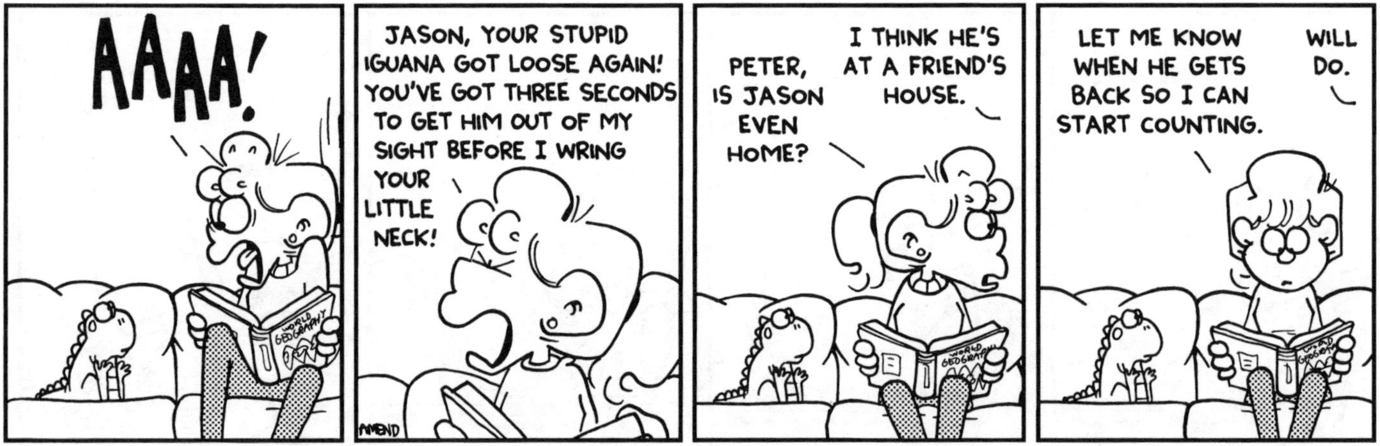
AAAA!
JASON, YOUR STUPID IGUANA GOT LOOSE AGAIN! YOU'VE GOT THREE SECONDS TO GET HIM OUT OF MY SIGHT BEFORE I WRING YOUR LITTLE NECK!
AMEND
PETER, IS JASON EVEN HOME?
I THINK HE'S AT A FRIEND'S HOUSE.
LET ME KNOW WHEN HE GETS BACK SO I CAN START COUNTING.
WILL DO.

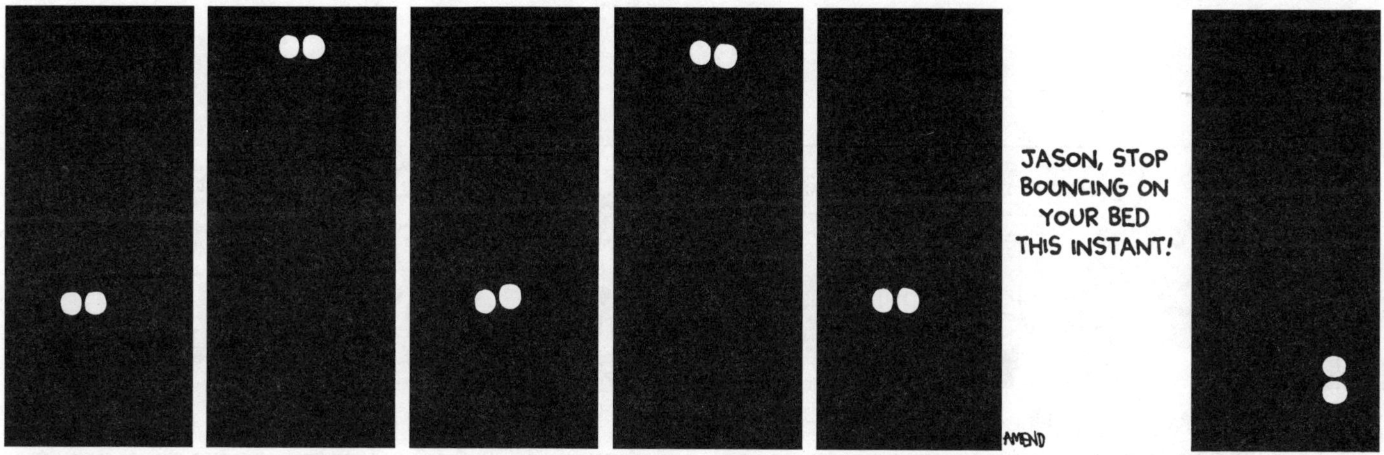
JASON, STOP BOUNCING ON YOUR BED THIS INSTANT!
AMEND

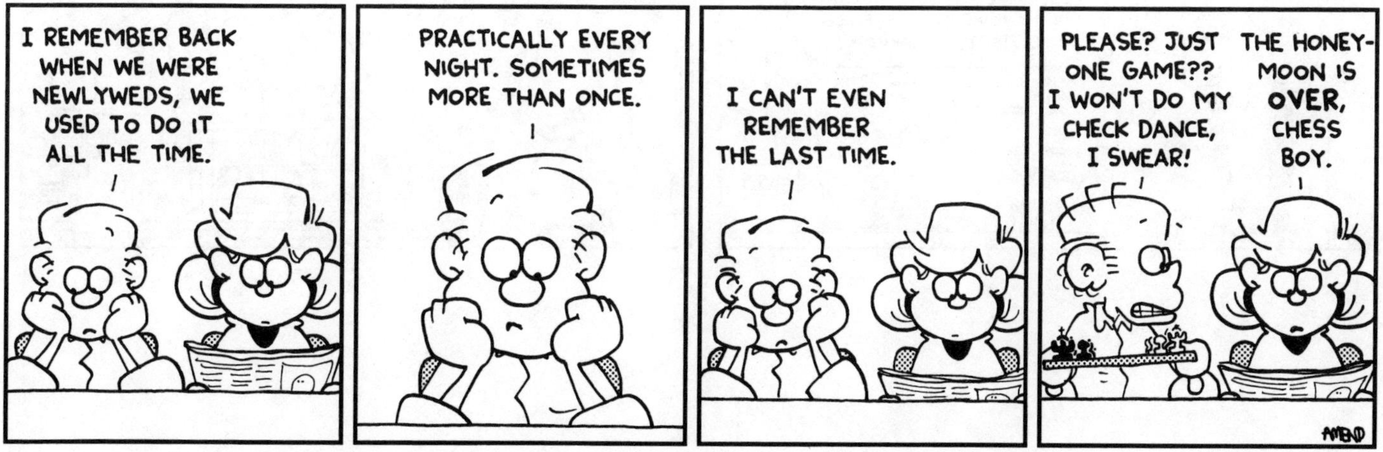
I REMEMBER BACK WHEN WE WERE NEWLYWEDS, WE USED TO DO IT ALL THE TIME.
PRACTICALLY EVERY NIGHT. SOMETIMES MORE THAN ONCE.
I CAN'T EVEN REMEMBER THE LAST TIME.
PLEASE? JUST ONE GAME?? I WON'T DO MY CHECK DANCE, I SWEAR!
THE HONEY-MOON IS **OVER**, CHESS BOY.
AMEND

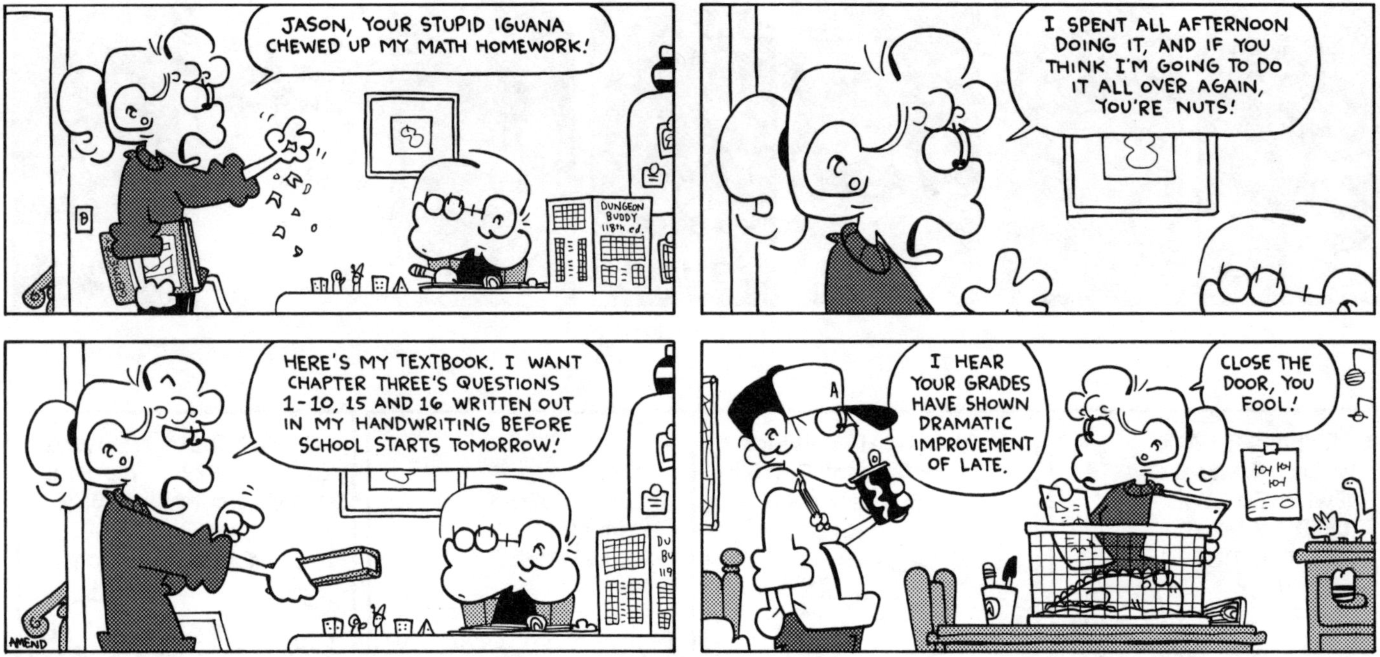
JASON, YOUR STUPID IGUANA CHEWED UP MY MATH HOMEWORK!
DUNGEON BUDDY 118th ed.
I SPENT ALL AFTERNOON DOING IT, AND IF YOU THINK I'M GOING TO DO IT ALL OVER AGAIN, YOU'RE NUTS!
HERE'S MY TEXTBOOK. I WANT CHAPTER THREE'S QUESTIONS 1-10, 15 AND 16 WRITTEN OUT IN MY HANDWRITING BEFORE SCHOOL STARTS TOMORROW!
AMEND
I HEAR YOUR GRADES HAVE SHOWN DRAMATIC IMPROVEMENT OF LATE.
CLOSE THE DOOR, YOU FOOL!

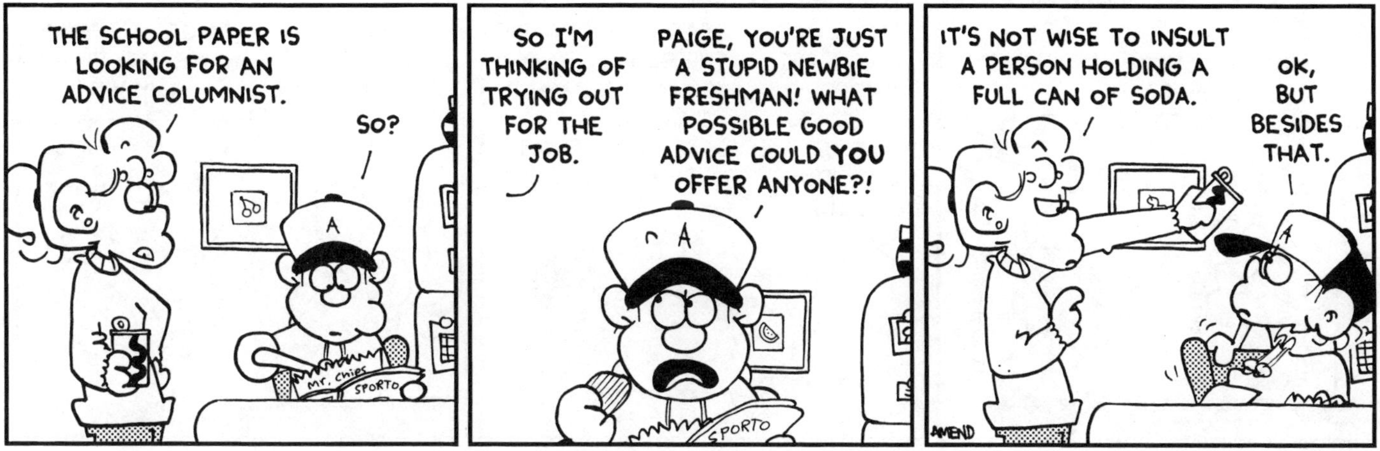
THE SCHOOL PAPER IS LOOKING FOR AN ADVICE COLUMNIST.
SO?
Mr. Chips
SPORTO
SO I'M THINKING OF TRYING OUT FOR THE JOB.
PAIGE, YOU'RE JUST A STUPID NEWBIE FRESHMAN! WHAT POSSIBLE GOOD ADVICE COULD **YOU** OFFER ANYONE?!
SPORTO
IT'S NOT WISE TO INSULT A PERSON HOLDING A FULL CAN OF SODA.
OK, BUT BESIDES THAT.
AMEND

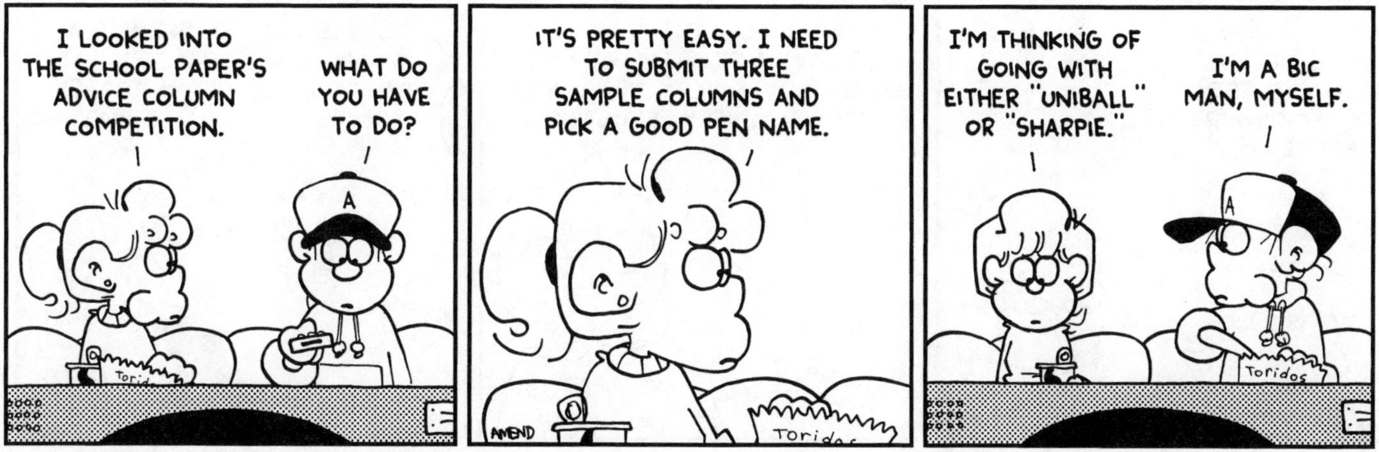
I LOOKED INTO THE SCHOOL PAPER'S ADVICE COLUMN COMPETITION.
WHAT DO YOU HAVE TO DO?
IT'S PRETTY EASY. I NEED TO SUBMIT THREE SAMPLE COLUMNS AND PICK A GOOD PEN NAME.
AMEND
I'M THINKING OF GOING WITH EITHER "UNIBALL" OR "SHARPIE."
I'M A BIC MAN, MYSELF.
Toridos

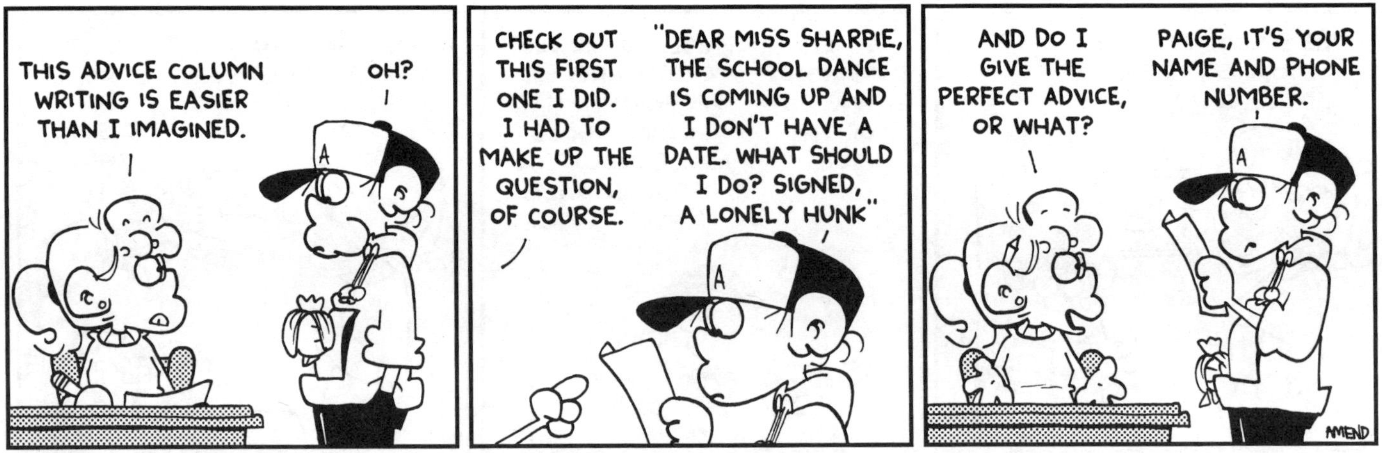
THIS ADVICE COLUMN WRITING IS EASIER THAN I IMAGINED.
OH?
CHECK OUT THIS FIRST ONE I DID. I HAD TO MAKE UP THE QUESTION, OF COURSE.
"DEAR MISS SHARPIE, THE SCHOOL DANCE IS COMING UP AND I DON'T HAVE A DATE. WHAT SHOULD I DO? SIGNED, A LONELY HUNK"
AND DO I GIVE THE PERFECT ADVICE, OR WHAT?
PAIGE, IT'S YOUR NAME AND PHONE NUMBER.
AMEND

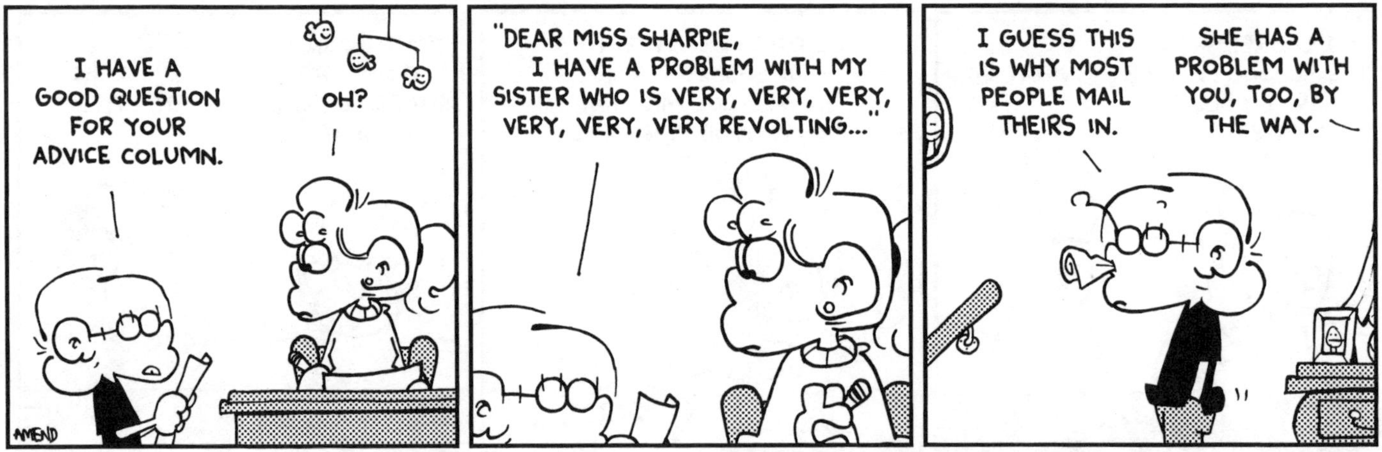
I HAVE A GOOD QUESTION FOR YOUR ADVICE COLUMN.
OH?
AMEND
"DEAR MISS SHARPIE, I HAVE A PROBLEM WITH MY SISTER WHO IS VERY, VERY, VERY, VERY, VERY, VERY REVOLTING..."
I GUESS THIS IS WHY MOST PEOPLE MAIL THEIRS IN.
SHE HAS A PROBLEM WITH YOU, TOO, BY THE WAY.

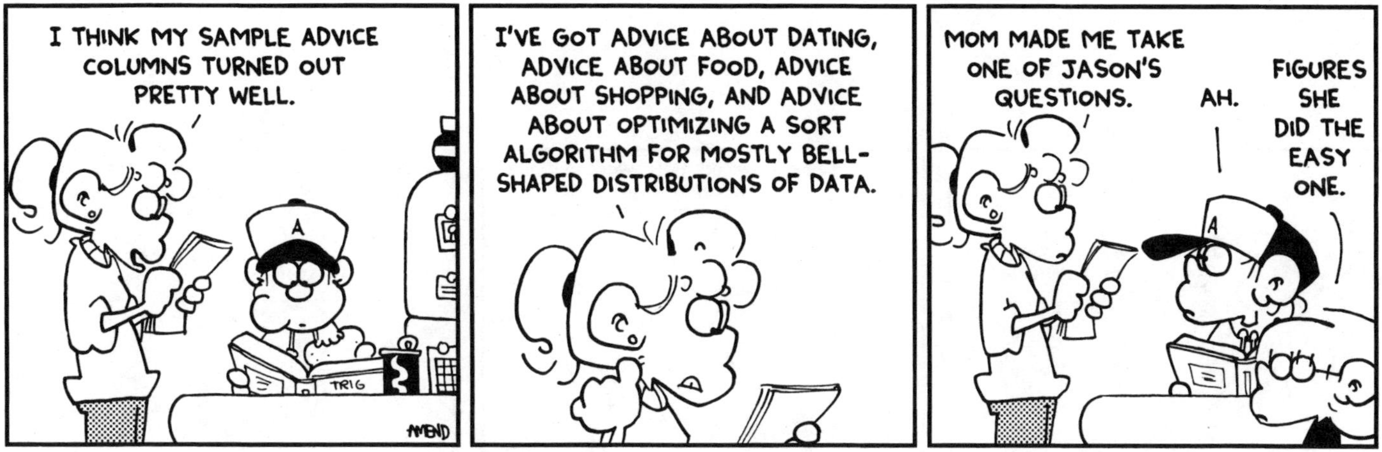
I THINK MY SAMPLE ADVICE COLUMNS TURNED OUT PRETTY WELL.
TRIG
AMEND
I'VE GOT ADVICE ABOUT DATING, ADVICE ABOUT FOOD, ADVICE ABOUT SHOPPING, AND ADVICE ABOUT OPTIMIZING A SORT ALGORITHM FOR MOSTLY BELL-SHAPED DISTRIBUTIONS OF DATA.
MOM MADE ME TAKE ONE OF JASON'S QUESTIONS.
AH.
FIGURES SHE DID THE EASY ONE.

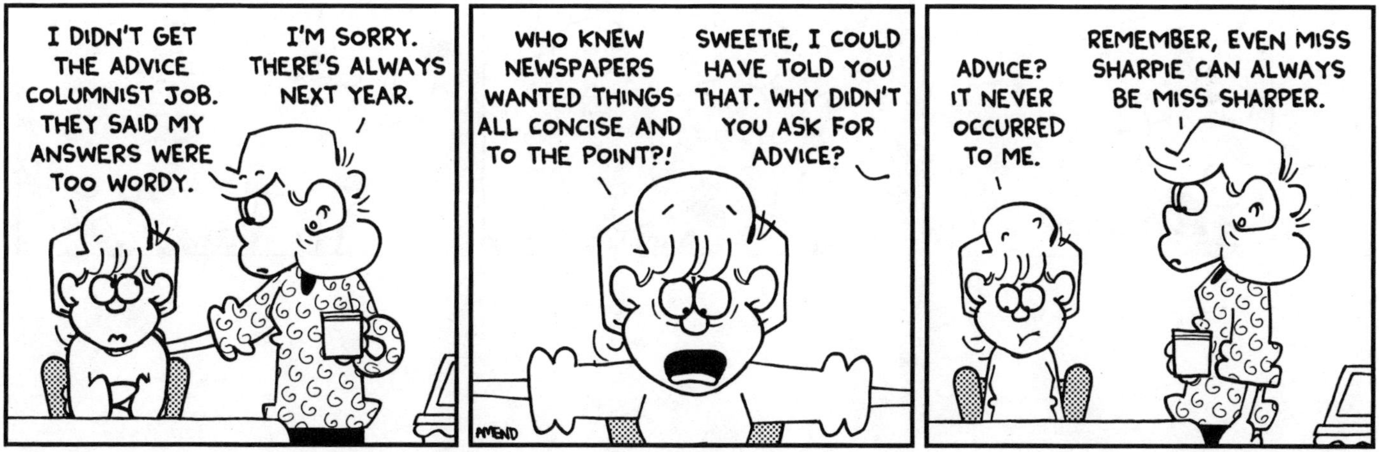
I DIDN'T GET THE ADVICE COLUMNIST JOB. THEY SAID MY ANSWERS WERE TOO WORDY.
I'M SORRY. THERE'S ALWAYS NEXT YEAR.
WHO KNEW NEWSPAPERS WANTED THINGS ALL CONCISE AND TO THE POINT?!
SWEETIE, I COULD HAVE TOLD YOU THAT. WHY DIDN'T YOU ASK FOR ADVICE?
AMEND
ADVICE? IT NEVER OCCURRED TO ME.
REMEMBER, EVEN MISS SHARPIE CAN ALWAYS BE MISS SHARPER.

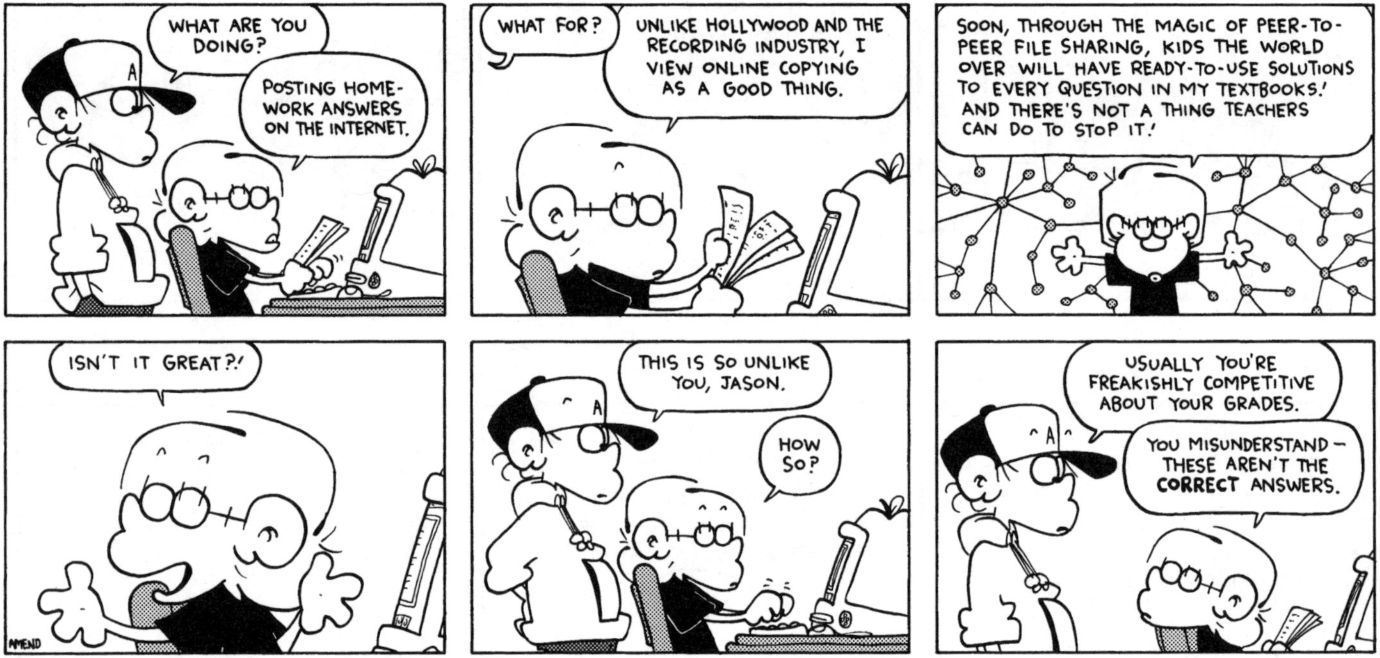
WHAT ARE YOU DOING?
POSTING HOMEWORK ANSWERS ON THE INTERNET.
WHAT FOR?
UNLIKE HOLLYWOOD AND THE RECORDING INDUSTRY, I VIEW ONLINE COPYING AS A GOOD THING.
SOON, THROUGH THE MAGIC OF PEER-TO-PEER FILE SHARING, KIDS THE WORLD OVER WILL HAVE READY-TO-USE SOLUTIONS TO EVERY QUESTION IN MY TEXTBOOKS! AND THERE'S NOT A THING TEACHERS CAN DO TO STOP IT!
ISN'T IT GREAT?!
AMEND
THIS IS SO UNLIKE YOU, JASON.
HOW SO?
USUALLY YOU'RE FREAKISHLY COMPETITIVE ABOUT YOUR GRADES.
YOU MISUNDERSTAND— THESE AREN'T THE **CORRECT** ANSWERS.

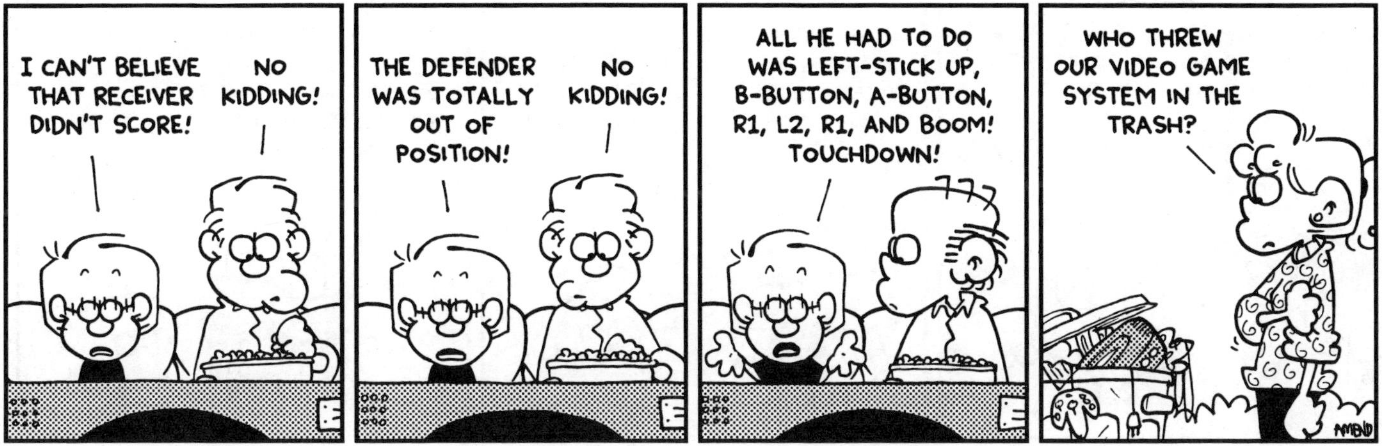
I CAN'T BELIEVE THAT RECEIVER DIDN'T SCORE!
NO KIDDING!
THE DEFENDER WAS TOTALLY OUT OF POSITION!
NO KIDDING!
ALL HE HAD TO DO WAS LEFT-STICK UP, B-BUTTON, A-BUTTON, R1, L2, R1, AND BOOM! TOUCHDOWN!
WHO THREW OUR VIDEO GAME SYSTEM IN THE TRASH?
AMEND

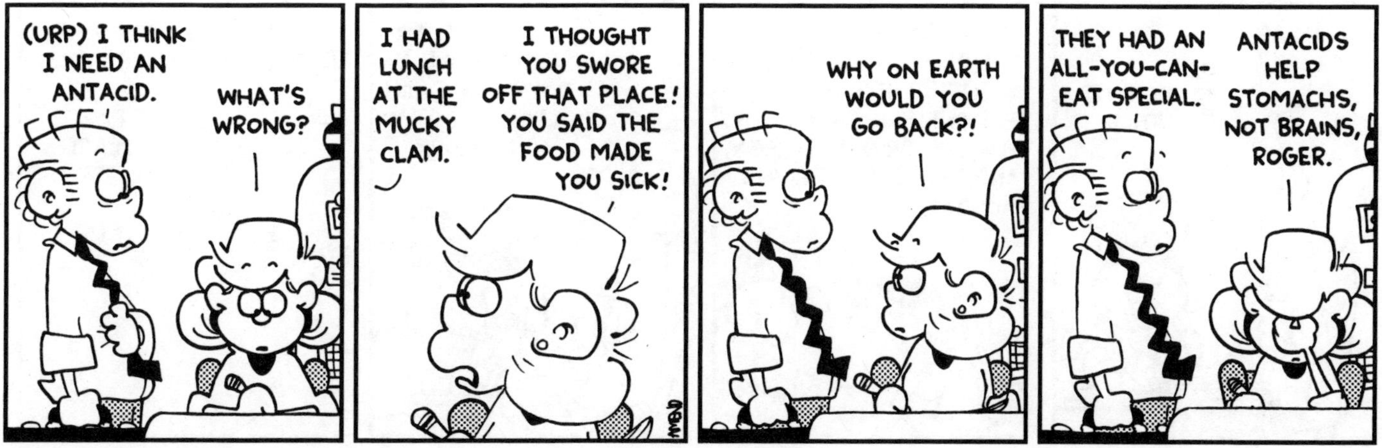
(URP) I THINK I NEED AN ANTACID.
WHAT'S WRONG?
I HAD LUNCH AT THE MUCKY CLAM.
I THOUGHT YOU SWORE OFF THAT PLACE! YOU SAID THE FOOD MADE YOU SICK!
AMEND
WHY ON EARTH WOULD YOU GO BACK?!
THEY HAD AN ALL-YOU-CAN-EAT SPECIAL.
ANTACIDS HELP STOMACHS, NOT BRAINS, ROGER.

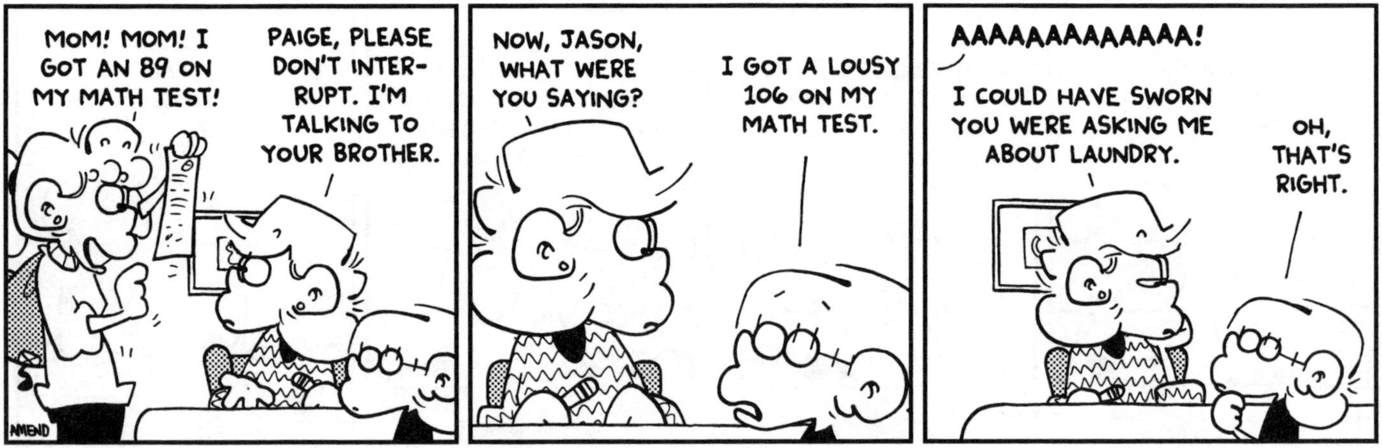
MOM! MOM! I GOT AN 89 ON MY MATH TEST!
PAIGE, PLEASE DON'T INTER-RUPT. I'M TALKING TO YOUR BROTHER.
AMEND
NOW, JASON, WHAT WERE YOU SAYING?
I GOT A LOUSY 106 ON MY MATH TEST.
AAAAAAAAAAAAA!
I COULD HAVE SWORN YOU WERE ASKING ME ABOUT LAUNDRY.
OH, THAT'S RIGHT.

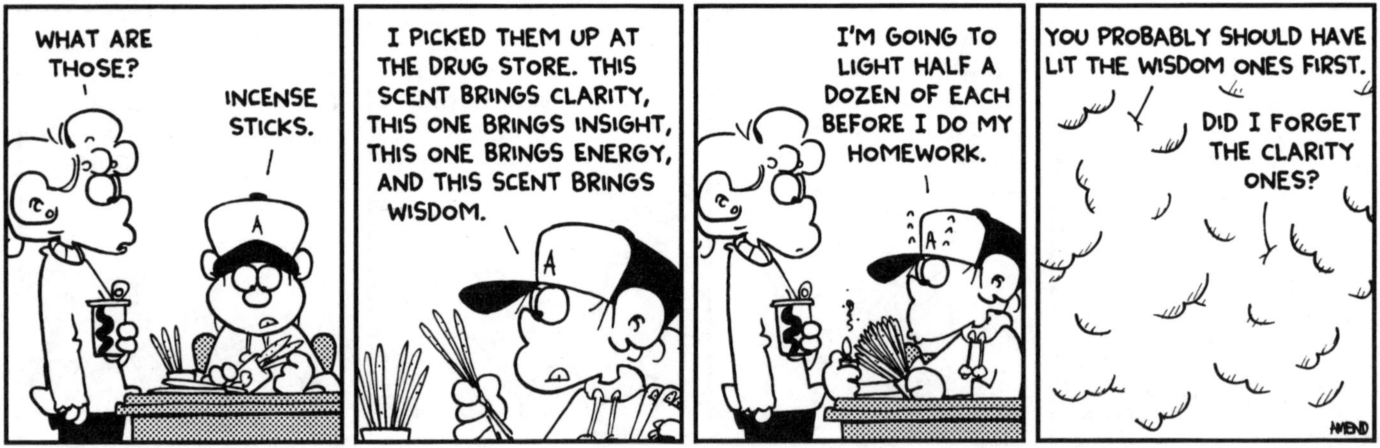
WHAT ARE THOSE?
INCENSE STICKS.
I PICKED THEM UP AT THE DRUG STORE. THIS SCENT BRINGS CLARITY, THIS ONE BRINGS INSIGHT, THIS ONE BRINGS ENERGY, AND THIS SCENT BRINGS WISDOM.
I'M GOING TO LIGHT HALF A DOZEN OF EACH BEFORE I DO MY HOMEWORK.
YOU PROBABLY SHOULD HAVE LIT THE WISDOM ONES FIRST.
DID I FORGET THE CLARITY ONES?
AMEND

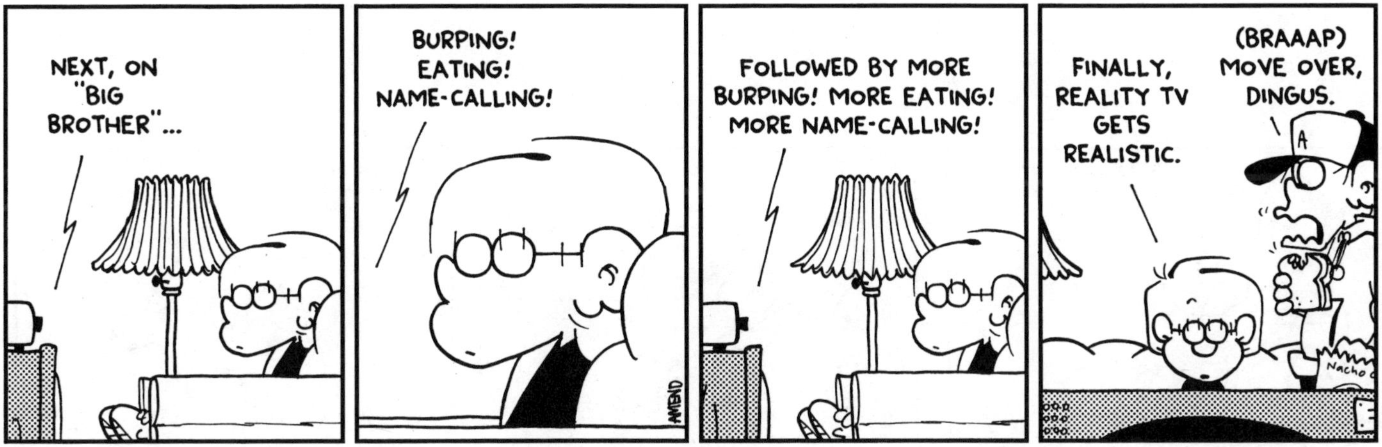
NEXT, ON "BIG BROTHER"...
BURPING! EATING! NAME-CALLING!
FOLLOWED BY MORE BURPING! MORE EATING! MORE NAME-CALLING!
FINALLY, REALITY TV GETS REALISTIC.
(BRAAAP) MOVE OVER, DINGUS.
AMEND

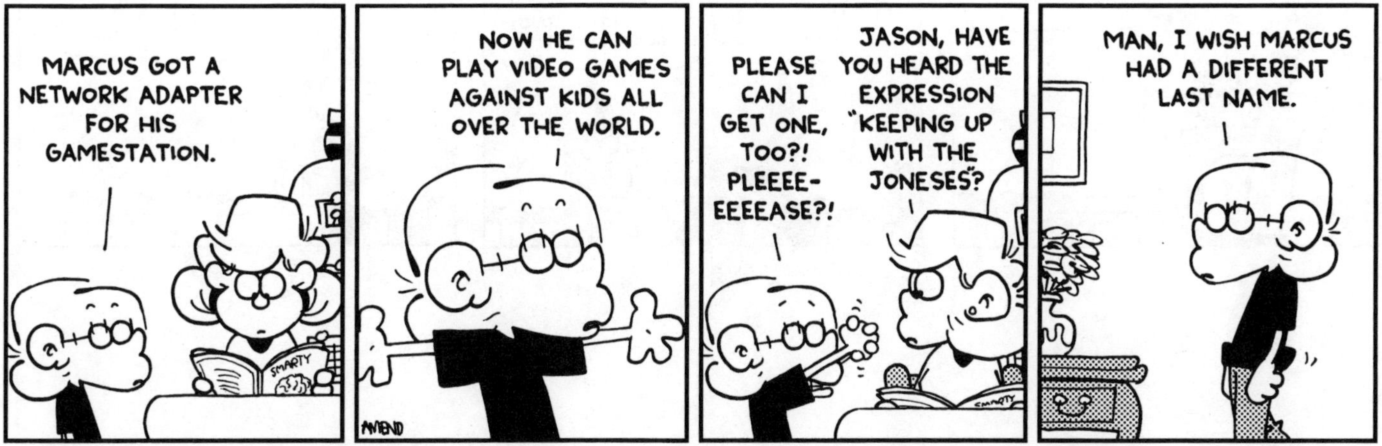
MARCUS GOT A NETWORK ADAPTER FOR HIS GAMESTATION.
SMARTY
NOW HE CAN PLAY VIDEO GAMES AGAINST KIDS ALL OVER THE WORLD.
AMEND
PLEASE CAN I GET ONE, TOO?! PLEEEE-EEEEASE?!
JASON, HAVE YOU HEARD THE EXPRESSION "KEEPING UP WITH THE JONESES"?
SMARTY
MAN, I WISH MARCUS HAD A DIFFERENT LAST NAME.

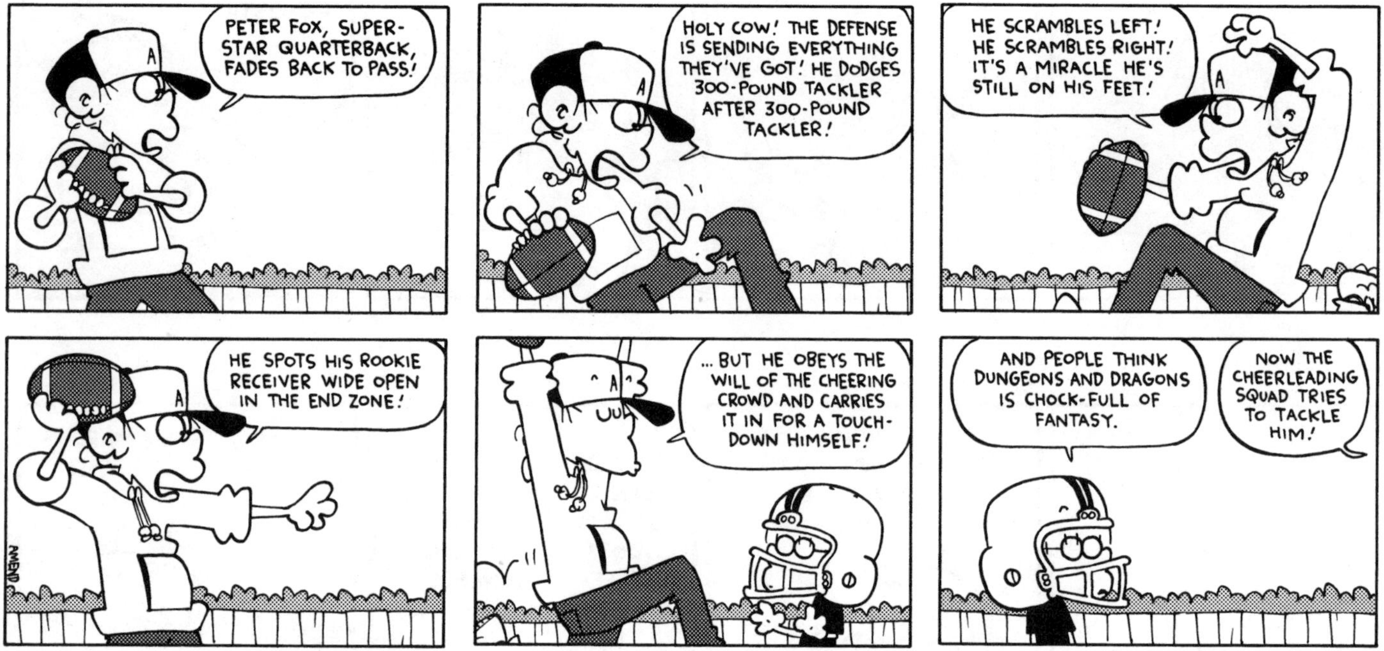
PETER FOX, SUPER-STAR QUARTERBACK, FADES BACK TO PASS!
HOLY COW! THE DEFENSE IS SENDING EVERYTHING THEY'VE GOT! HE DODGES 300-POUND TACKLER AFTER 300-POUND TACKLER!
HE SCRAMBLES LEFT! HE SCRAMBLES RIGHT! IT'S A MIRACLE HE'S STILL ON HIS FEET!
HE SPOTS HIS ROOKIE RECEIVER WIDE OPEN IN THE END ZONE!
AMEND
... BUT HE OBEYS THE WILL OF THE CHEERING CROWD AND CARRIES IT IN FOR A TOUCH-DOWN HIMSELF!
AND PEOPLE THINK DUNGEONS AND DRAGONS IS CHOCK-FULL OF FANTASY.
NOW THE CHEERLEADING SQUAD TRIES TO TACKLE HIM!

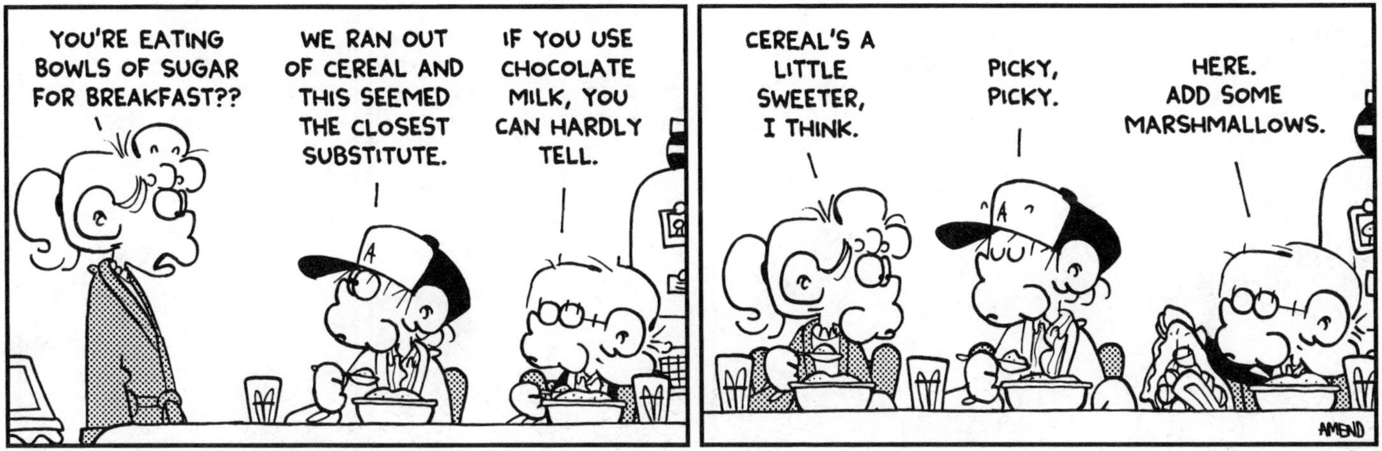
YOU'RE EATING BOWLS OF SUGAR FOR BREAKFAST??
WE RAN OUT OF CEREAL AND THIS SEEMED THE CLOSEST SUBSTITUTE.
IF YOU USE CHOCOLATE MILK, YOU CAN HARDLY TELL.
CEREAL'S A LITTLE SWEETER, I THINK.
PICKY, PICKY.
HERE. ADD SOME MARSHMALLOWS.
AMEND

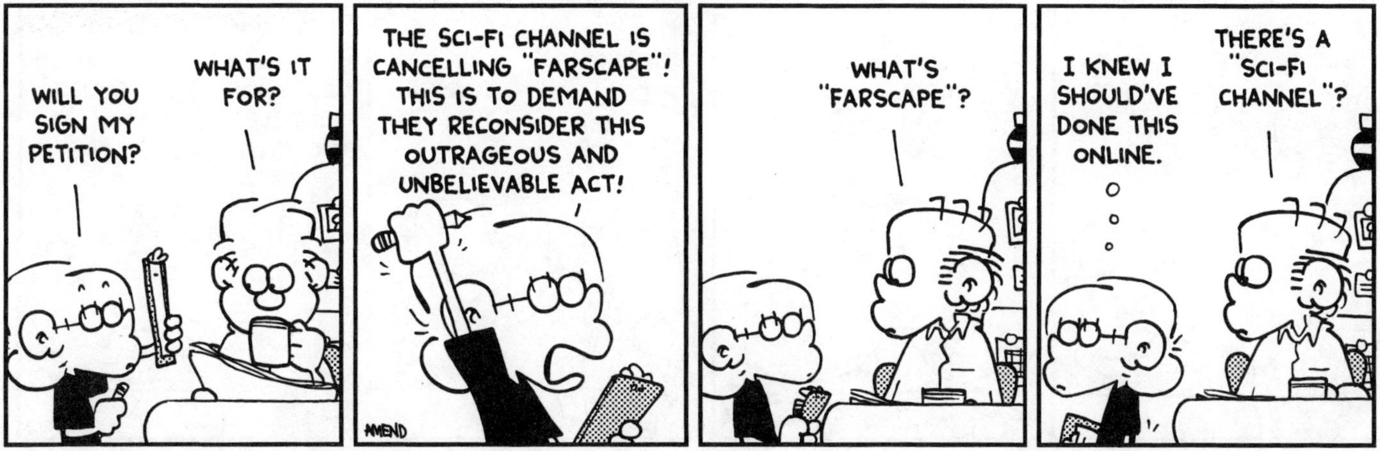
WILL YOU SIGN MY PETITION?
WHAT'S IT FOR?
THE SCI-FI CHANNEL IS CANCELLING "FARSCAPE"! THIS IS TO DEMAND THEY RECONSIDER THIS OUTRAGEOUS AND UNBELIEVABLE ACT!
AMEND
WHAT'S "FARSCAPE"?
I KNEW I SHOULD'VE DONE THIS ONLINE.
THERE'S A "SCI-FI CHANNEL"?

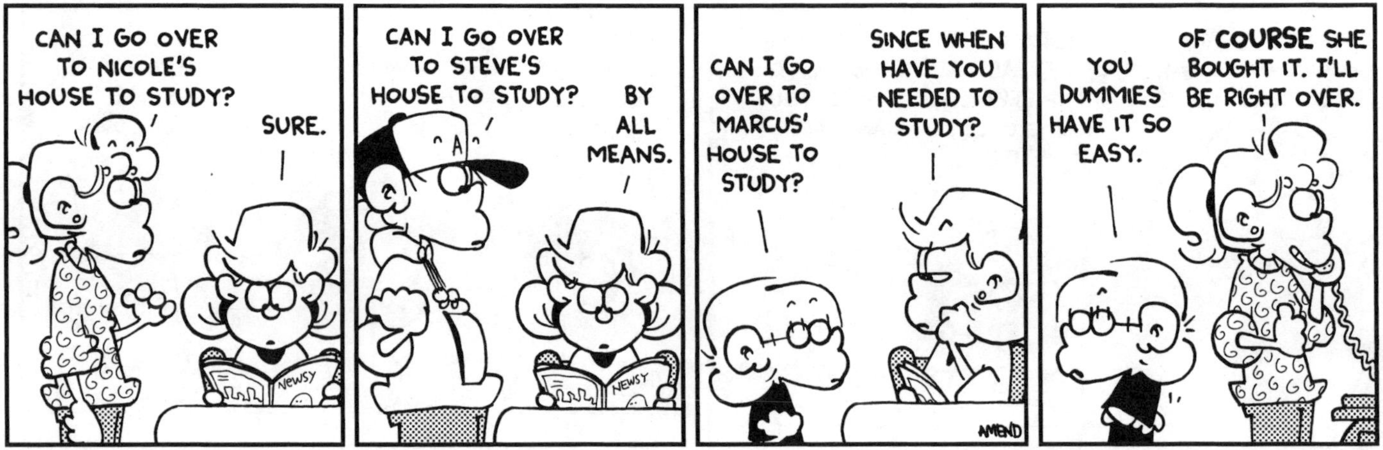
CAN I GO OVER TO NICOLE'S HOUSE TO STUDY?
SURE.
NEWSY
CAN I GO OVER TO STEVE'S HOUSE TO STUDY?
BY ALL MEANS.
NEWSY
CAN I GO OVER TO MARCUS' HOUSE TO STUDY?
SINCE WHEN HAVE YOU NEEDED TO STUDY?
AMEND
YOU DUMMIES HAVE IT SO EASY.
OF COURSE SHE BOUGHT IT. I'LL BE RIGHT OVER.

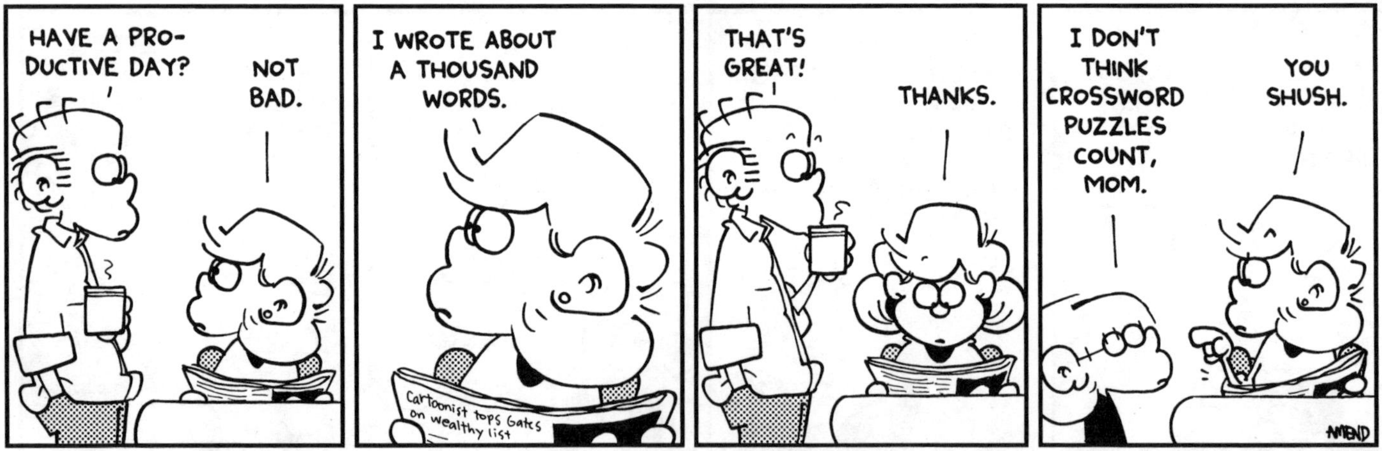
HAVE A PRODUCTIVE DAY?
NOT BAD.
I WROTE ABOUT A THOUSAND WORDS.
Cartoonist tops Gates on wealthy list
THAT'S GREAT!
THANKS.
I DON'T THINK CROSSWORD PUZZLES COUNT, MOM.
YOU SHUSH.
AMEND

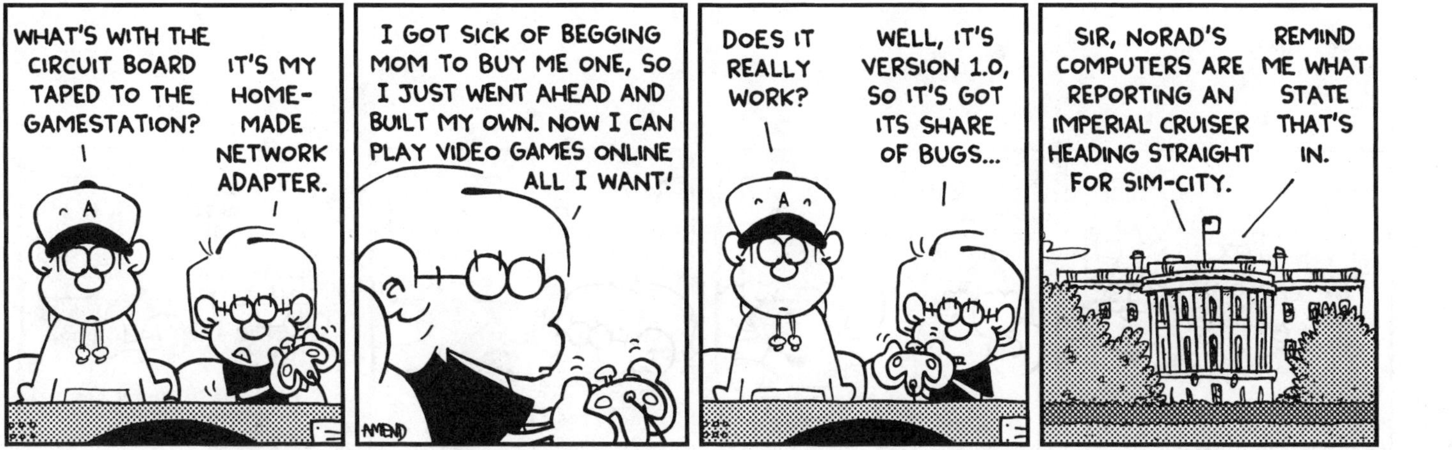
WHAT'S WITH THE CIRCUIT BOARD TAPED TO THE GAMESTATION?
IT'S MY HOME-MADE NETWORK ADAPTER.
I GOT SICK OF BEGGING MOM TO BUY ME ONE, SO I JUST WENT AHEAD AND BUILT MY OWN. NOW I CAN PLAY VIDEO GAMES ONLINE ALL I WANT!
AMEND
DOES IT REALLY WORK?
WELL, IT'S VERSION 1.0, SO IT'S GOT ITS SHARE OF BUGS...
SIR, NORAD'S COMPUTERS ARE REPORTING AN IMPERIAL CRUISER HEADING STRAIGHT FOR SIM-CITY.
REMIND ME WHAT STATE THAT'S IN.

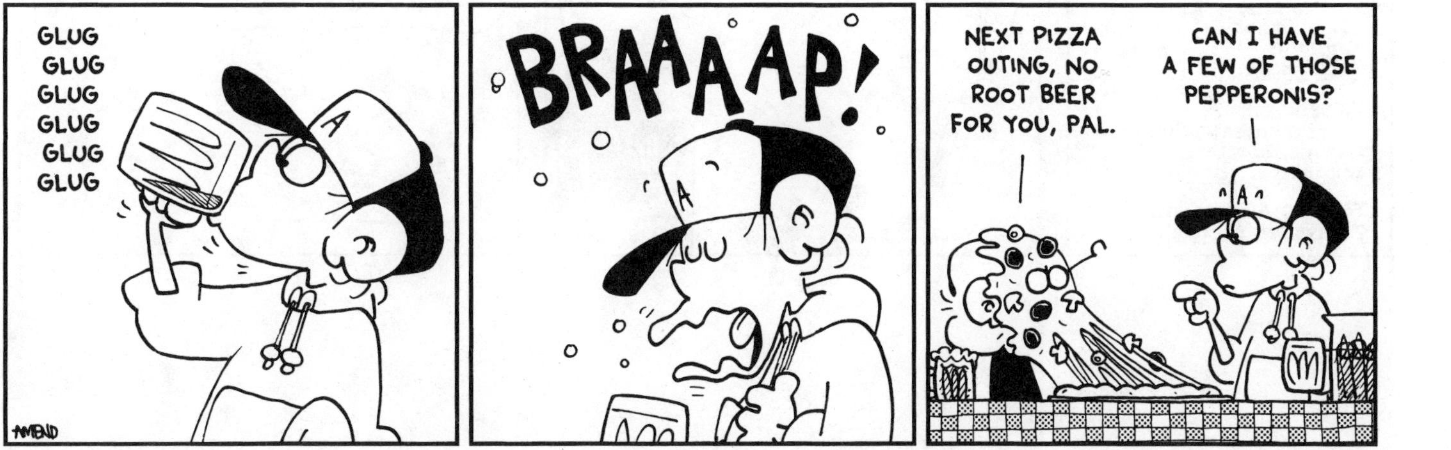
GLUG
GLUG
GLUG
GLUG
GLUG
GLUG
AMEND
BRAAAAP!
NEXT PIZZA OUTING, NO ROOT BEER FOR YOU, PAL.
CAN I HAVE A FEW OF THOSE PEPPERONIS?

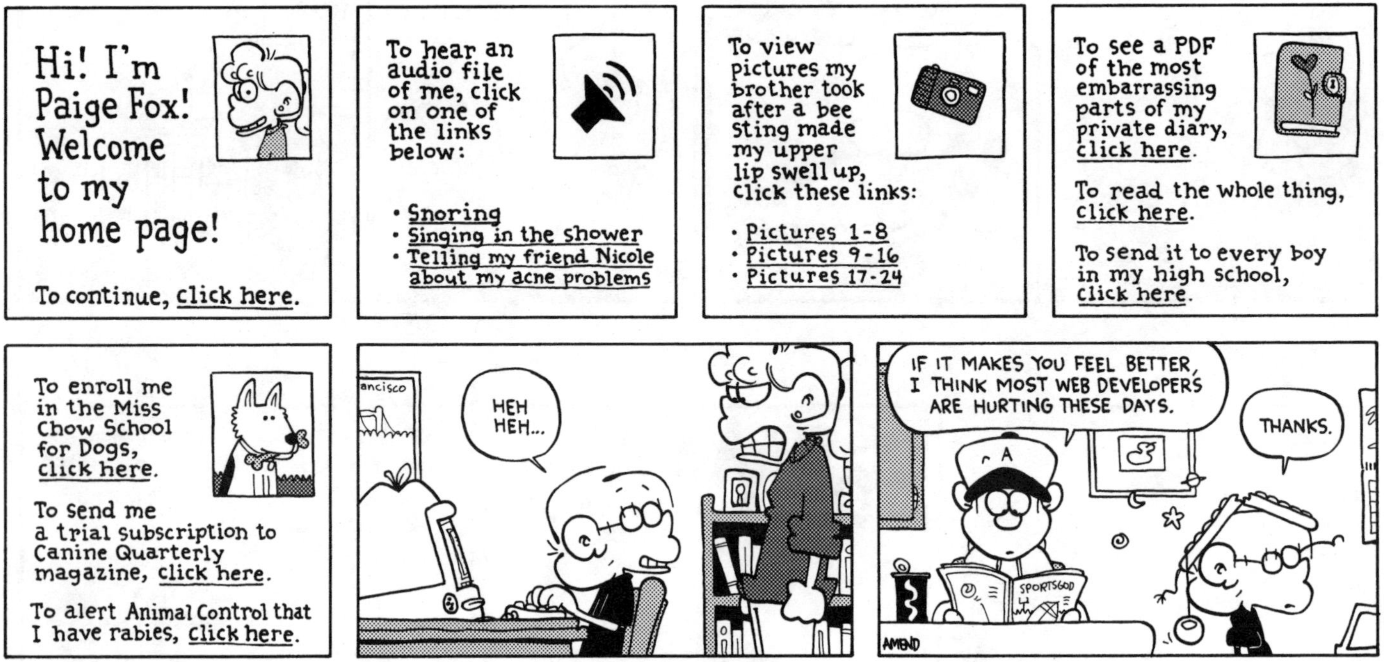
Hi! I'm Paige Fox! Welcome to my home page!
To continue, click here.
To hear an audio file of me, click on one of the links below:
• Snoring
• Singing in the shower
• Telling my friend Nicole about my acne problems
To view pictures my brother took after a bee sting made my upper lip swell up, click these links:
• Pictures 1-8
• Pictures 9-16
• Pictures 17-24
To see a PDF of the most embarrassing parts of my private diary, click here.
To read the whole thing, click here.
To send it to every boy in my high school, click here.
To enroll me in the Miss Chow School for Dogs, click here.
To send me a trial subscription to Canine Quarterly magazine, click here.
To alert Animal Control that I have rabies, click here.
HEH HEH...
IF IT MAKES YOU FEEL BETTER, I THINK MOST WEB DEVELOPERS ARE HURTING THESE DAYS.
THANKS.
SPORTSGOD
AMEND

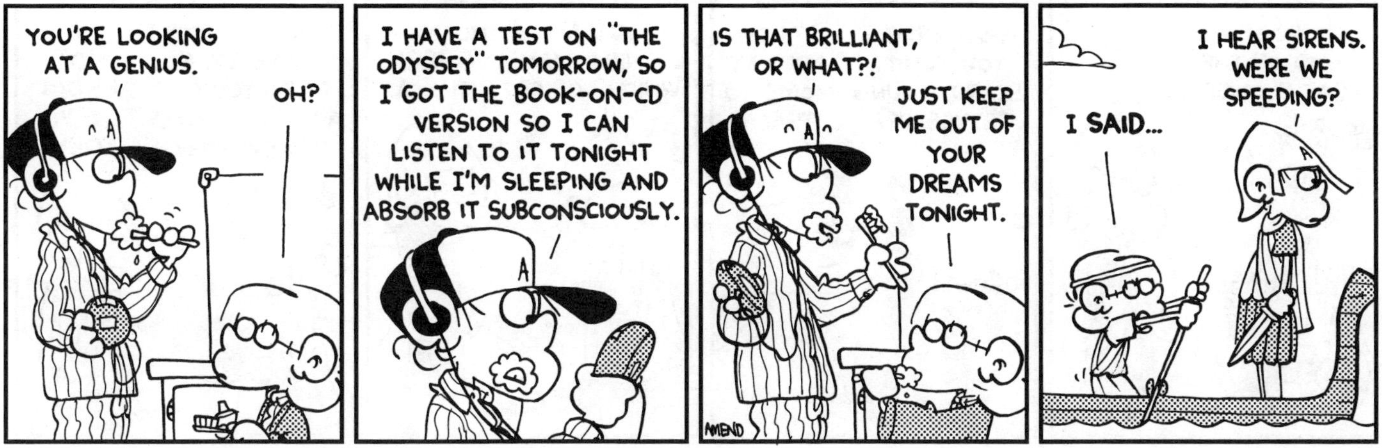
YOU'RE LOOKING AT A GENIUS.
OH?
I HAVE A TEST ON "THE ODYSSEY" TOMORROW, SO I GOT THE BOOK-ON-CD VERSION SO I CAN LISTEN TO IT TONIGHT WHILE I'M SLEEPING AND ABSORB IT SUBCONSCIOUSLY.
IS THAT BRILLIANT, OR WHAT?!
JUST KEEP ME OUT OF YOUR DREAMS TONIGHT.
AMEND
I HEAR SIRENS. WERE WE SPEEDING?
I SAID...

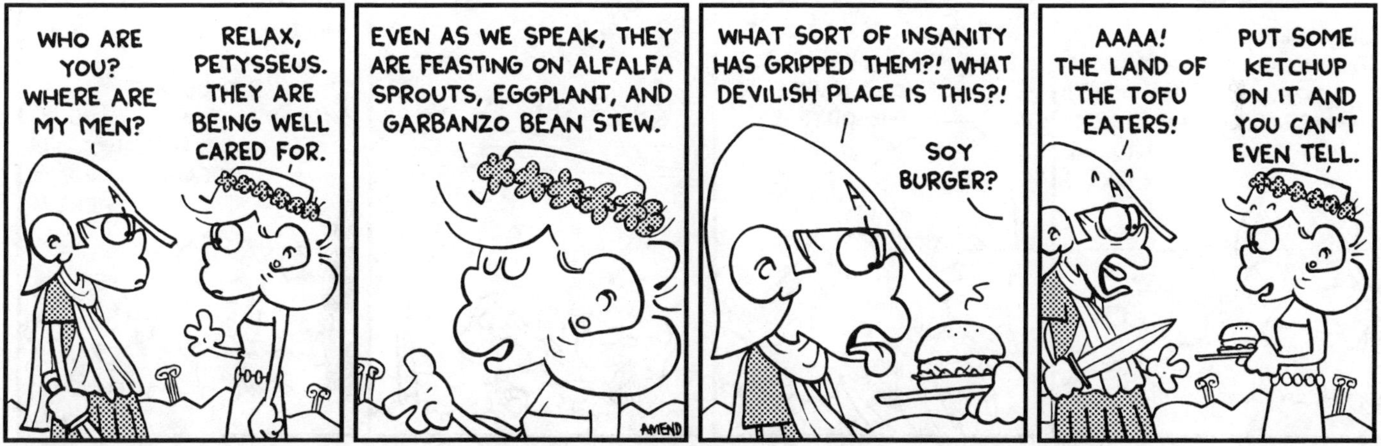
WHO ARE YOU? WHERE ARE MY MEN?
RELAX, PETYSSEUS. THEY ARE BEING WELL CARED FOR.
EVEN AS WE SPEAK, THEY ARE FEASTING ON ALFALFA SPROUTS, EGGPLANT, AND GARBANZO BEAN STEW.
AMEND
WHAT SORT OF INSANITY HAS GRIPPED THEM?! WHAT DEVILISH PLACE IS THIS?!
SOY BURGER?
AAAA! THE LAND OF THE TOFU EATERS!
PUT SOME KETCHUP ON IT AND YOU CAN'T EVEN TELL.

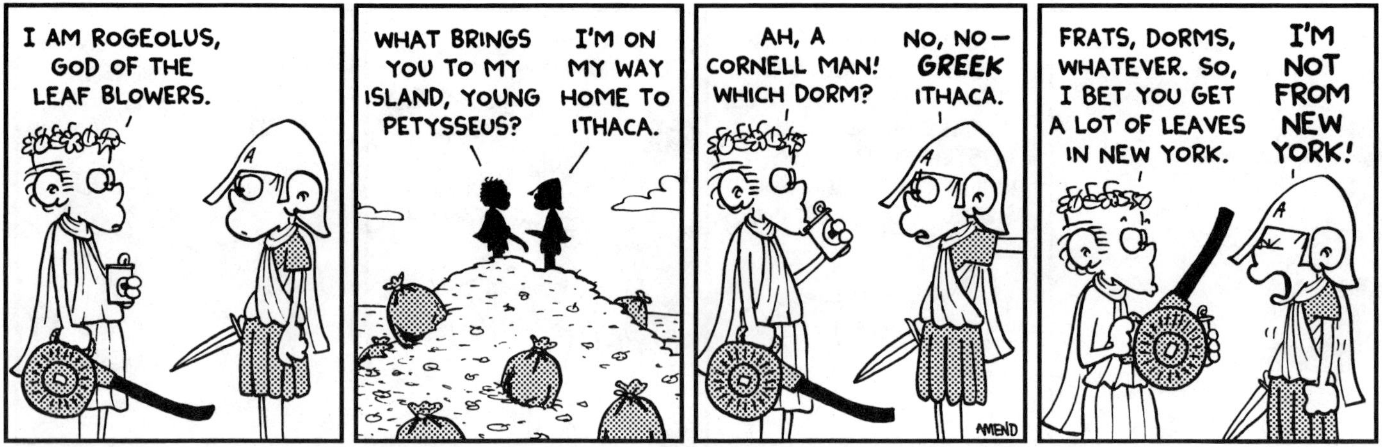
I AM ROGEOLUS, GOD OF THE LEAF BLOWERS.
WHAT BRINGS YOU TO MY ISLAND, YOUNG PETYSSEUS?
I'M ON MY WAY HOME TO ITHACA.
AH, A CORNELL MAN! WHICH DORM?
NO, NO— GREEK ITHACA.
FRATS, DORMS, WHATEVER. SO, I BET YOU GET A LOT OF LEAVES IN NEW YORK.
I'M NOT FROM NEW YORK!
AMEND

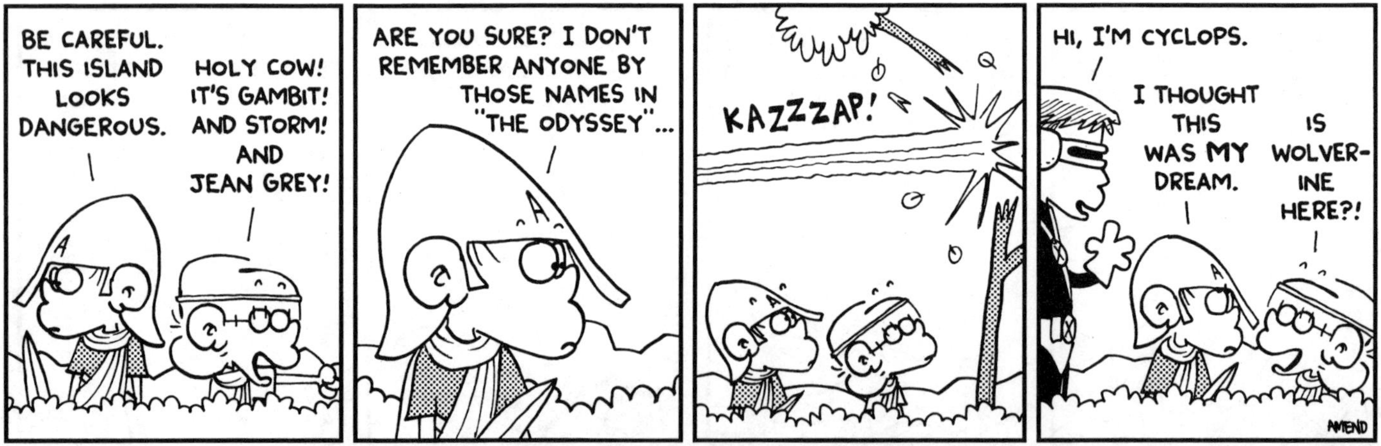
BE CAREFUL. THIS ISLAND LOOKS DANGEROUS.
HOLY COW! IT'S GAMBIT! AND STORM! AND JEAN GREY!
ARE YOU SURE? I DON'T REMEMBER ANYONE BY THOSE NAMES IN "THE ODYSSEY"...
KAZZZAP!
HI, I'M CYCLOPS.
I THOUGHT THIS WAS MY DREAM.
IS WOLVER-INE HERE?!
AMEND

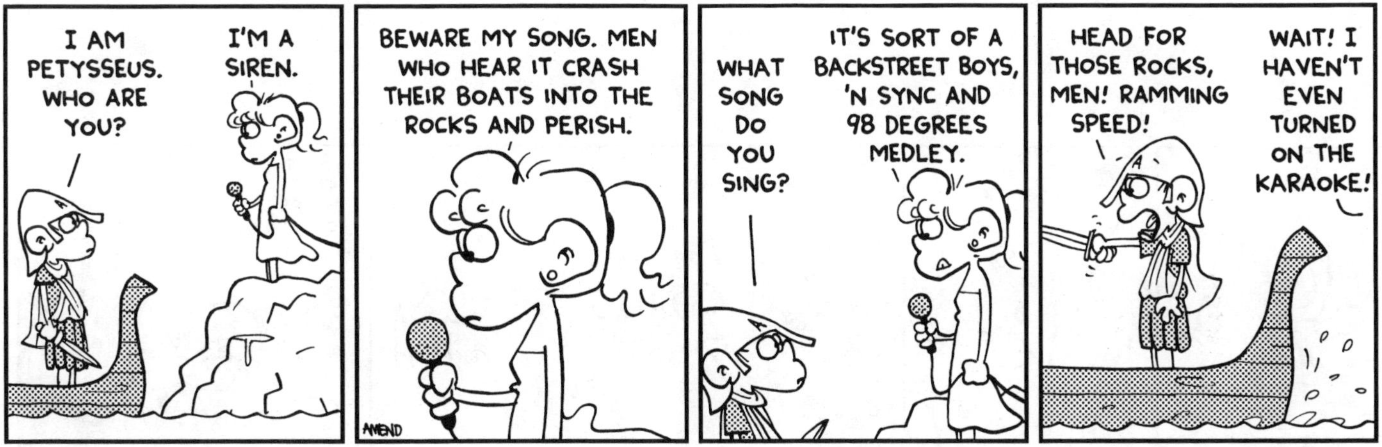
I AM PETYSSEUS. WHO ARE YOU?
I'M A SIREN.
BEWARE MY SONG. MEN WHO HEAR IT CRASH THEIR BOATS INTO THE ROCKS AND PERISH.
AMEND
WHAT SONG DO YOU SING?
IT'S SORT OF A BACKSTREET BOYS, 'N SYNC AND 98 DEGREES MEDLEY.
HEAD FOR THOSE ROCKS, MEN! RAMMING SPEED!
WAIT! I HAVEN'T EVEN TURNED ON THE KARAOKE!

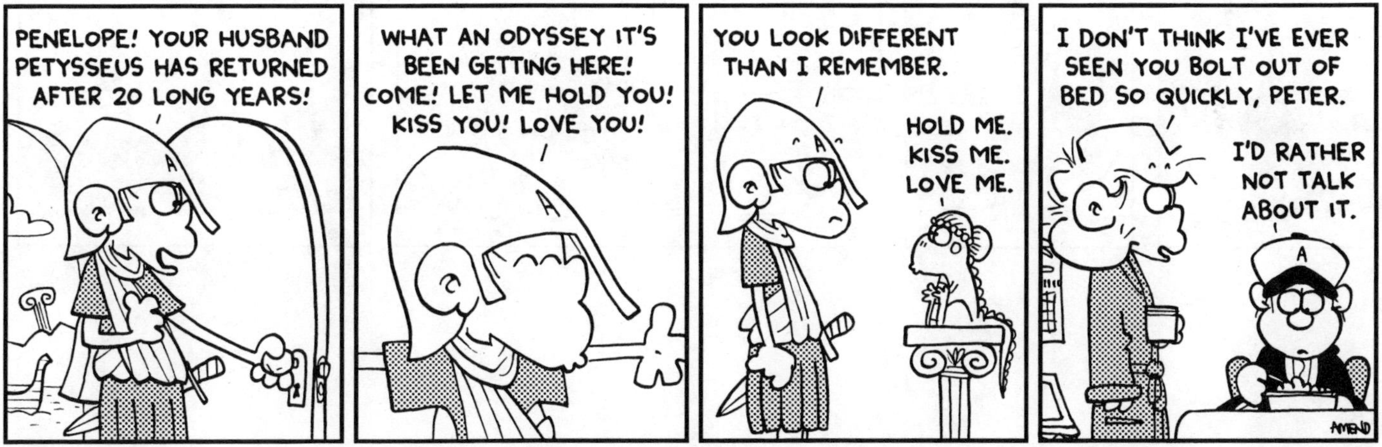
PENELOPE! YOUR HUSBAND PETYSSEUS HAS RETURNED AFTER 20 LONG YEARS!
WHAT AN ODYSSEY IT'S BEEN GETTING HERE! COME! LET ME HOLD YOU! KISS YOU! LOVE YOU!
YOU LOOK DIFFERENT THAN I REMEMBER.
HOLD ME. KISS ME. LOVE ME.
I DON'T THINK I'VE EVER SEEN YOU BOLT OUT OF BED SO QUICKLY, PETER.
I'D RATHER NOT TALK ABOUT IT.
AMEND

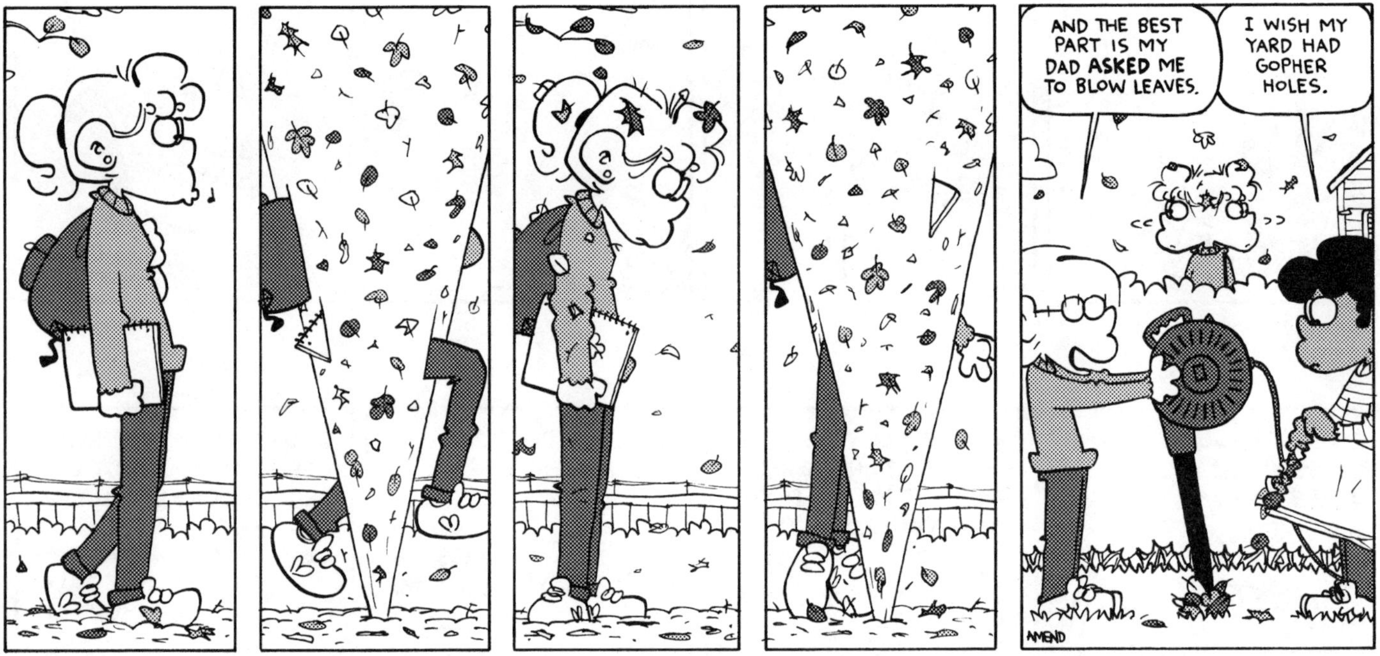
AND THE BEST PART IS MY DAD **ASKED** ME TO BLOW LEAVES.
I WISH MY YARD HAD GOPHER HOLES.
AMEND

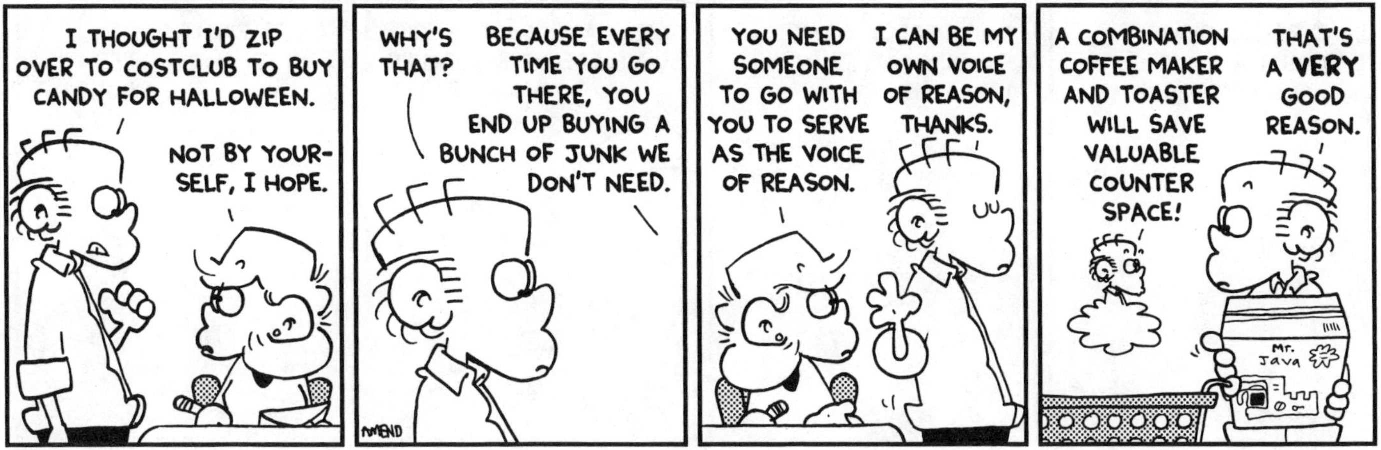
I THOUGHT I'D ZIP OVER TO COSTCLUB TO BUY CANDY FOR HALLOWEEN.
NOT BY YOURSELF, I HOPE.
WHY'S THAT?
BECAUSE EVERY TIME YOU GO THERE, YOU END UP BUYING A BUNCH OF JUNK WE DON'T NEED.
AMEND
YOU NEED SOMEONE TO GO WITH YOU TO SERVE AS THE VOICE OF REASON.
I CAN BE MY OWN VOICE OF REASON, THANKS.
A COMBINATION COFFEE MAKER AND TOASTER WILL SAVE VALUABLE COUNTER SPACE!
THAT'S A **VERY** GOOD REASON.
Mr. Java

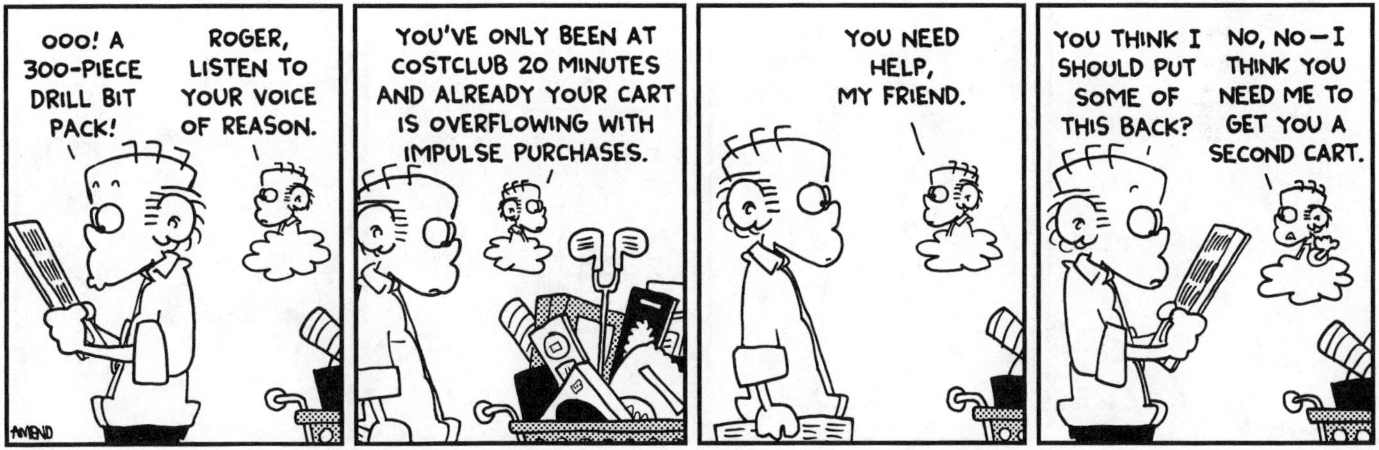
OOO! A 300-PIECE DRILL BIT PACK!
ROGER, LISTEN TO YOUR VOICE OF REASON.
AMEND
YOU'VE ONLY BEEN AT COSTCLUB 20 MINUTES AND ALREADY YOUR CART IS OVERFLOWING WITH IMPULSE PURCHASES.
YOU NEED HELP, MY FRIEND.
YOU THINK I SHOULD PUT SOME OF THIS BACK?
NO, NO—I THINK YOU NEED ME TO GET YOU A SECOND CART.

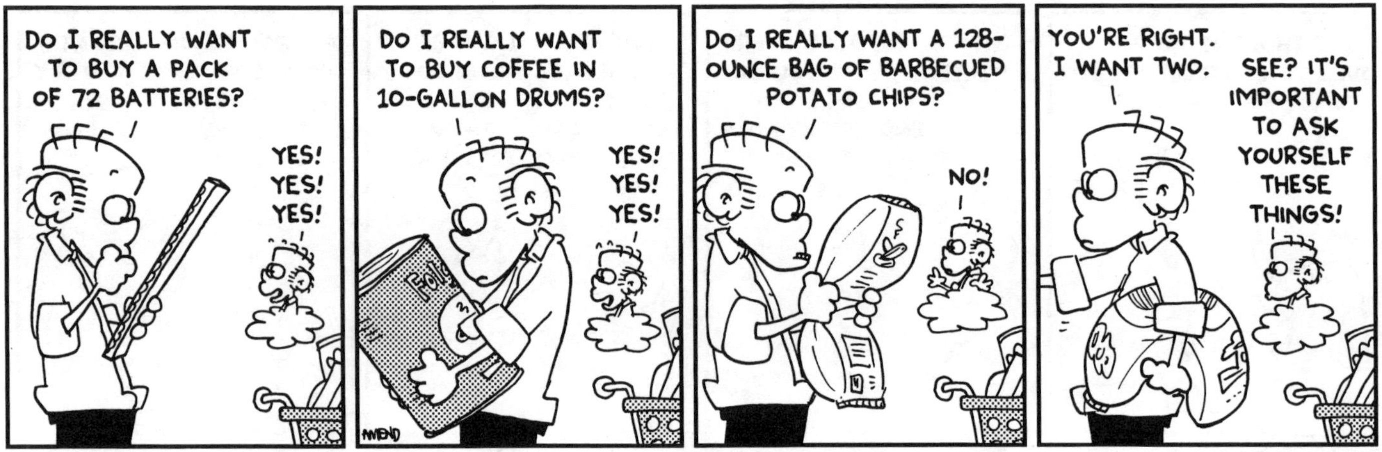
DO I REALLY WANT TO BUY A PACK OF 72 BATTERIES?
YES! YES! YES!
DO I REALLY WANT TO BUY COFFEE IN 10-GALLON DRUMS?
YES! YES! YES!
DO I REALLY WANT A 128-OUNCE BAG OF BARBECUED POTATO CHIPS?
NO!
YOU'RE RIGHT. I WANT TWO.
SEE? IT'S IMPORTANT TO ASK YOURSELF THESE THINGS!
AMEND

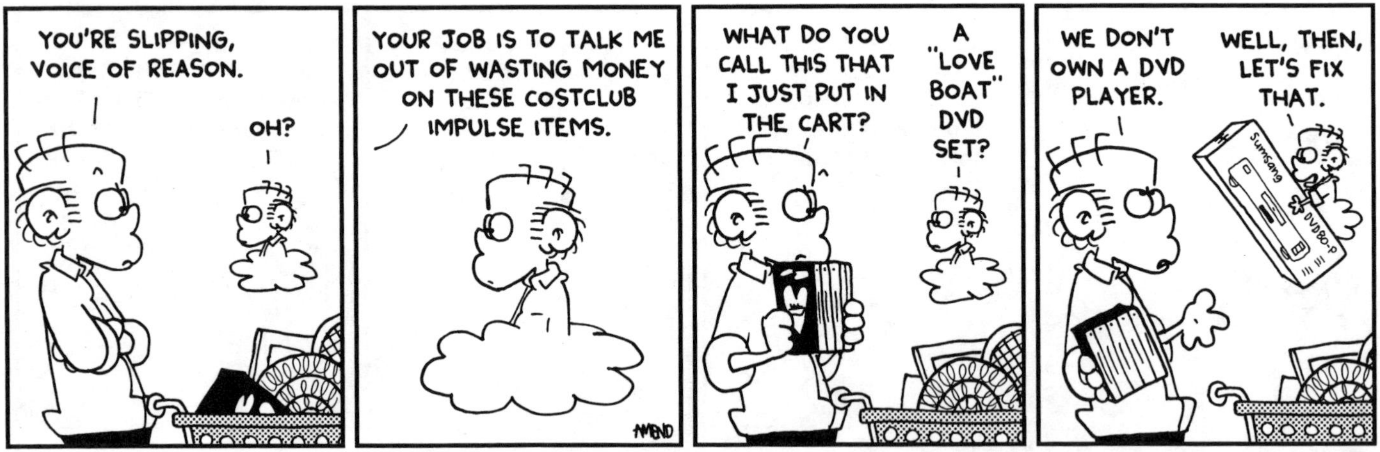
YOU'RE SLIPPING, VOICE OF REASON.
OH?
YOUR JOB IS TO TALK ME OUT OF WASTING MONEY ON THESE COSTCLUB IMPULSE ITEMS.
AMEND
WHAT DO YOU CALL THIS THAT I JUST PUT IN THE CART?
A "LOVE BOAT" DVD SET?
WE DON'T OWN A DVD PLAYER.
WELL, THEN, LET'S FIX THAT.
SumSang

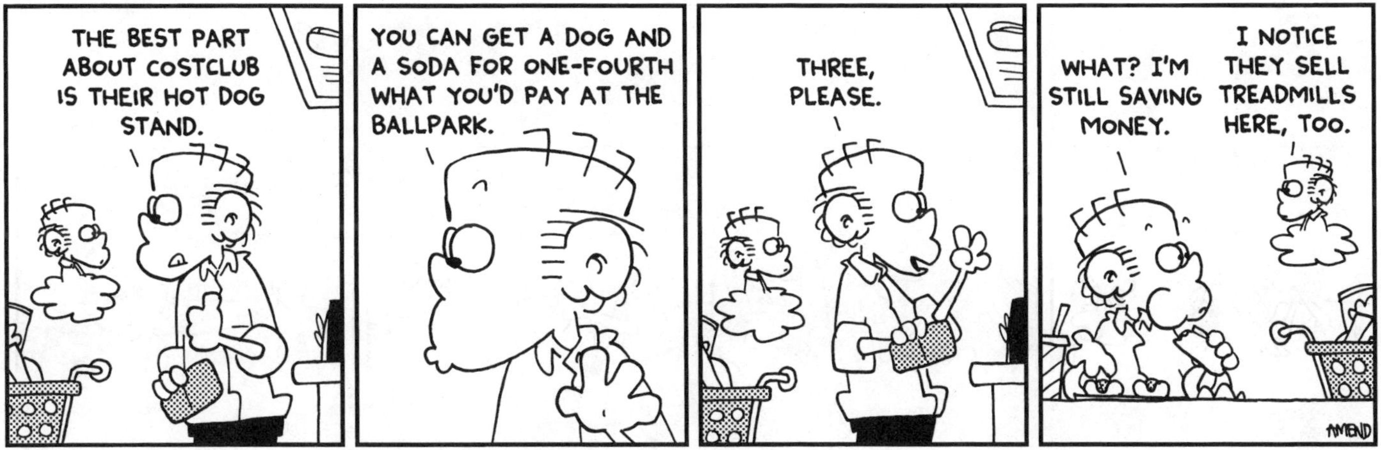
THE BEST PART ABOUT COSTCLUB IS THEIR HOT DOG STAND.
YOU CAN GET A DOG AND A SODA FOR ONE-FOURTH WHAT YOU'D PAY AT THE BALLPARK.
THREE, PLEASE.
WHAT? I'M STILL SAVING MONEY.
I NOTICE THEY SELL TREADMILLS HERE, TOO.
AMEND

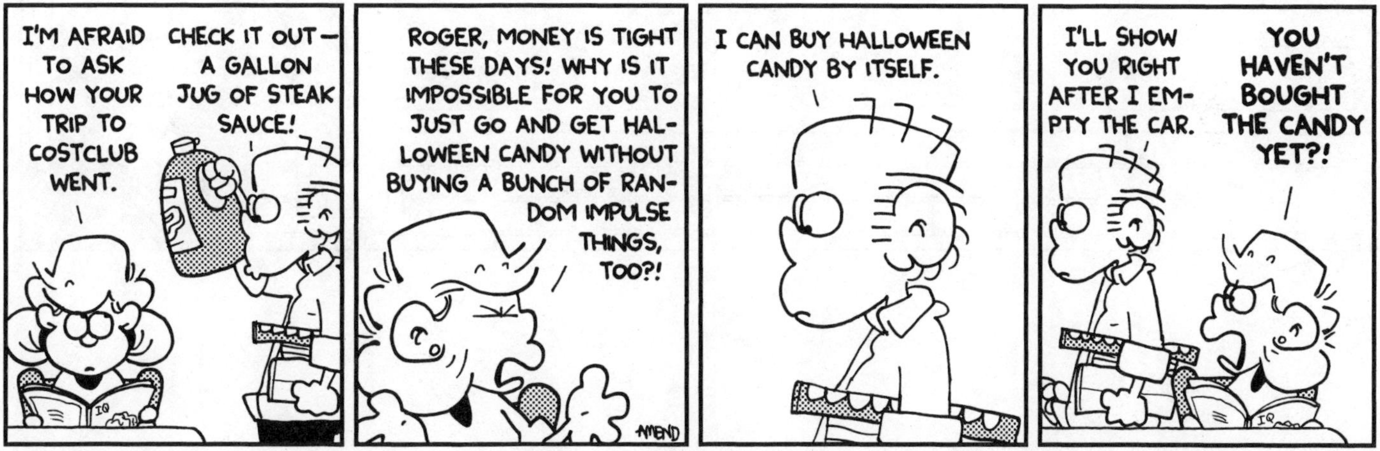
I'M AFRAID TO ASK HOW YOUR TRIP TO COSTCLUB WENT.
CHECK IT OUT— A GALLON JUG OF STEAK SAUCE!
ROGER, MONEY IS TIGHT THESE DAYS! WHY IS IT IMPOSSIBLE FOR YOU TO JUST GO AND GET HAL-LOWEEN CANDY WITHOUT BUYING A BUNCH OF RAN-DOM IMPULSE THINGS, TOO?!
AMEND
I CAN BUY HALLOWEEN CANDY BY ITSELF.
I'LL SHOW YOU RIGHT AFTER I EM-PTY THE CAR.
YOU HAVEN'T BOUGHT THE CANDY YET?!

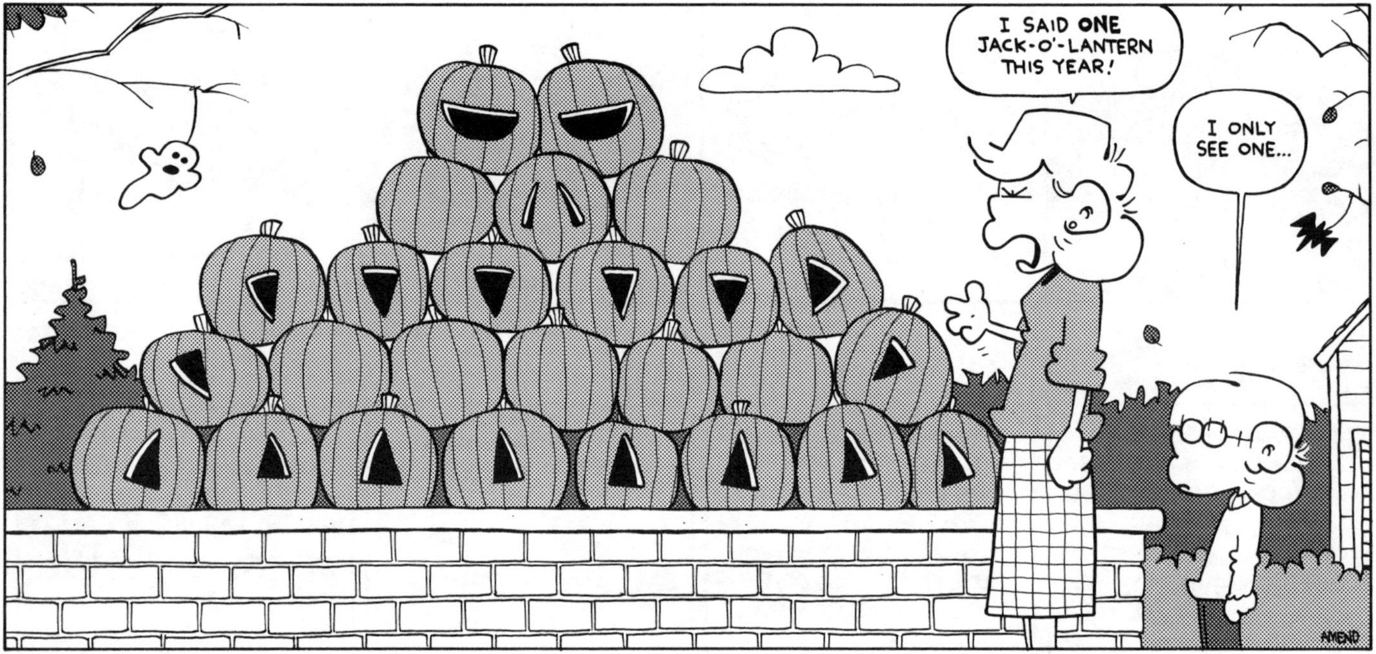
I SAID ONE JACK-O'-LANTERN THIS YEAR!
I ONLY SEE ONE...
AMEND

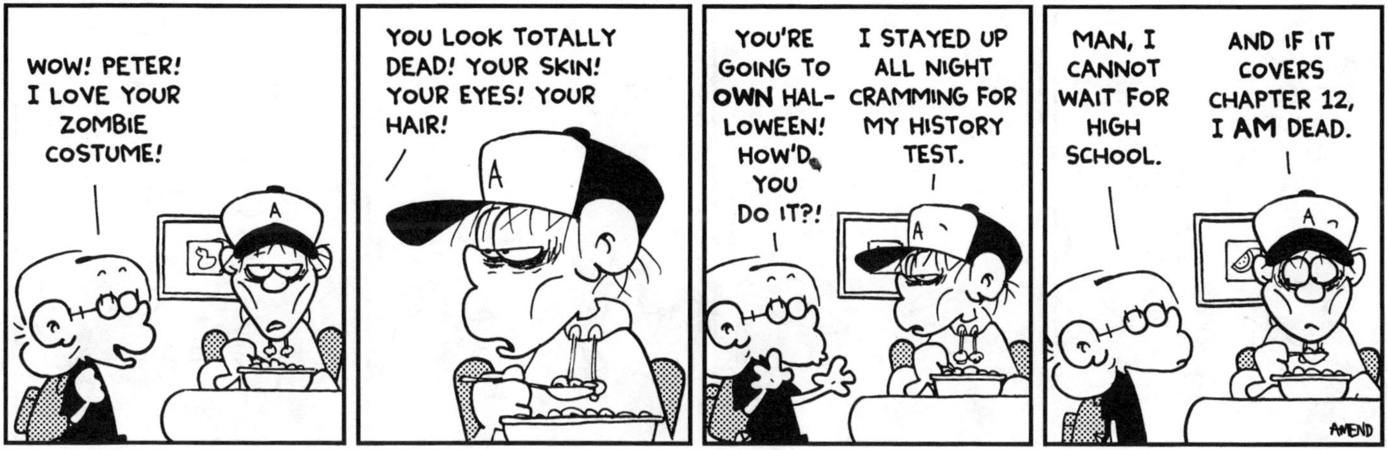
WOW! PETER! I LOVE YOUR ZOMBIE COSTUME!
YOU LOOK TOTALLY DEAD! YOUR SKIN! YOUR EYES! YOUR HAIR!
YOU'RE GOING TO OWN HALLOWEEN! HOW'D YOU DO IT?!
I STAYED UP ALL NIGHT CRAMMING FOR MY HISTORY TEST.
MAN, I CANNOT WAIT FOR HIGH SCHOOL.
AND IF IT COVERS CHAPTER 12, I AM DEAD.
AMEND

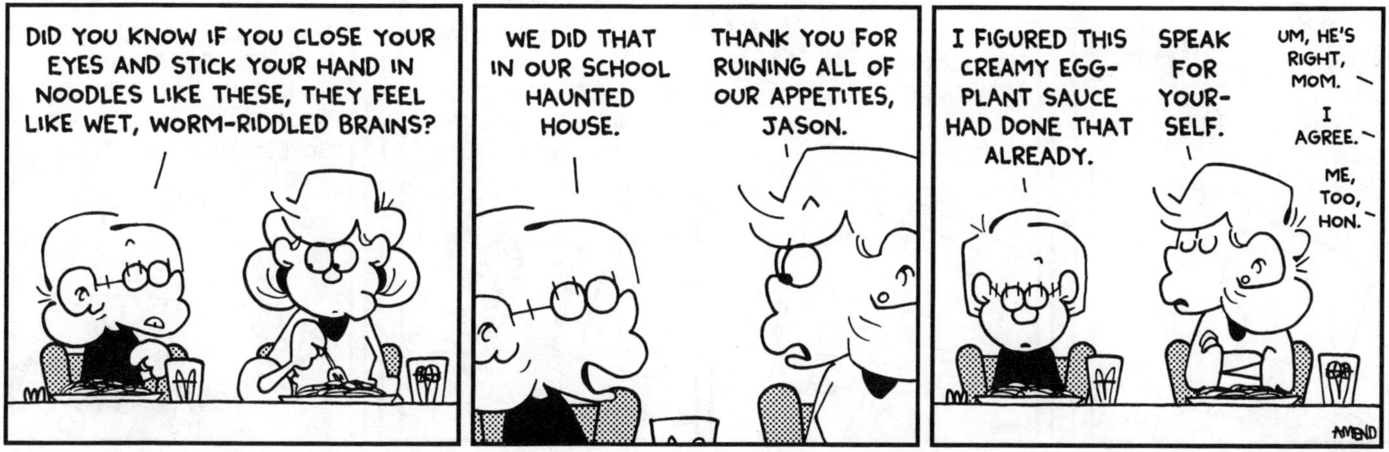
DID YOU KNOW IF YOU CLOSE YOUR EYES AND STICK YOUR HAND IN NOODLES LIKE THESE, THEY FEEL LIKE WET, WORM-RIDDLED BRAINS?
WE DID THAT IN OUR SCHOOL HAUNTED HOUSE.
THANK YOU FOR RUINING ALL OF OUR APPETITES, JASON.
I FIGURED THIS CREAMY EGGPLANT SAUCE HAD DONE THAT ALREADY.
SPEAK FOR YOURSELF.
UM, HE'S RIGHT, MOM.
I AGREE.
ME, TOO, HON.
AMEND

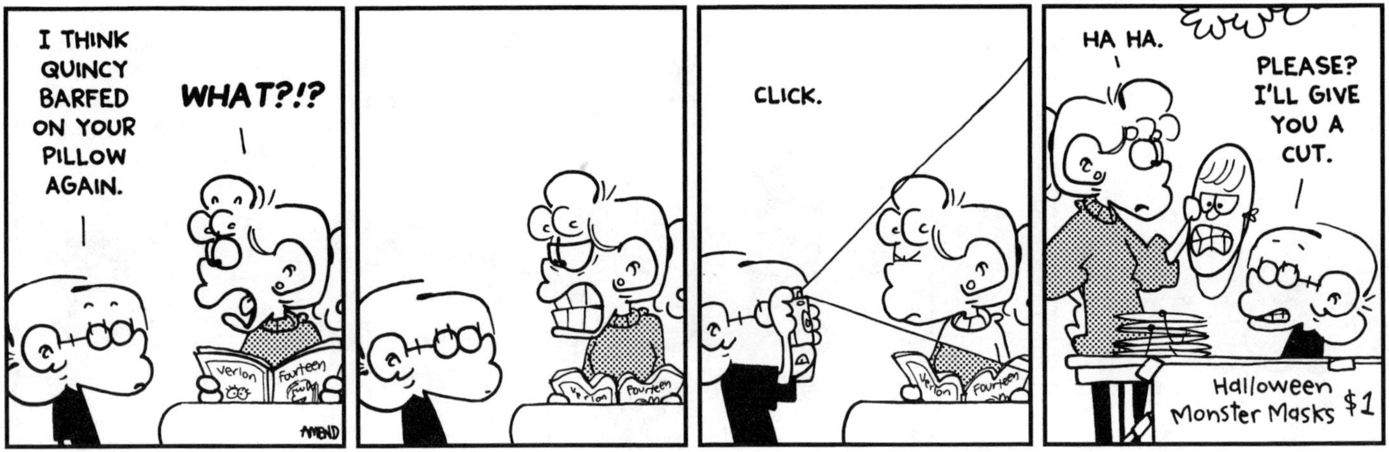
I THINK QUINCY BARFED ON YOUR PILLOW AGAIN.
WHAT?!?
Verlon Fourteen
AMEND
CLICK.
HA HA.
PLEASE? I'LL GIVE YOU A CUT.
Halloween Monster Masks $1

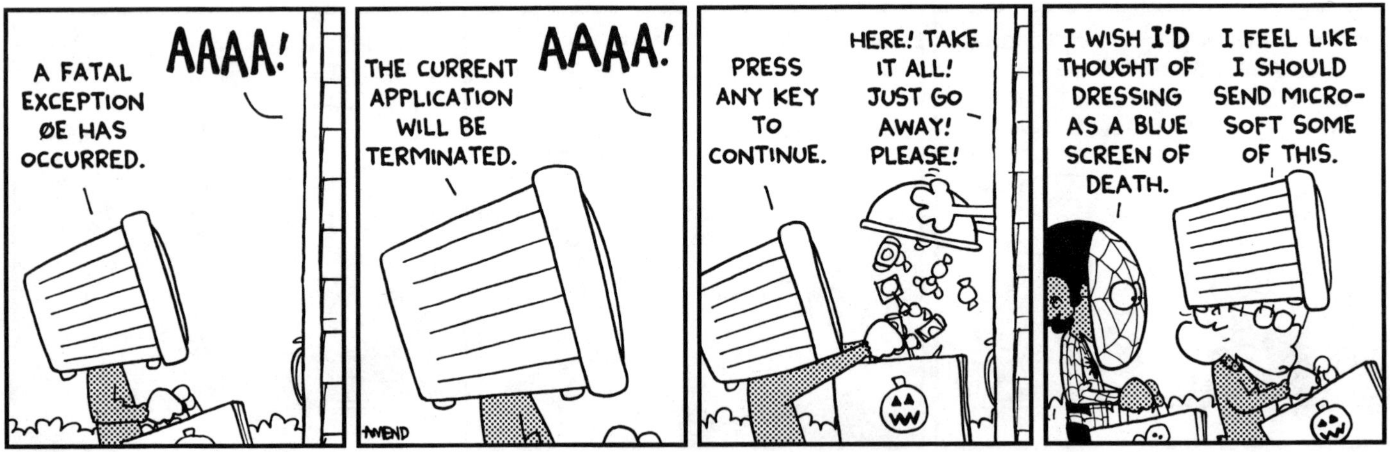
A FATAL EXCEPTION ØE HAS OCCURRED.
AAAA!
THE CURRENT APPLICATION WILL BE TERMINATED.
AAAA!
AMEND
PRESS ANY KEY TO CONTINUE.
HERE! TAKE IT ALL! JUST GO AWAY! PLEASE!
I WISH I'D THOUGHT OF DRESSING AS A BLUE SCREEN OF DEATH.
I FEEL LIKE I SHOULD SEND MICRO-SOFT SOME OF THIS.

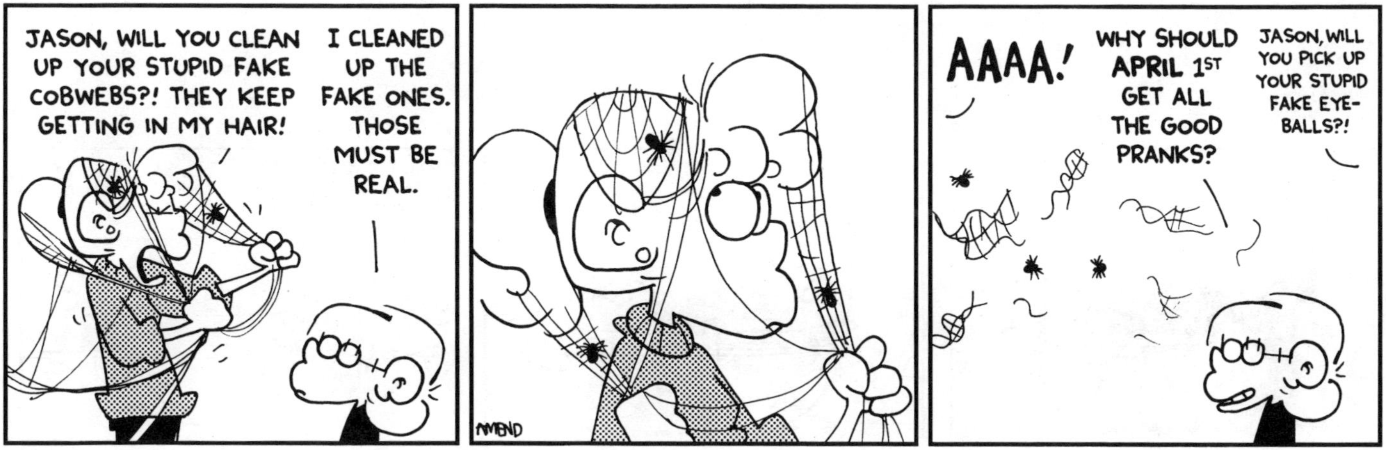
JASON, WILL YOU CLEAN UP YOUR STUPID FAKE COBWEBS?! THEY KEEP GETTING IN MY HAIR!
I CLEANED UP THE FAKE ONES. THOSE MUST BE REAL.
AMEND
AAAA!
WHY SHOULD APRIL 1ST GET ALL THE GOOD PRANKS?
JASON, WILL YOU PICK UP YOUR STUPID FAKE EYE-BALLS?!

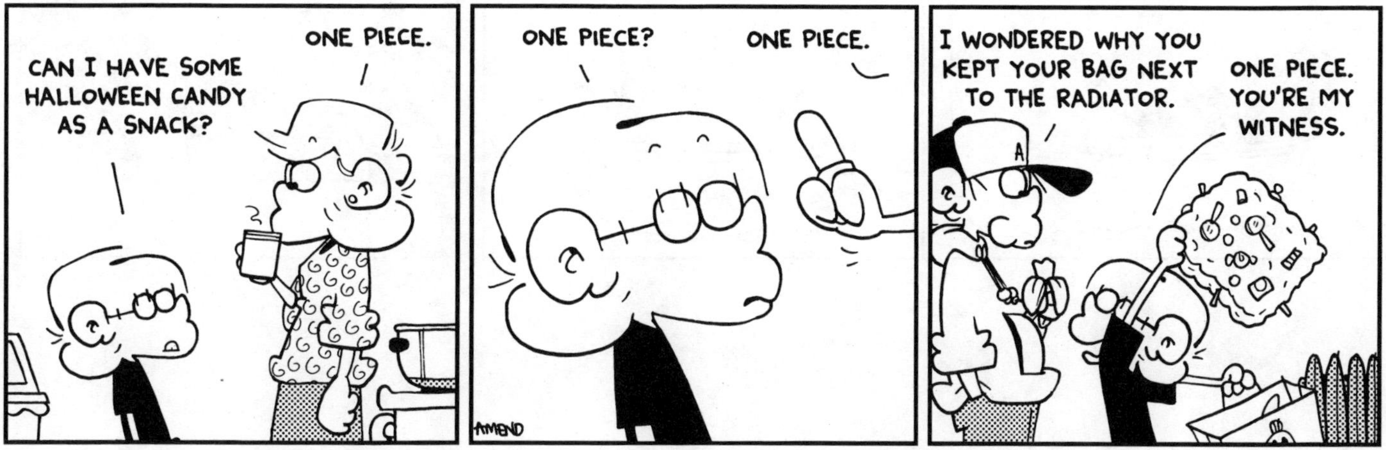
CAN I HAVE SOME HALLOWEEN CANDY AS A SNACK?
ONE PIECE.
ONE PIECE?
ONE PIECE.
AMEND
I WONDERED WHY YOU KEPT YOUR BAG NEXT TO THE RADIATOR.
ONE PIECE. YOU'RE MY WITNESS.

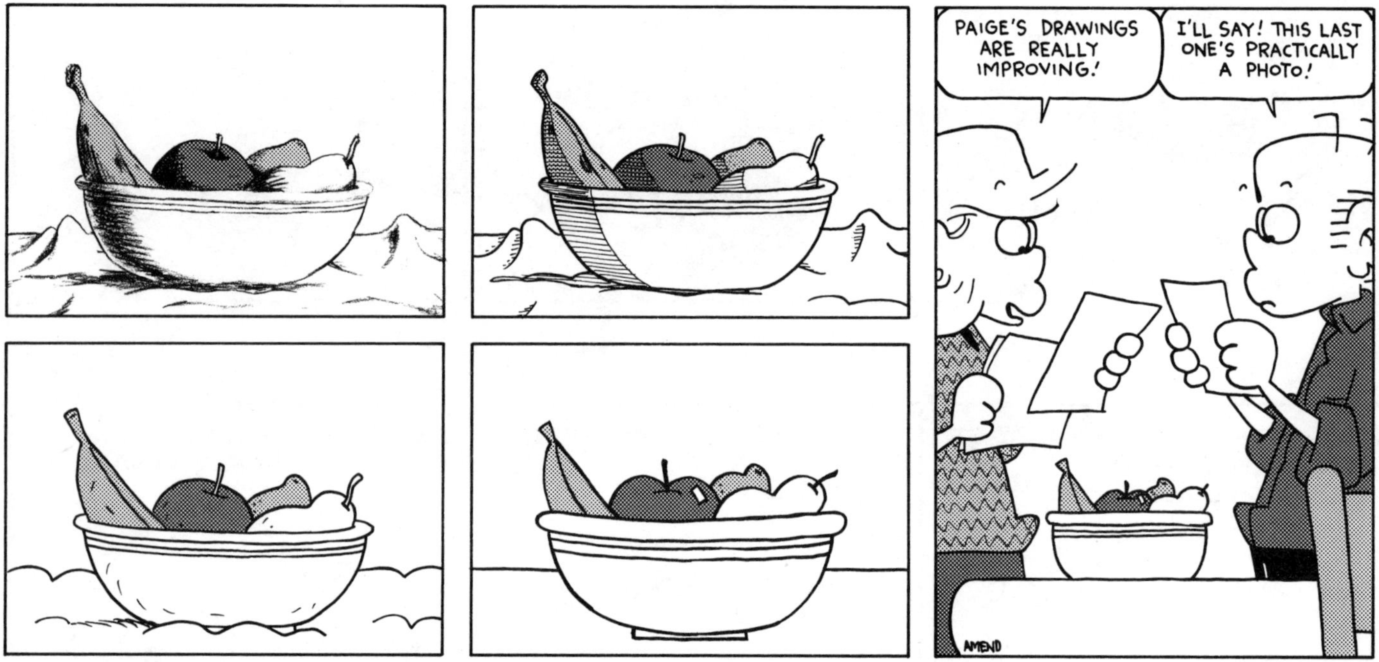
PAIGE'S DRAWINGS ARE REALLY IMPROVING!
I'LL SAY! THIS LAST ONE'S PRACTICALLY A PHOTO!
AMEND

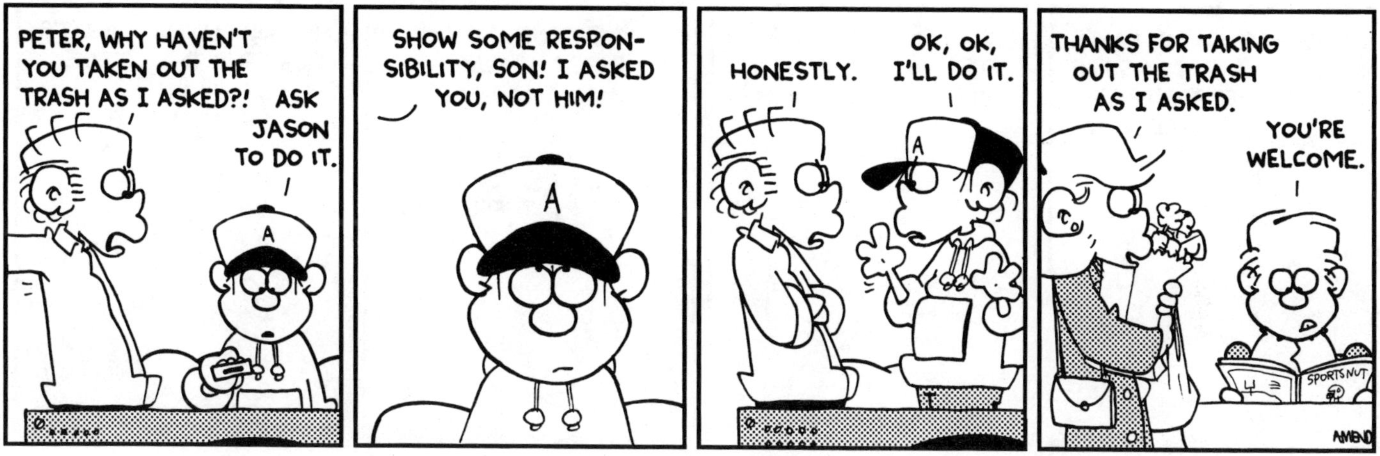
PETER, WHY HAVEN'T YOU TAKEN OUT THE TRASH AS I ASKED?!
ASK JASON TO DO IT.
SHOW SOME RESPONSIBILITY, SON! I ASKED YOU, NOT HIM!
HONESTLY.
OK, OK, I'LL DO IT.
THANKS FOR TAKING OUT THE TRASH AS I ASKED.
YOU'RE WELCOME.
SPORTS NUT
AMEND

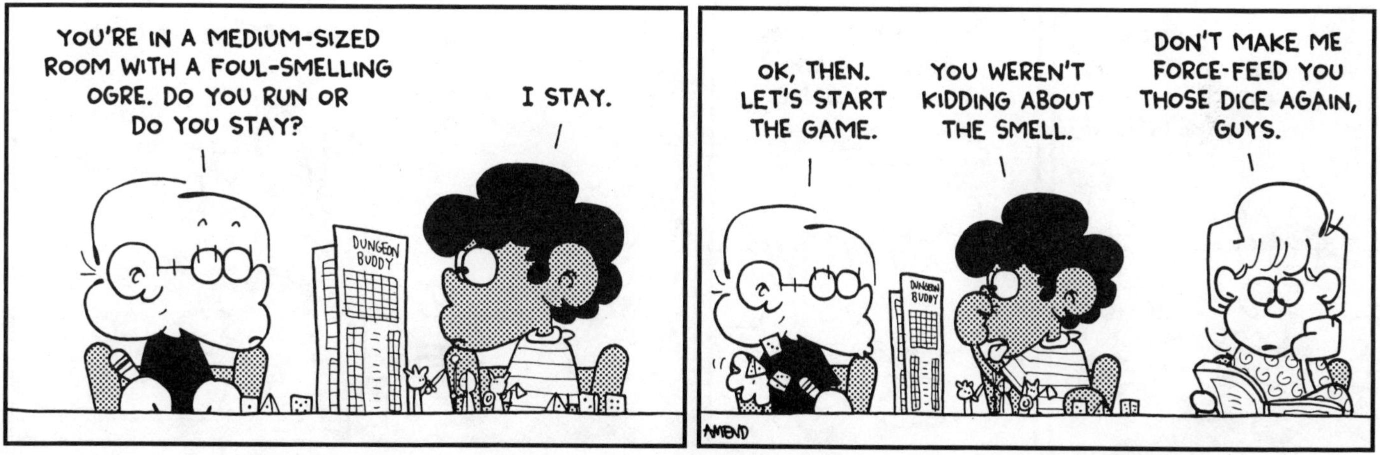
YOU'RE IN A MEDIUM-SIZED ROOM WITH A FOUL-SMELLING OGRE. DO YOU RUN OR DO YOU STAY?
I STAY.
DUNGEON BUDDY
OK, THEN. LET'S START THE GAME.
YOU WEREN'T KIDDING ABOUT THE SMELL.
DON'T MAKE ME FORCE-FEED YOU THOSE DICE AGAIN, GUYS.
AMEND

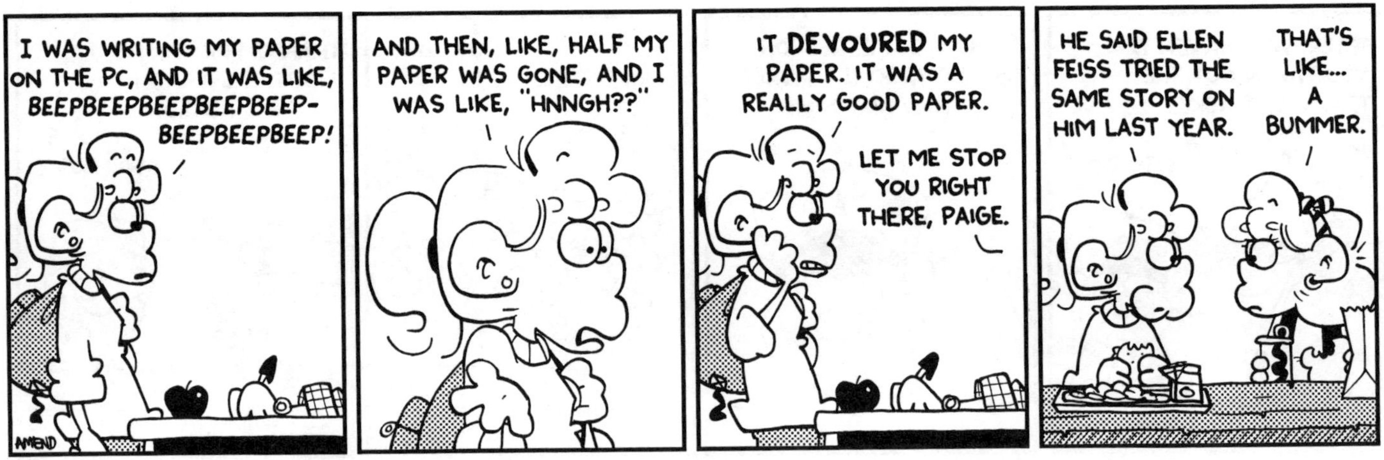
I WAS WRITING MY PAPER ON THE PC, AND IT WAS LIKE, BEEPBEEPBEEPBEEPBEEP-BEEPBEEPBEEP!
AMEND
AND THEN, LIKE, HALF MY PAPER WAS GONE, AND I WAS LIKE, "HNNGH??"
IT DEVOURED MY PAPER. IT WAS A REALLY GOOD PAPER.
LET ME STOP YOU RIGHT THERE, PAIGE.
HE SAID ELLEN FEISS TRIED THE SAME STORY ON HIM LAST YEAR.
THAT'S LIKE... A BUMMER.

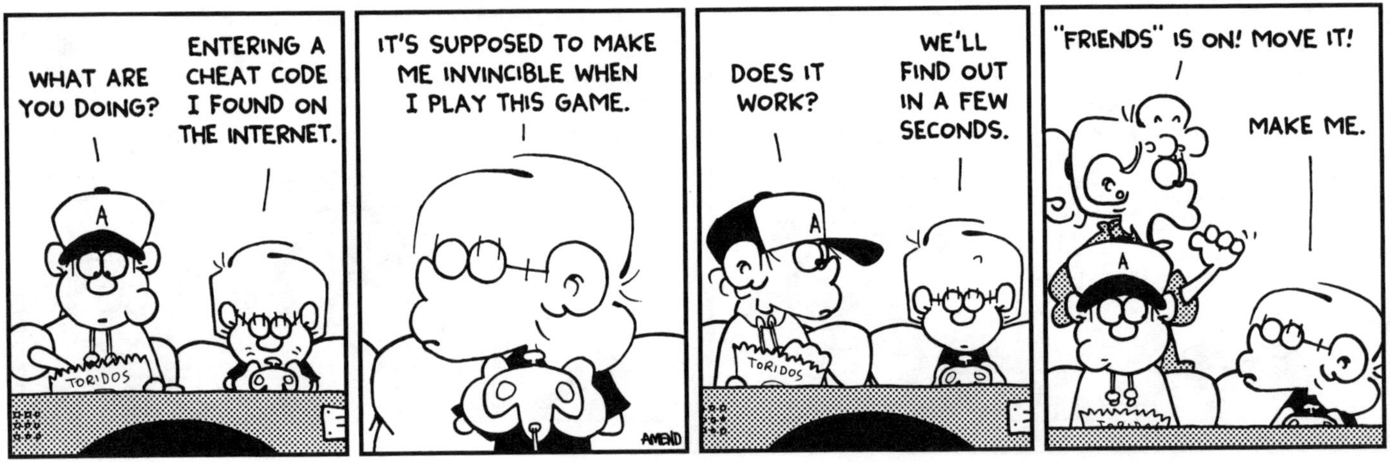
WHAT ARE YOU DOING?
ENTERING A CHEAT CODE I FOUND ON THE INTERNET.
TORIDOS
IT'S SUPPOSED TO MAKE ME INVINCIBLE WHEN I PLAY THIS GAME.
AMEND
DOES IT WORK?
WE'LL FIND OUT IN A FEW SECONDS.
TORIDOS
"FRIENDS" IS ON! MOVE IT!
MAKE ME.

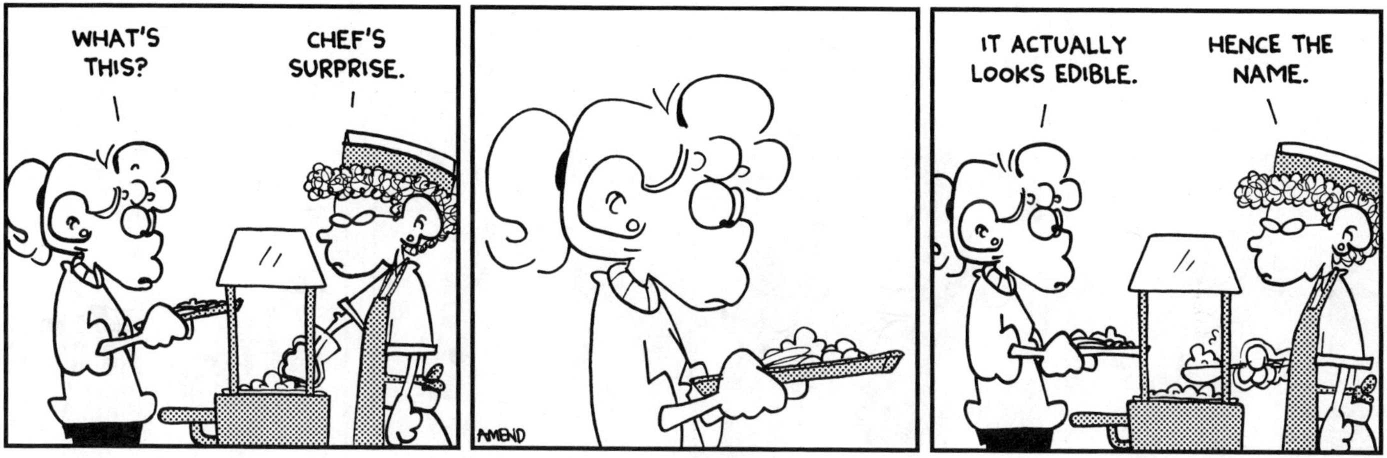
WHAT'S THIS?
CHEF'S SURPRISE.
IT ACTUALLY LOOKS EDIBLE.
HENCE THE NAME.
AMEND

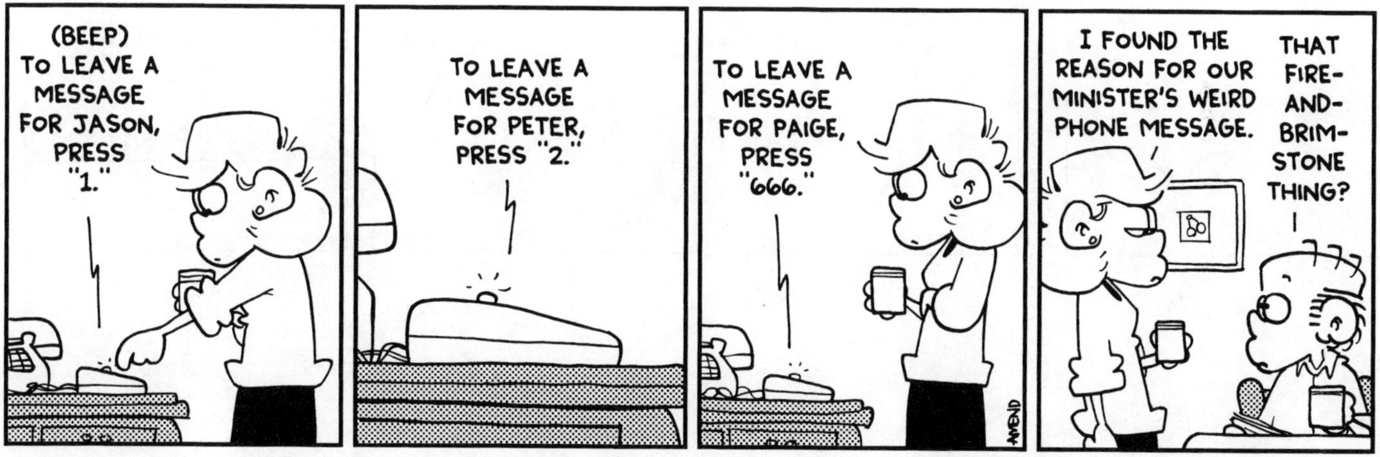
(BEEP) TO LEAVE A MESSAGE FOR JASON, PRESS "1."
TO LEAVE A MESSAGE FOR PETER, PRESS "2."
TO LEAVE A MESSAGE FOR PAIGE, PRESS "666."
AMEND
I FOUND THE REASON FOR OUR MINISTER'S WEIRD PHONE MESSAGE.
THAT FIRE-AND-BRIMSTONE THING?

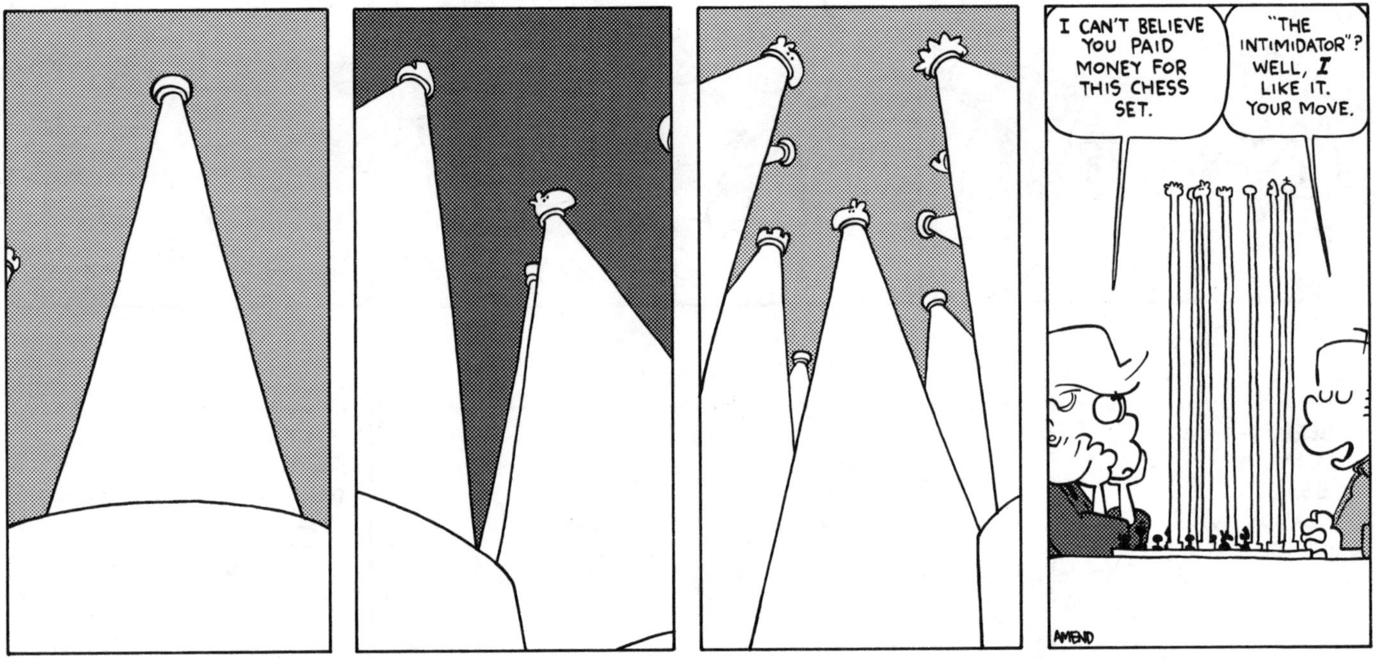
I CAN'T BELIEVE YOU PAID MONEY FOR THIS CHESS SET.
"THE INTIMIDATOR"? WELL, *I* LIKE IT. YOUR MOVE.
AMEND

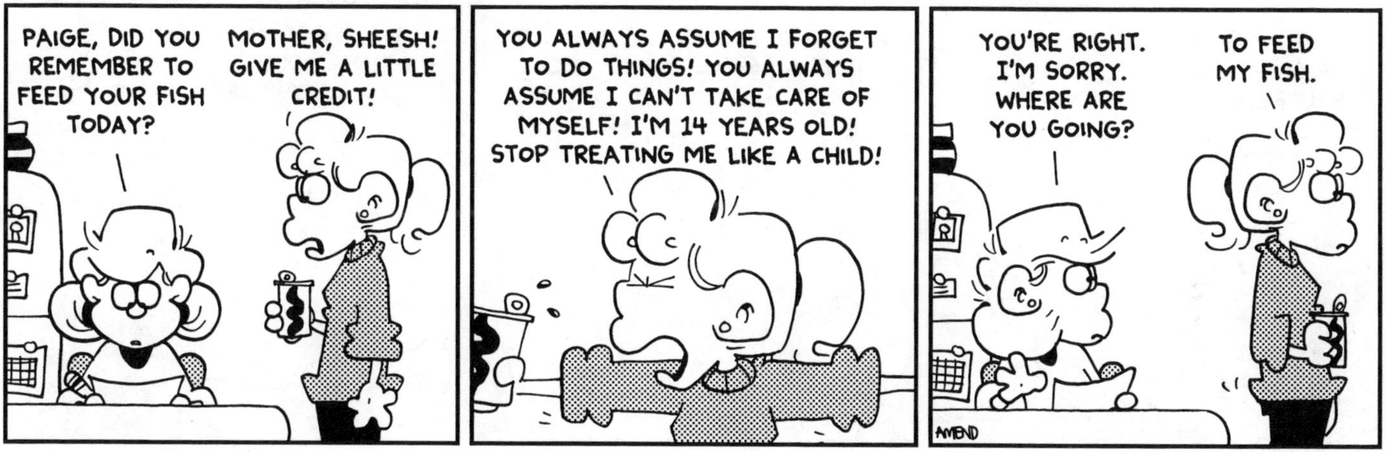
PAIGE, DID YOU REMEMBER TO FEED YOUR FISH TODAY?
MOTHER, SHEESH! GIVE ME A LITTLE CREDIT!
YOU ALWAYS ASSUME I FORGET TO DO THINGS! YOU ALWAYS ASSUME I CAN'T TAKE CARE OF MYSELF! I'M 14 YEARS OLD! STOP TREATING ME LIKE A CHILD!
YOU'RE RIGHT. I'M SORRY. WHERE ARE YOU GOING?
TO FEED MY FISH.
AMEND

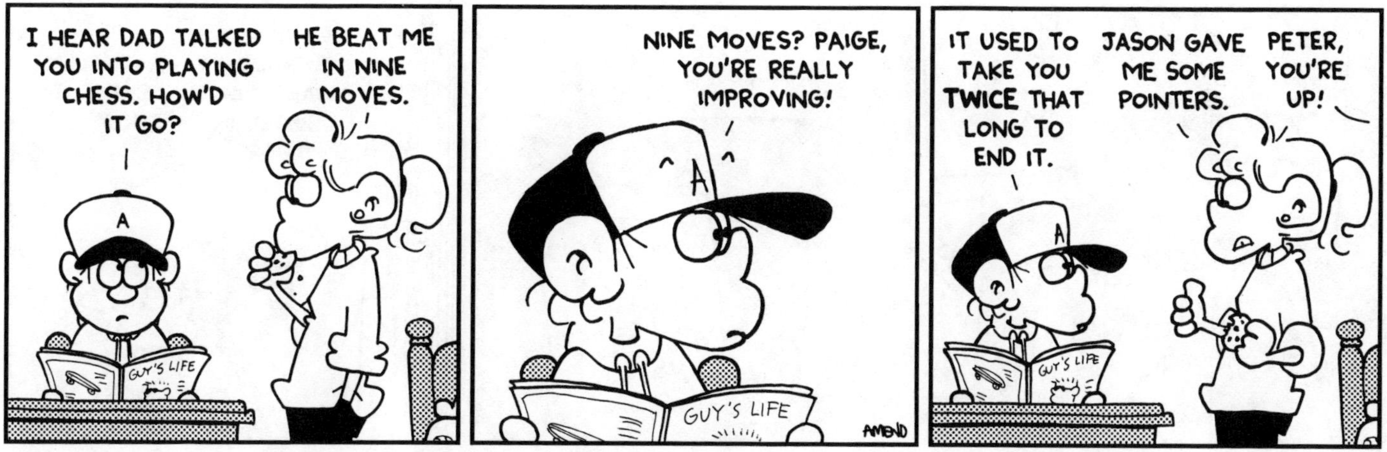
I HEAR DAD TALKED YOU INTO PLAYING CHESS. HOW'D IT GO?
HE BEAT ME IN NINE MOVES.
GUY'S LIFE
NINE MOVES? PAIGE, YOU'RE REALLY IMPROVING!
GUY'S LIFE
AMEND
IT USED TO TAKE YOU **TWICE** THAT LONG TO END IT.
JASON GAVE ME SOME POINTERS.
PETER, YOU'RE UP!
GUY'S LIFE

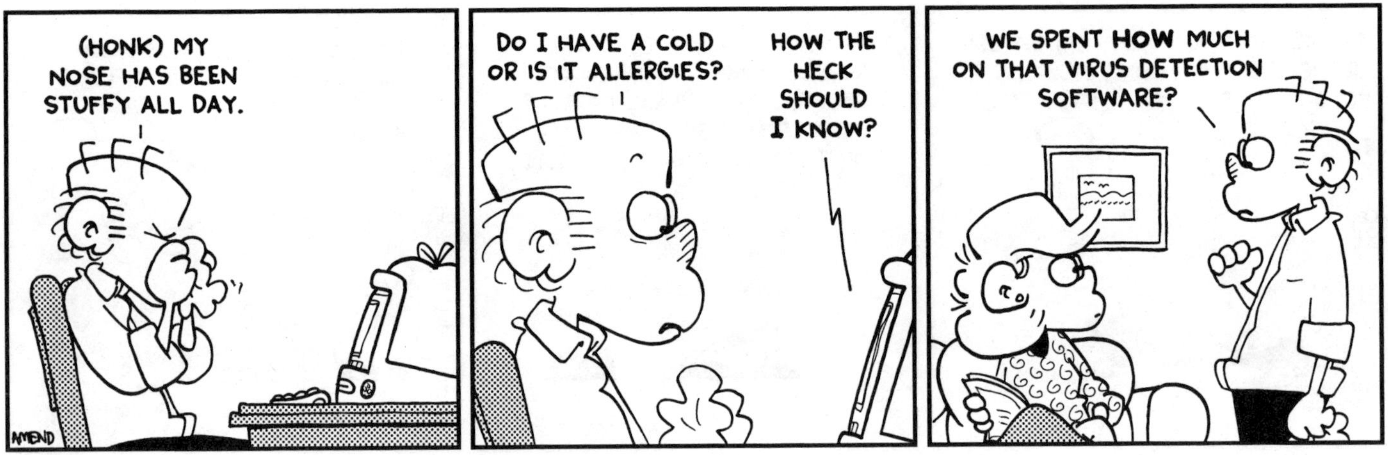
(HONK) MY NOSE HAS BEEN STUFFY ALL DAY.
DO I HAVE A COLD OR IS IT ALLERGIES?
HOW THE HECK SHOULD I KNOW?
WE SPENT HOW MUCH ON THAT VIRUS DETECTION SOFTWARE?
AMEND

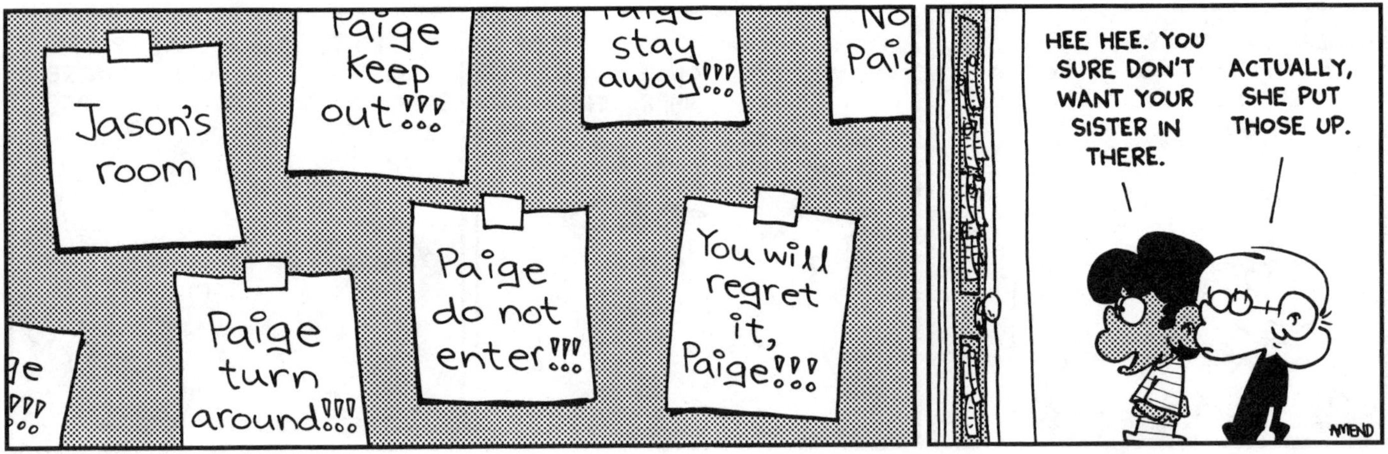
Paige keep out!!!
stay away!!!
Jason's room
Paige turn around!!!
Paige do not enter!!!
You will regret it, Paige!!!
HEE HEE. YOU SURE DON'T WANT YOUR SISTER IN THERE.
ACTUALLY, SHE PUT THOSE UP.
AMEND

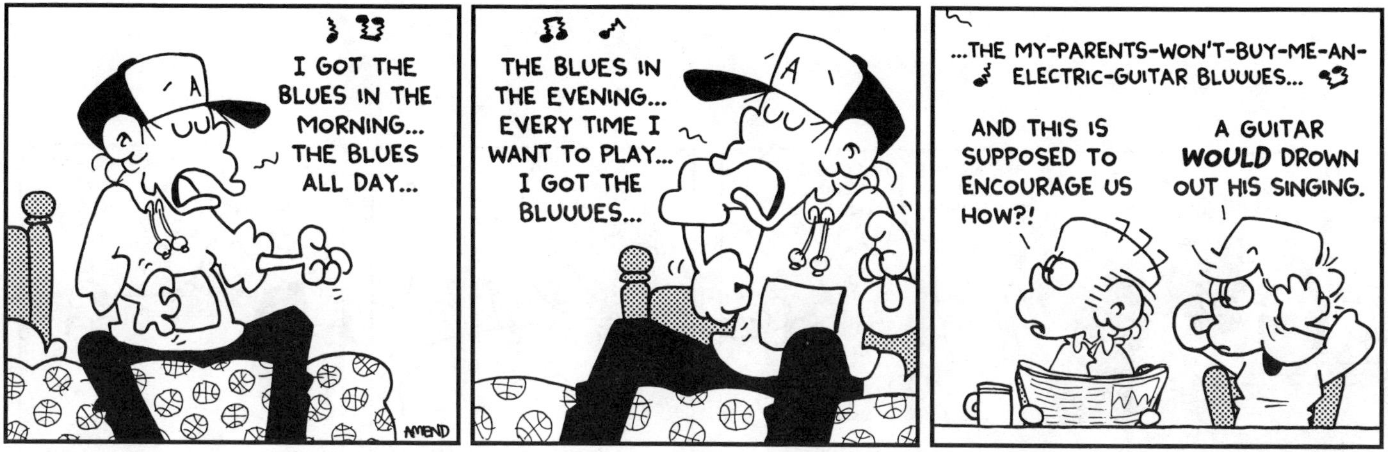
I GOT THE BLUES IN THE MORNING... THE BLUES ALL DAY...
THE BLUES IN THE EVENING... EVERY TIME I WANT TO PLAY... I GOT THE BLUUUES...
...THE MY-PARENTS-WON'T-BUY-ME-AN-ELECTRIC-GUITAR BLUUUES...
AND THIS IS SUPPOSED TO ENCOURAGE US HOW?!
A GUITAR WOULD DROWN OUT HIS SINGING.
AMEND

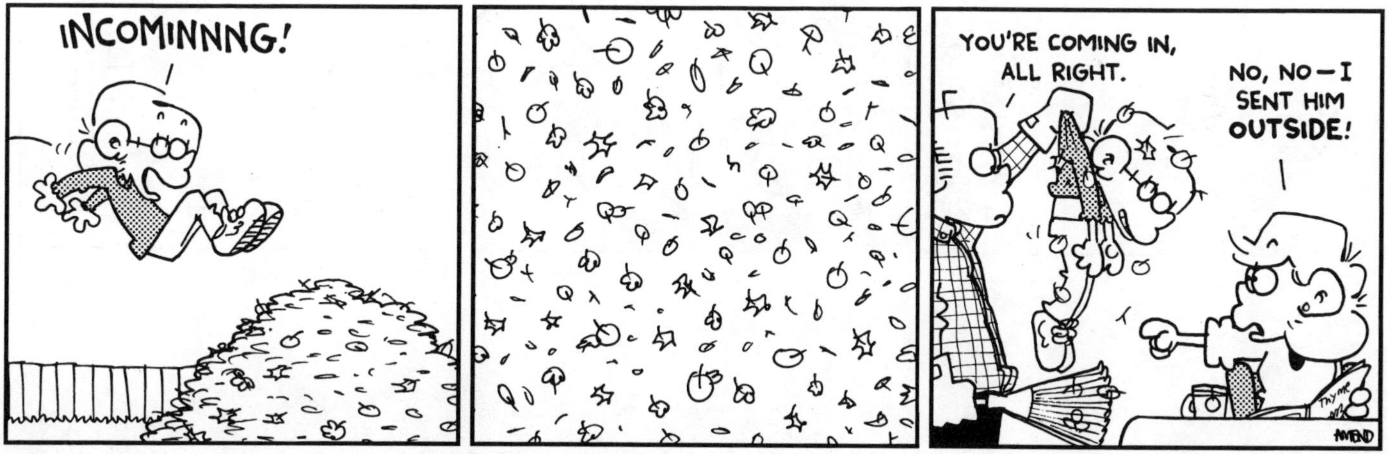
INCOMINNNG!
YOU'RE COMING IN, ALL RIGHT.
NO, NO—I SENT HIM OUTSIDE!
AMEND

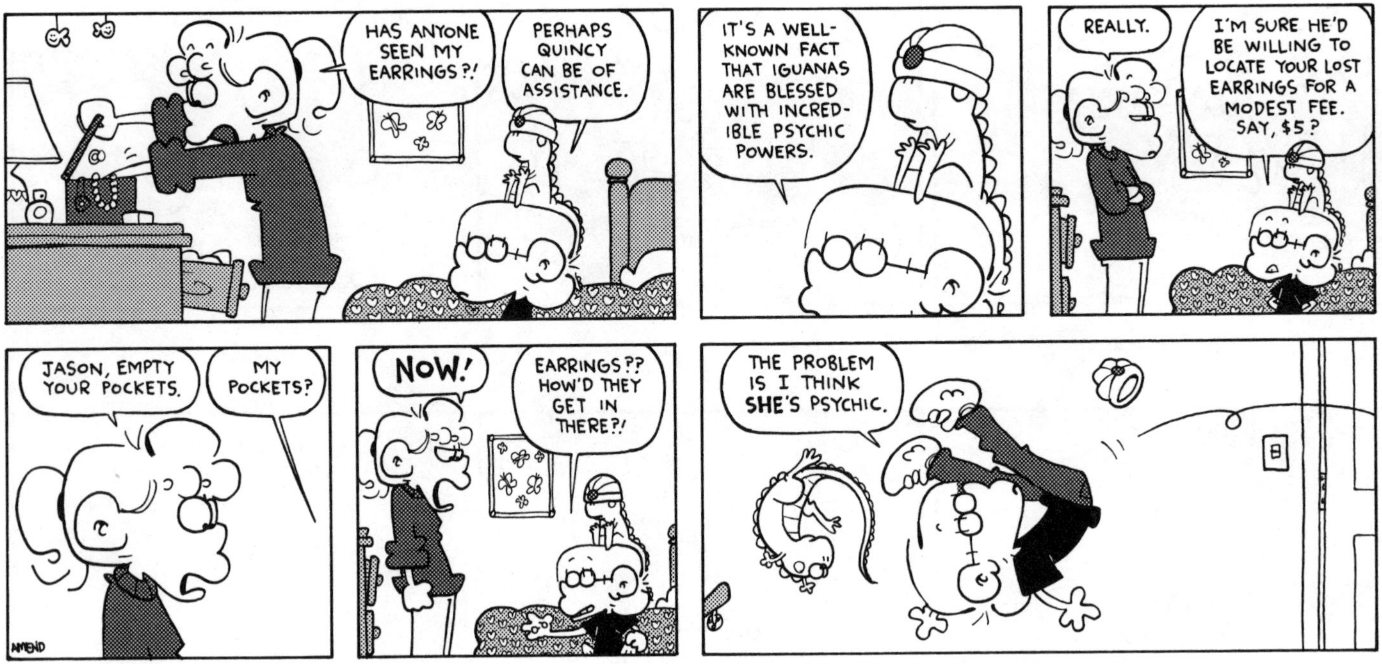
HAS ANYONE SEEN MY EARRINGS?!
PERHAPS QUINCY CAN BE OF ASSISTANCE.
IT'S A WELL-KNOWN FACT THAT IGUANAS ARE BLESSED WITH INCREDIBLE PSYCHIC POWERS.
REALLY.
I'M SURE HE'D BE WILLING TO LOCATE YOUR LOST EARRINGS FOR A MODEST FEE. SAY, $5?
JASON, EMPTY YOUR POCKETS.
MY POCKETS?
NOW!
EARRINGS?? HOW'D THEY GET IN THERE?!
THE PROBLEM IS I THINK SHE'S PSYCHIC.
AMEND

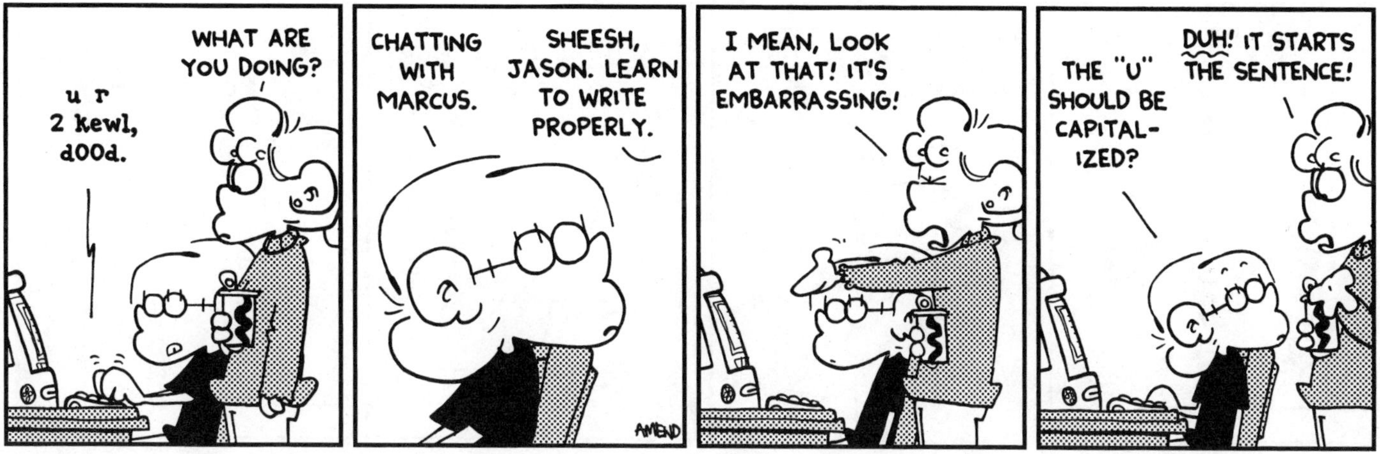
WHAT ARE YOU DOING?
u r 2 kewl, d00d.
CHATTING WITH MARCUS.
SHEESH, JASON. LEARN TO WRITE PROPERLY.
I MEAN, LOOK AT THAT! IT'S EMBARRASSING!
THE "U" SHOULD BE CAPITAL-IZED?
DUH! IT STARTS THE SENTENCE!
AMEND

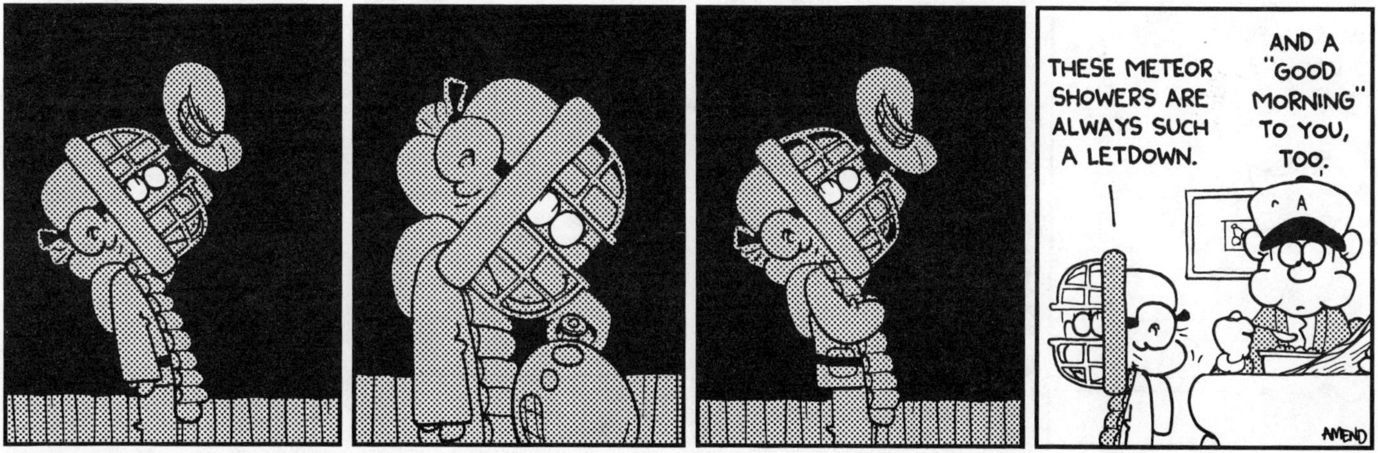
THESE METEOR SHOWERS ARE ALWAYS SUCH A LETDOWN.
AND A "GOOD MORNING" TO YOU, TOO.
AMEND

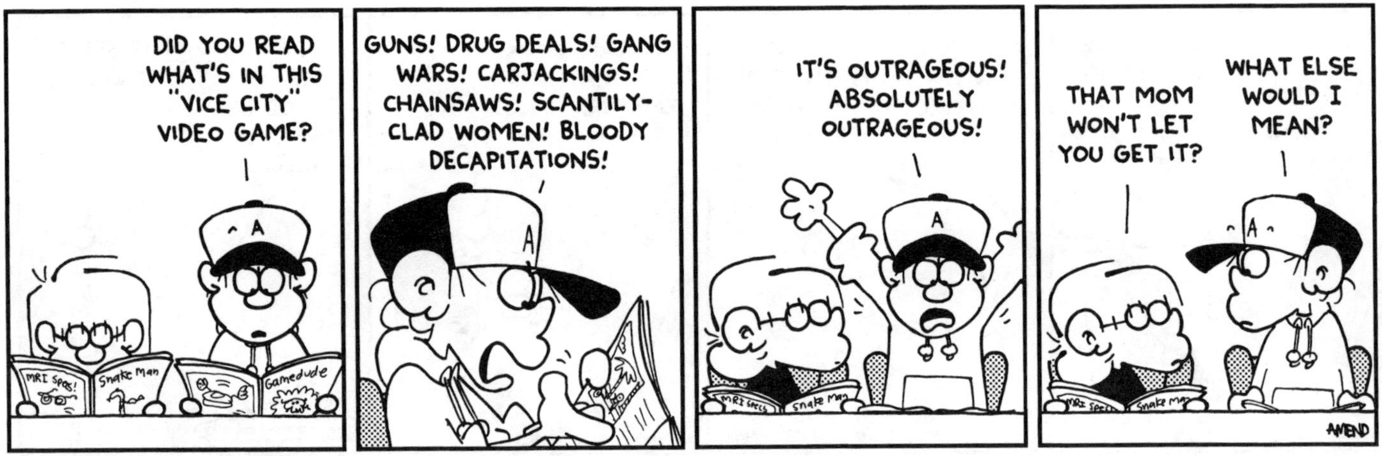
DID YOU READ WHAT'S IN THIS "VICE CITY" VIDEO GAME?
MRI Specs!
Snake Man
Gamedude
GUNS! DRUG DEALS! GANG WARS! CARJACKINGS! CHAINSAWS! SCANTILY-CLAD WOMEN! BLOODY DECAPITATIONS!
IT'S OUTRAGEOUS! ABSOLUTELY OUTRAGEOUS!
THAT MOM WON'T LET YOU GET IT?
WHAT ELSE WOULD I MEAN?
AMEND

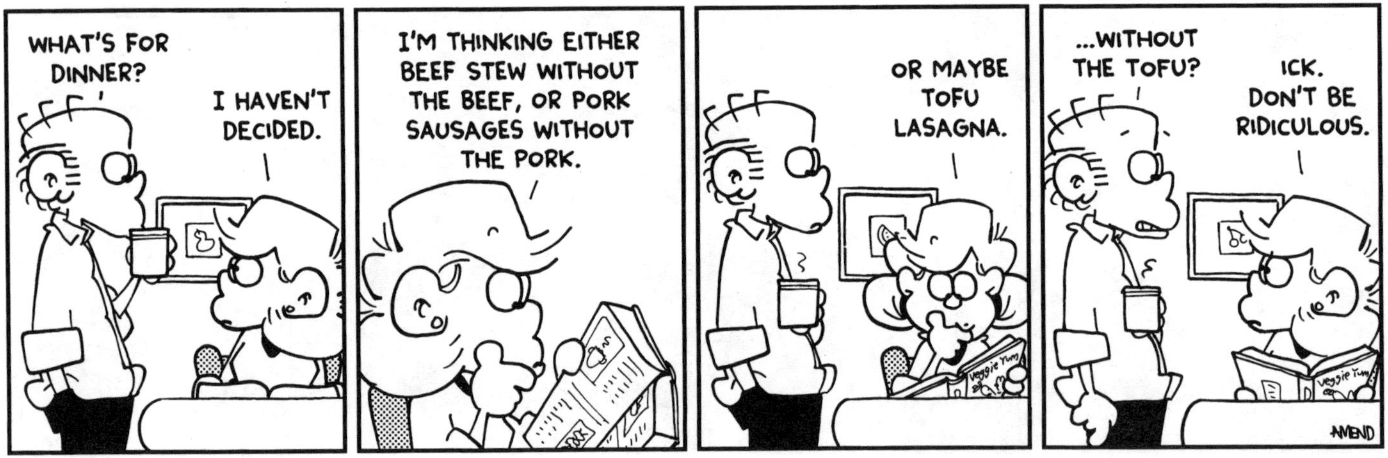
WHAT'S FOR DINNER?
I HAVEN'T DECIDED.
I'M THINKING EITHER BEEF STEW WITHOUT THE BEEF, OR PORK SAUSAGES WITHOUT THE PORK.
OR MAYBE TOFU LASAGNA.
Veggie Yum
...WITHOUT THE TOFU?
ICK. DON'T BE RIDICULOUS.
AMEND

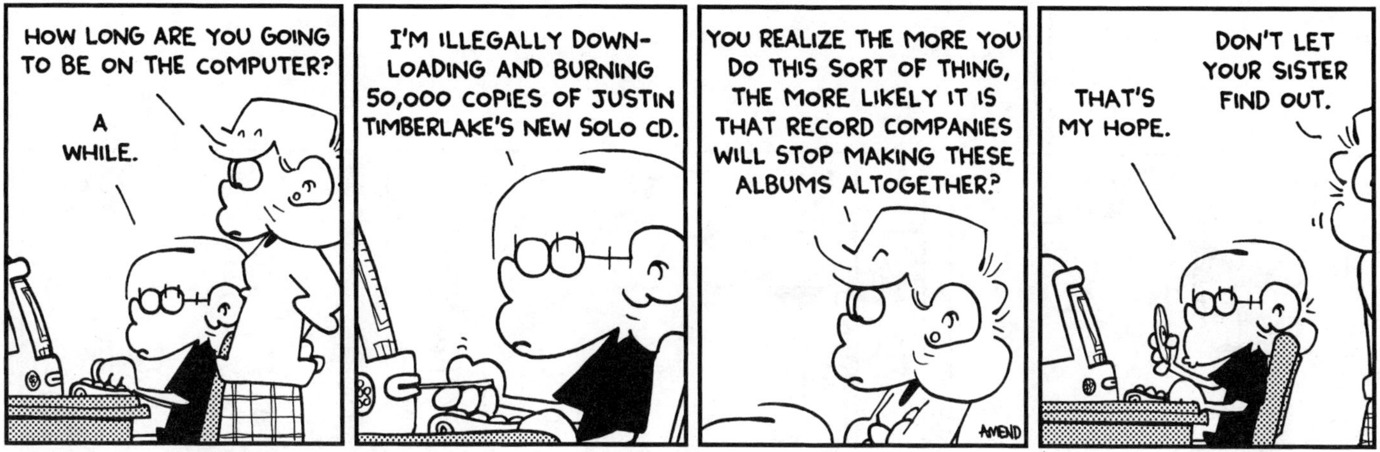
HOW LONG ARE YOU GOING TO BE ON THE COMPUTER?
A WHILE.
I'M ILLEGALLY DOWN-LOADING AND BURNING 50,000 COPIES OF JUSTIN TIMBERLAKE'S NEW SOLO CD.
YOU REALIZE THE MORE YOU DO THIS SORT OF THING, THE MORE LIKELY IT IS THAT RECORD COMPANIES WILL STOP MAKING THESE ALBUMS ALTOGETHER?
AMEND
THAT'S MY HOPE.
DON'T LET YOUR SISTER FIND OUT.

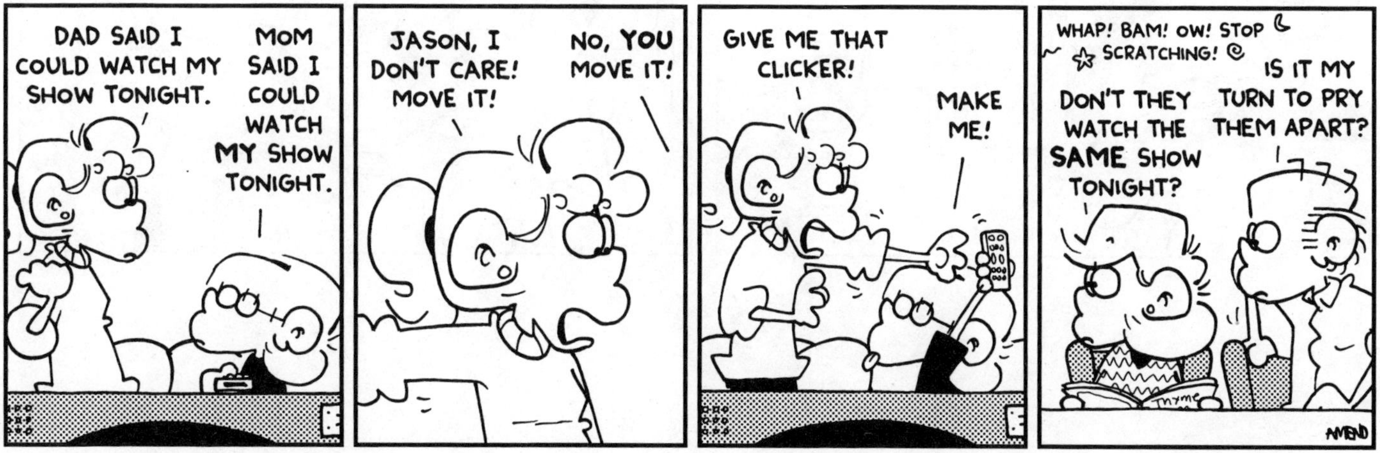
DAD SAID I COULD WATCH MY SHOW TONIGHT.
MOM SAID I COULD WATCH **MY** SHOW TONIGHT.
JASON, I DON'T CARE! MOVE IT!
NO, **YOU** MOVE IT!
GIVE ME THAT CLICKER!
MAKE ME!
WHAP! BAM! OW! STOP SCRATCHING!
DON'T THEY WATCH THE **SAME** SHOW TONIGHT?
IS IT MY TURN TO PRY THEM APART?
Thyme
AMEND

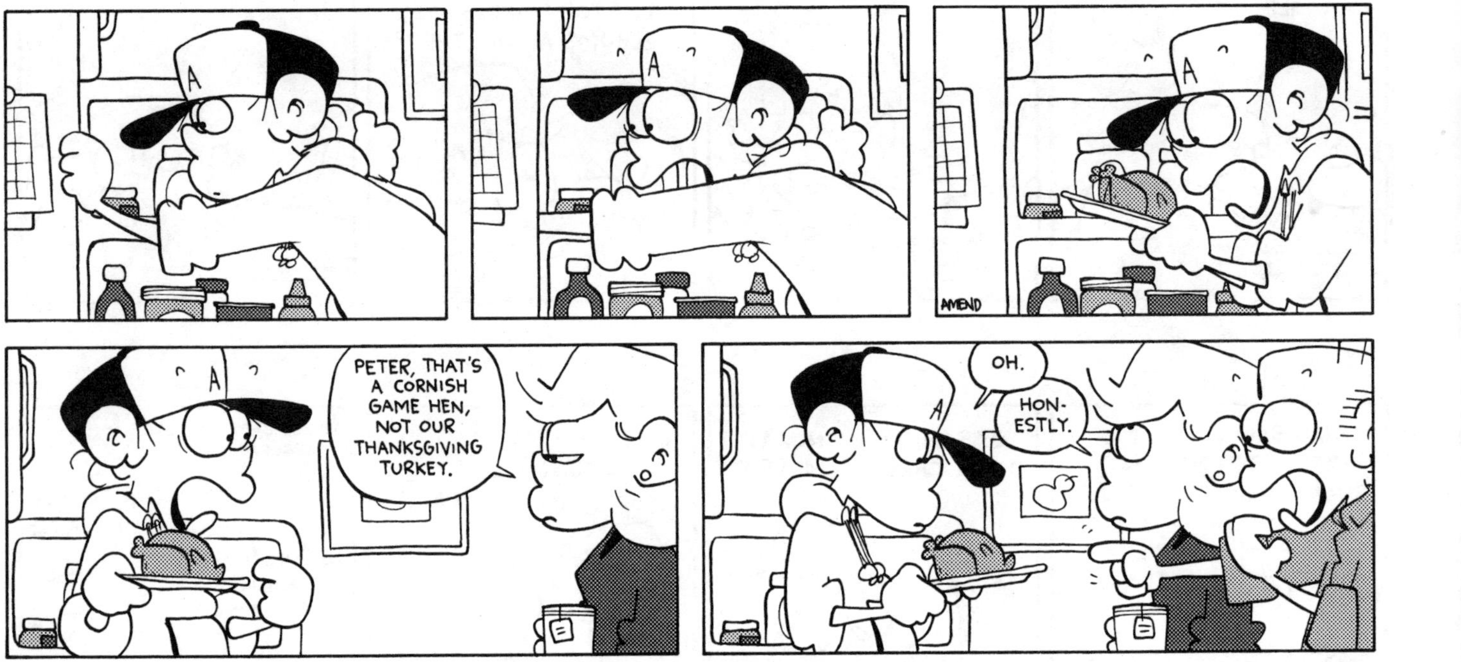
AMEND
PETER, THAT'S A CORNISH GAME HEN, NOT OUR THANKSGIVING TURKEY.
OH.
HON-ESTLY.

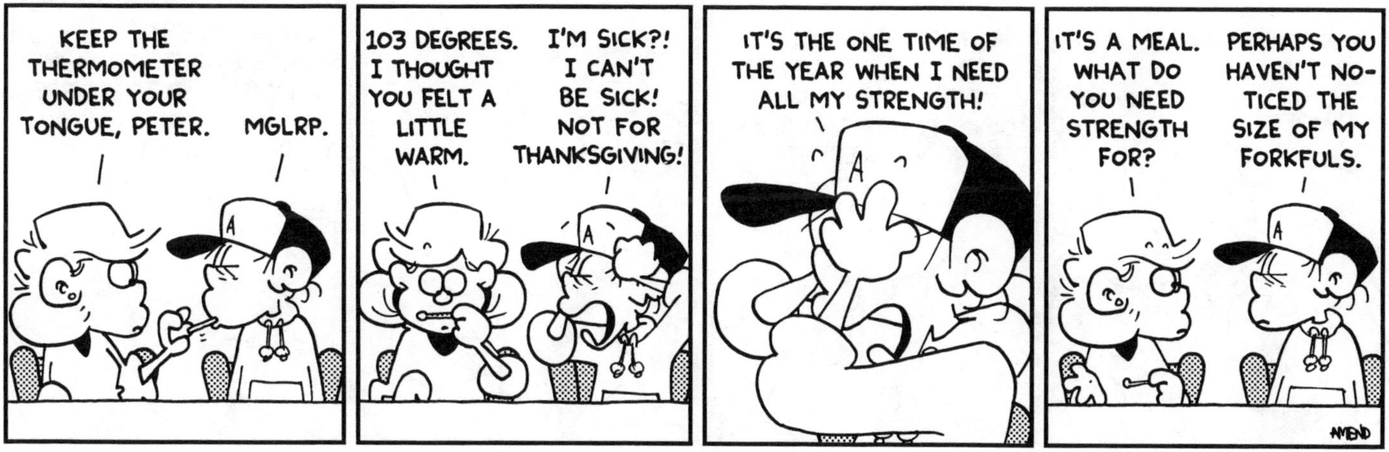
KEEP THE THERMOMETER UNDER YOUR TONGUE, PETER.
MGLRP.
103 DEGREES. I THOUGHT YOU FELT A LITTLE WARM.
I'M SICK?! I CAN'T BE SICK! NOT FOR THANKSGIVING!
IT'S THE ONE TIME OF THE YEAR WHEN I NEED ALL MY STRENGTH!
IT'S A MEAL. WHAT DO YOU NEED STRENGTH FOR?
PERHAPS YOU HAVEN'T NOTICED THE SIZE OF MY FORKFULS.
AMEND

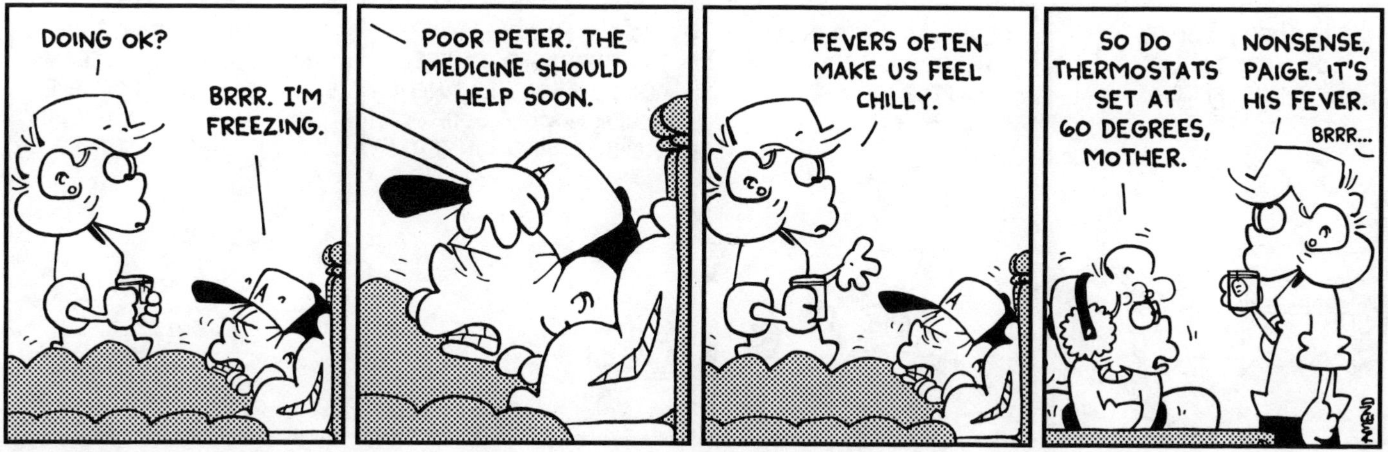
DOING OK?
BRRR. I'M FREEZING.
POOR PETER. THE MEDICINE SHOULD HELP SOON.
FEVERS OFTEN MAKE US FEEL CHILLY.
SO DO THERMOSTATS SET AT 60 DEGREES, MOTHER.
NONSENSE, PAIGE. IT'S HIS FEVER.
BRRR...
AMEND

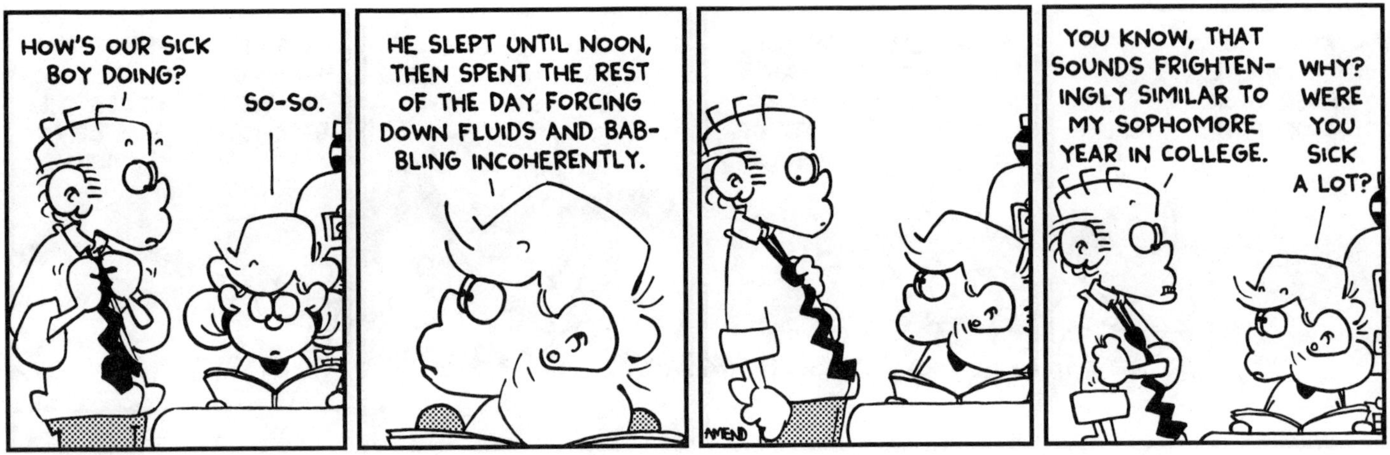
HOW'S OUR SICK BOY DOING?
SO-SO.
HE SLEPT UNTIL NOON, THEN SPENT THE REST OF THE DAY FORCING DOWN FLUIDS AND BABBLING INCOHERENTLY.
AMEND
YOU KNOW, THAT SOUNDS FRIGHTENINGLY SIMILAR TO MY SOPHOMORE YEAR IN COLLEGE.
WHY? WERE YOU SICK A LOT?

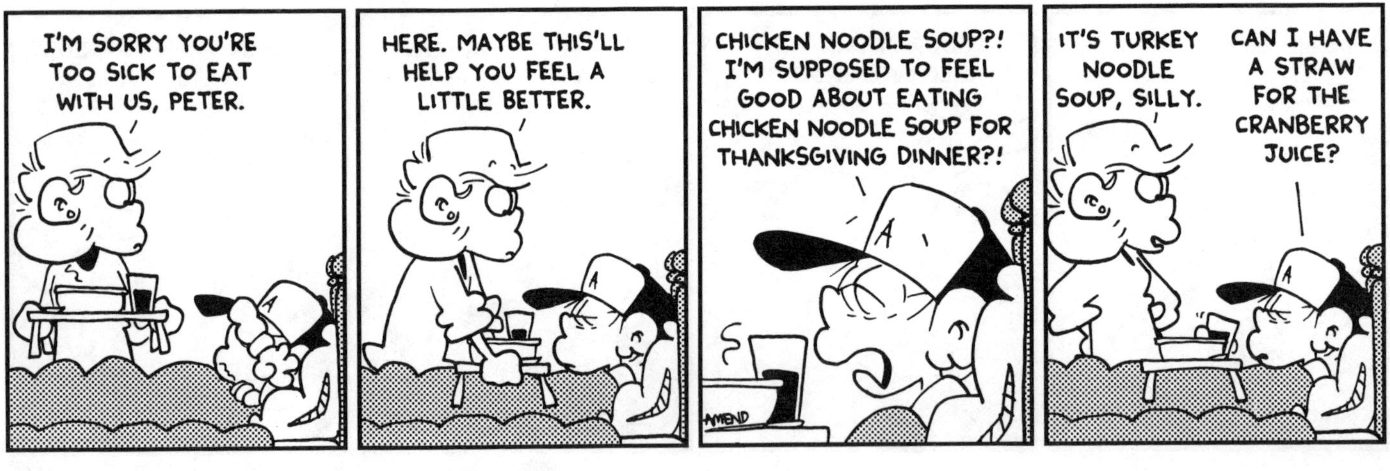
I'M SORRY YOU'RE TOO SICK TO EAT WITH US, PETER.
HERE. MAYBE THIS'LL HELP YOU FEEL A LITTLE BETTER.
CHICKEN NOODLE SOUP?! I'M SUPPOSED TO FEEL GOOD ABOUT EATING CHICKEN NOODLE SOUP FOR THANKSGIVING DINNER?!
AMEND
IT'S TURKEY NOODLE SOUP, SILLY.
CAN I HAVE A STRAW FOR THE CRANBERRY JUICE?

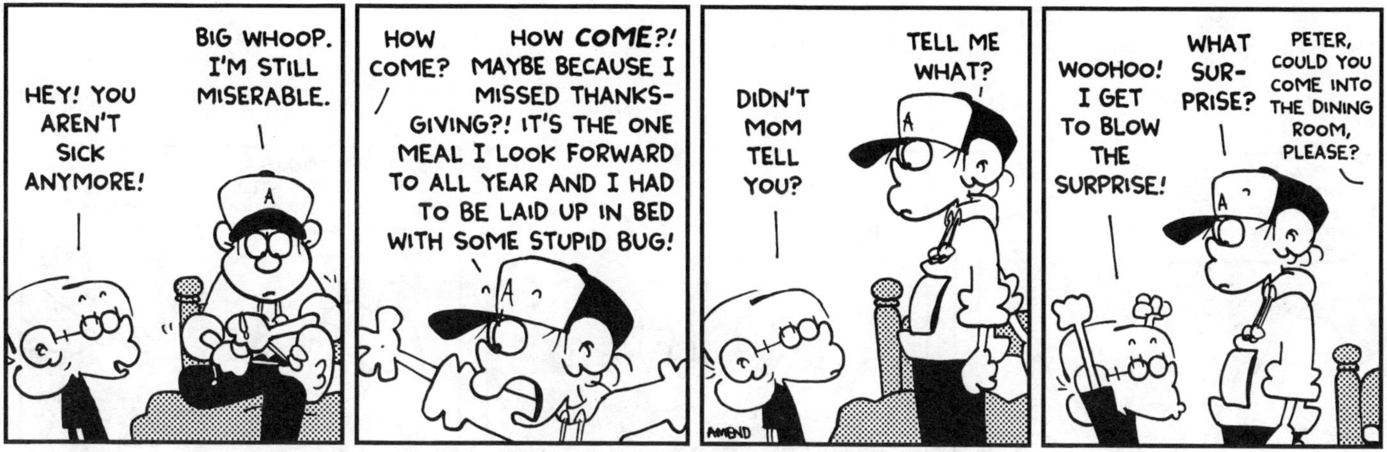
HEY! YOU AREN'T SICK ANYMORE!
BIG WHOOP. I'M STILL MISERABLE.
HOW COME?
HOW COME?! MAYBE BECAUSE I MISSED THANKSGIVING?! IT'S THE ONE MEAL I LOOK FORWARD TO ALL YEAR AND I HAD TO BE LAID UP IN BED WITH SOME STUPID BUG!
DIDN'T MOM TELL YOU?
TELL ME WHAT?
AMEND
WOOHOO! I GET TO BLOW THE SURPRISE!
WHAT SURPRISE?
PETER, COULD YOU COME INTO THE DINING ROOM, PLEASE?

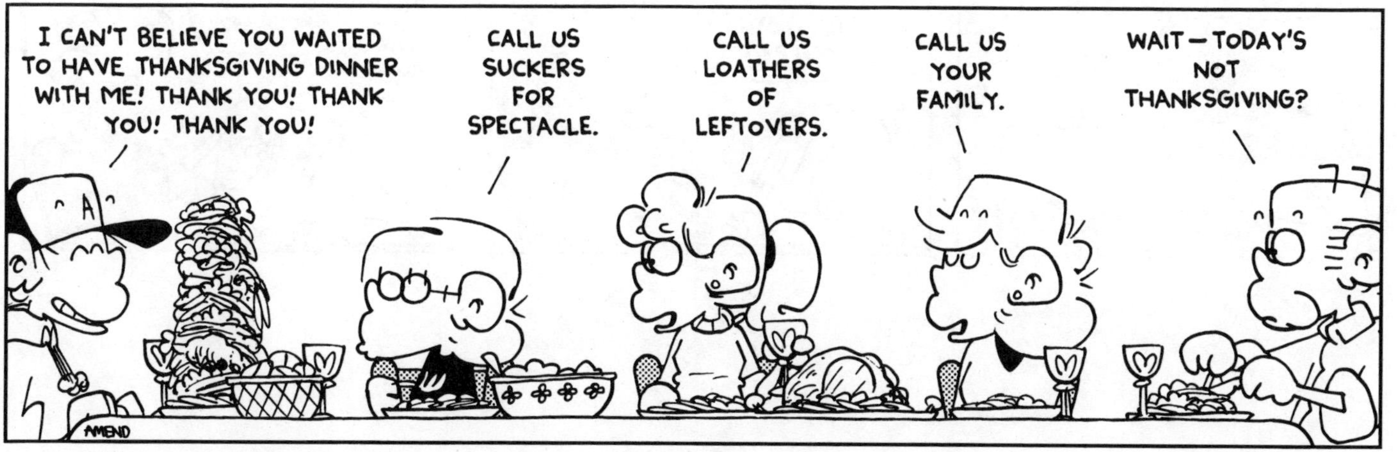
I CAN'T BELIEVE YOU WAITED TO HAVE THANKSGIVING DINNER WITH ME! THANK YOU! THANK YOU! THANK YOU!
CALL US SUCKERS FOR SPECTACLE.
CALL US LOATHERS OF LEFTOVERS.
CALL US YOUR FAMILY.
WAIT — TODAY'S NOT THANKSGIVING?
AMEND

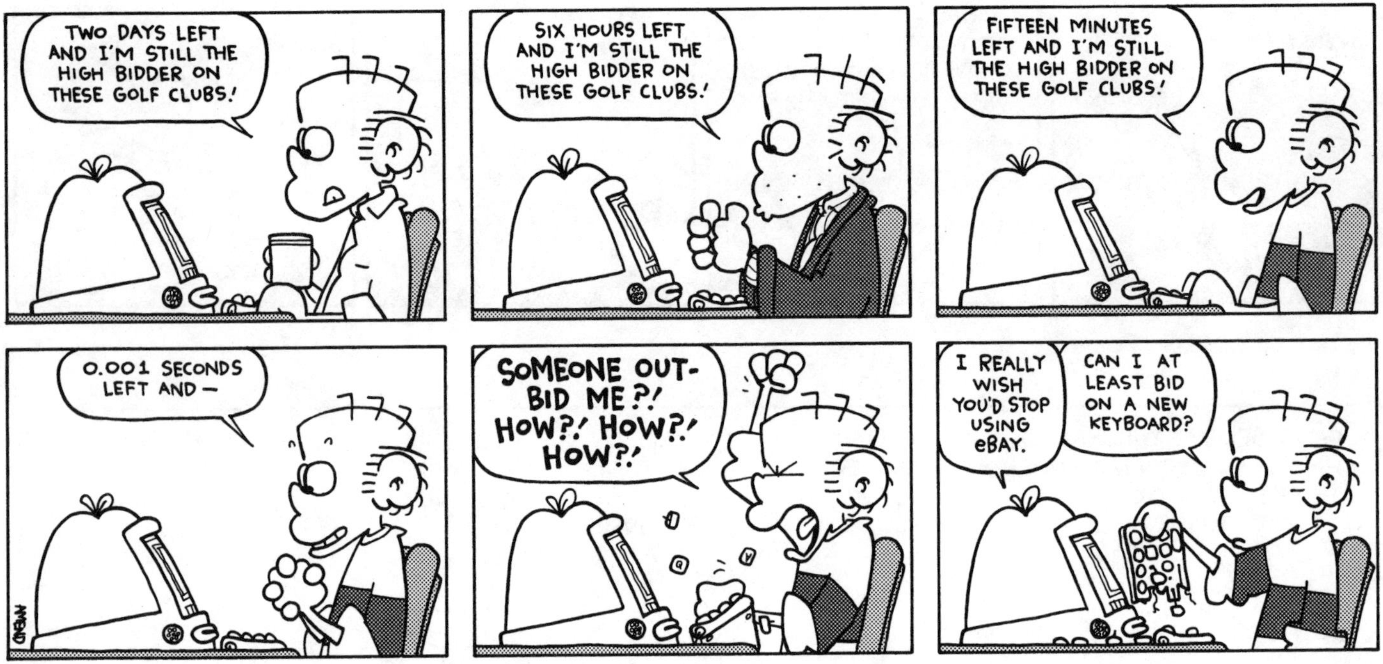
TWO DAYS LEFT AND I'M STILL THE HIGH BIDDER ON THESE GOLF CLUBS!
SIX HOURS LEFT AND I'M STILL THE HIGH BIDDER ON THESE GOLF CLUBS!
FIFTEEN MINUTES LEFT AND I'M STILL THE HIGH BIDDER ON THESE GOLF CLUBS!
0.001 SECONDS LEFT AND —
SOMEONE OUT-BID ME?! HOW?! HOW?! HOW?!
I REALLY WISH YOU'D STOP USING eBAY.
CAN I AT LEAST BID ON A NEW KEYBOARD?